HIGH IMPACT

— INTERNAL EVALUATION —

A PRACTITIONER'S GUIDE TO

EVALUATING AND CONSULTING

INSIDE ORGANIZATIONS

RICHARD C. SONNICHSEN

Sage Publications, Inc.
International Educational and Professional Publisher
Thousand Oaks ▪ London ▪ New Delhi

For information:

Sage Publications, Inc.
2455 Teller Road
Thousand Oaks, California 91320
E-mail: order@sagepub.com

Sage Publications Ltd.
1 Olivers Yard, 55 City Road
London EC1Y 1SP

SAGE Publications India Pvt Ltd
B-42 Panchsheel Enclave
PO Box 4109
New Delhi 110 017

Printed in the United States of America

Library of Congress Cataloging-in-Publication Data

Sonnichsen, Richard C.
   High impact internal evaluation: A practitioner's guide to
evaluating and consulting inside organizations / by Richard C. Sonnichsen.
      p. cm.
   Includes bibliographical references and index.
   ISBN 0-7619-1152-9 (cloth: acid-free paper)
   ISBN 0-7619-1153-7 (pbk.: acid-free paper)
      1. Organizational effectiveness—Evaluation.
   2. Industrial management. I. Title.
      HD58.9 .S67 2000
      658.4′013—dc21   99-6668

00   01   02   03   04   05   06   7   6   5   4   3   2   1

Acquiring Editor:	C. Deborah Laughton
Editorial Assistant:	Eileen Carr
Production Editor:	Astrid Virding
Editorial Assistant:	Nevair Kabakian
Copy Editor:	Kate Peterson
Typesetter/Designer:	Marion Warren
Cover Designer:	Candice Harman
Cover Art:	Jennifer Sonnichsen-Parker

HIGH IMPACT

INTERNAL EVALUATION

This book is dedicated to my wife and best friend
Sally
in thanks for her love and friendship.

Brief Contents

Detailed Contents

Preface

Unbeknownst to me at the time, the germination of this book began in the fall of 1974, when I was transferred from a field office assignment to the Office of Planning and Evaluation (OPE) at Federal Bureau of Investigation (FBI) headquarters in Washington, D.C. This new assignment began my evaluation experience. For the next five years, I evaluated programs, studied policy issues, observed how large organizations functioned, and became actively involved in the implementation of evaluation recommendations that called for a major revision of the FBI's approach to its investigative activities. My fascination with organizational structure, policy formulation, organizational change, information distribution dynamics, personnel behavior and management, and the value of independent evaluative activities and their affect on organizations, begun over two decades ago, continues to this day and is the primary rationale for engaging in this writing exercise.

In 1979, I was assigned as the assistant special agent in charge (ASAC) of the FBI's San Francisco office for two years, then after a tour of duty on the FBI inspection staff, I was appointed director of OPE in 1982. As I began the task of managing OPE, I was struck by the lack of training opportunities and available information on internal evaluation. Although the most conspicuous taxonomic distinction in the field of evaluation is internal/external, I discovered that a dearth of material existed about the theory and practice of internal evaluation. Inquiry among evaluation professionals led me to conclude that the majority of the evaluation literature was created by academics writing about their experiences as external evaluation contractors. Few incentives existed for internal evaluators to write about their experiences because organizational reward systems did not attach any significant value to authoring journal articles nor did most organizations wish to expose their internal operations to the outside world. Fortunately, during the past decade, some growth in the internal evaluation literature has occurred, albeit incremental, and this book is an attempt to build on that limited literature. One of the motivations for my commentary about internal evaluation is the hope that it will encourage other internal evaluators to write and publish their experiences and contribute to the development of an internal evaluation literature, a rapidly growing and significant segment of the evaluation community.

The goal of this book is to present a philosophical, administrative, methodological, and ethical framework for the practice of internal evaluation that results in high-quality evaluations with positive impacts on organizations. The content of the book draws on my experience as an evaluator in the FBI for five years, as the director of the FBI's Office of Planning, Evaluation, and Audits (OPEA) for 12 years, my management and evaluation consulting activities, research I conducted during graduate school, and feedback from master's and doctoral students in evaluation classes I taught at the University of Southern California's Washington Public Affairs Center (WPAC). This book also represents an accumulation of knowledge gathered from my association with scholars and practitioners in the American Evaluation Association (AEA) and the International Working Group on Evaluation (INTEVAL),[1] who have freely shared their wisdom with me. My substantial debt to these colleagues is best expressed in the elegant prose of Henry David Thoreau, who wrote: "I think it will be found that he who speaks with most authority on a given subject is not ignorant of what has been said by his predecessors. He will take his place in a regular order, and substantially add his own knowledge to the knowledge of previous generations."

I owe a great deal of gratitude to numerous friends, relatives, and colleagues who have encouraged and advised me during my work and growth as an evaluator, organizational observer, and manager. Although I am fully responsible for the content and any errors in this book, without the guidance and camaraderie of these associates, this effort would have never begun or been completed. It was in graduate school at the University of Southern California, WPAC, where I began learning about the craft of evaluation from Joe Wholey, who graciously shared his time and extensive knowledge of evaluation with me. It was also at WPAC where Chris Bellavita challenged me to examine and begin to understand the rationale and theoretical implications behind my management behavior as an FBI executive. His thoughtful insights ignited my interest in organizational theory and human behavior and was instrumental in changing my conception of managing people. Without the friendly prodding of my FBI boss and friend John Glover, I never would have attended graduate school. His friendship, support, and joint attendance with me at WPAC helped make that a rewarding experience. Ray Rist, then at the General Accounting Office (GAO) and now at the World Bank, invited me to learn about the international aspects of evaluation by joining INTEVAL, which he chairs, and participating in its annual conferences. This 10-year association with a worldwide community of evaluation practitioners and scholars has expanded my evaluation horizons and cemented personal and professional friendships on five continents.

Attendance at American and Canadian annual evaluation conferences for over a decade also contributed to my understanding of the craft of evaluation. My evaluation education was further supplemented by attending meetings of Washington Evaluators (WE), a group of evaluation practitioners in the Washington, D.C. area founded by Mike Hendricks, and "brown bag lunches" sponsored by Joe Wholey at WPAC, where evaluation practitioners and scholars discussed how to improve government programs and practice effective public management.

I am substantially indebted to Arnold Love, Joe Wholey, and Ray Rist, who devoted considerable time, talent, and energy to reviewing a preliminary draft of this book. Their constructive criticism and valuable suggestions for improvement helped focus my thinking. I also received helpful comments from the following reviewers: Arnold Love, Robert T. Golembiewski, Michael Hendricks, Joseph S. Wholey, and Jonathan A. Morell. Over the past decade, Mike Patton has shared his evaluation expertise with me, offering his friendship, guidance, and astute counsel. His pragmatic approach to the use of evaluation has influenced my thinking and affected my practice. In addition to the persons mentioned above, other colleagues who have been helpful and influenced my evaluation career and the content of this book include Kathryn Newcomer, Mike Hendricks, Midge Smith, Ernie House, Pablo Guerrero, and my associates from AEA and INTEVAL.

I also want to express my deep appreciation to the federal government evaluation office directors who helped in the research for this book. Chris Wye, Jake Barkdoll, Mike Mangano, Mike Dole, and Glenn Freeman gave me unrestricted access to their evaluation staffs, office documents, and agency personnel. My thanks also go to George Grob, Oliver Cummings, Racqueline Shelton, and Bob Diegelman, internal evaluation office directors who kindly updated me on their current evaluation practices. Thanks go to Sage editor C. Deborah Laughton, who offered me a book contract after reading a draft of the first chapter. The Sage commitment was an incentive to finish a writing project that was beginning to develop an inertia problem. I am also indebted to Kate Peterson at Sage. Her considerable copyediting skills made the book more readable.

This book has been somewhat of a family affair. My daughter Susan Sonnichsen-Wilson and son-in-law David Wilson used their formidable computer talents to advise me how to overcome computer glitches; my other daughter, Jennifer Sonnichsen-Parker, designed the cover. My wife and best friend, Sally, has tolerated my many hours at the computer. Her love and friendship has created a family and home environment that I never imagined possible, enabling me to devote a significant amount of time to writing.

Because of the insular nature of internal evaluation, the extent of its practice can only be estimated and its quality and impact subject to speculation. The development and evolution of internal evaluation practice will flourish only when its practitioners begin writing, publishing, and sharing their experiences and begin the public dialogue that is important for the advancement of any professional endeavor. Through public discussion and critique, the quality, impact, and influence of internal evaluation on organizations can be promulgated and debated, clarifying some of the mystery surrounding its practice. I hope that this book will stimulate other internal evaluation practitioners to share their expertise and experiences.

For those who practice the craft of internal evaluation, we are crossing a threshold into exciting times. The demand for evaluative services is growing, and the practice of internal evaluation is undergoing a paradigmatic reframing. As we approach the 21st century, the advent of the knowledge-based organization, the demand for articulate and measurable performance data, and the information technology revolution have combined to create enormous opportunities for internal evaluators. Producing useful knowledge and constructively evaluating and consulting inside organizations will enable internal evaluators to contribute to improved decision making and more productive, effective, and efficient organizations. This book outlines some of the approaches to these tasks that will aid in the recognition of the value of evaluative efforts, the building of evaluation capacity, and the eventual institutionalization of evaluation as an essential component in modern organizations.

RICHARD C. SONNICHSEN

Note

1. INTEVAL is a group of international evaluation scholars and practitioners from North America, Europe, and Asia who conduct evaluation research and publish the results in books. They began meeting in 1986 under the auspices of the International Institute of Administrative Sciences (IIAS). In 1997, they became independent but continue their research and publishing activities.

Chapter 1

❧❧❧

Opportunities, Obstacles, and Observations

KEY CHAPTER TOPICS

- ◇ Description of internal evaluation and definition of terms
- ◇ Central themes of the book
- ◇ Internal evaluation trends
- ◇ Preconditions for high impact internal evaluation
- ◇ Purpose and genesis of the book
- ◇ Organization of the book

The practice of internal evaluation is on the threshold of exciting new developments and expanded recognition of the value of evaluative activity initiated inside organizations. An emerging internal evaluation paradigm, characterized by heightened evaluator sensitivity to client needs and interests and increased participation in the organizational decision-making process, is changing the relationship between internal evaluators and the organizations they serve. Internal evaluators

1

are identifying new strategies for problem solving and reframing the traditional notion of internal evaluation. At least three significant developments will affect the future of internal evaluation: (1) the increasing complexity of managing modern organizations, (2) the availability of sophisticated information processing technology to gather and process voluminous data, and (3) the demands for improved performance and service delivery by organizations. The combination of these factors creates a need for increased analytical and evaluative capacity in modern organizations.

This book will present a practical, administrative, methodological, philosophical, and ethical framework for the practice of internal evaluation that results in high impact and a positive influence on the host organization. My firm conviction, and the main premise of this book, is that internal evaluators, with senior management's support, can build an organizational tradition of systematic, critical review and reflection on organizational issues and problems with positive consequences in terms of improved performance. Internal evaluation has the potential to become a useful and integral tool of management but only if it maintains a commitment to basic scientific principles while adapting to the unique conditions inside organizations.

Internal evaluators have the opportunity to challenge entrenched organizational preconceptions, biases, and misunderstandings. They can develop methodological and administrative approaches and demonstrate that positive evaluation outcomes are possible when evaluators and senior managers work cooperatively, respectful of each other's views and needs. Notwithstanding the potential benefit of evaluation to organizations, internal evaluators will have to continue to overcome the inherent resistance—because if its judgmental nature—to evaluation. This chapter will summarize the central themes of the book, review the major preconditions for high impact internal evaluation, highlight significant trends, and examine and reflect on internal evaluation opportunities and obstacles.

What Is Internal Evaluation?

Internal evaluation is a systematic process for collecting and analyzing reliable performance data and interpreting the results to inform and clarify issues that will illuminate and facilitate the decision-making process within organizations. Internal evaluation is a process of reviewing administrative, operational, and environmental activities of organizations to develop independent, empirical information that can be used for program improvement, decision making, and coping with change. Internal evaluation is a striving for empirical rationality in a political and emotional environment. Internal evaluation is action oriented, focused on the use of findings and recommendations to improve organizational performance. As opposed to evaluation research, action-oriented evaluation includes analytical and management-related activities aimed at influencing organizational behavior (Mayne, 1992b).

Internal evaluation is, above all, a practical enterprise. Practicing internal evaluation in organizations is the art of merging science with management, applying research principles and techniques to the conduct of business to determine effectiveness, efficiency, economy, and performance. "Evaluators working in the public or nonprofit sector need a bias for the pragmatic" (Bellavita, Wholey, & Abramson, 1986, p. 289). Internal evaluators are fundamentally problem solvers and change agents. Functioning essentially in a formative mode, they provide feedback to managers and decisionmakers. The primary goal for the vast majority of internal evaluators is to ascertain, for a predetermined client, how programs are working: Have they been effectively implemented and operating as originally intended with predicted results? Internal evaluators can recommend alternative solutions and options to achieve the program's goals.

Internal evaluators have the opportunity to challenge assumptions and confront entrenched organizational traditions and policies, subjecting them to empirical testing. Their goal is to examine issues and programs and present credible evidentiary material supporting plausible and understandable explanations for organizational phenomena, unencumbered by traditional preconceptions. However, it would be absurd to advocate evaluation as a panacea for all organizational shortcomings. Internal evaluation is not decision making. Evaluators gather and analyze data, present findings, and issue recommendations containing judgments, but evaluation is not a substitute for decision making. It is an applied research enterprise within an organization designed to assist the organization in accomplishing its mission. Pawson and Tilley (1997) emphasize the "realistic" nature of evaluation: "The whole point is that it [evaluation] is a form of applied research, *not* [italics in the original] performed for the benefit of science as such, but pursued in order to inform the thinking of policymakers, practitioners, program participants, and public" (p. xiii).

Internal evaluation is fundamentally a sense-making process. Given sufficient latitude and freedom within the organization, it can become an organizational learning mechanism. Internal evaluation is not an insular activity; it requires a linkage with the organization. It is an ongoing consulting arrangement with evaluators inside organizations to identify and process data and supply information. Successful internal evaluators will become consultants to the organization, performing a variety of management roles pivoting around the axis of independent assessment. "[Without empirical, objective data on organizational issues, actions, and their consequences] there is no body of evidence that can be investigated to mediate the multiple opinions, subjective interpretations and assumptions, or strictly ideological beliefs that frame judgments" (Boyle, Lemaire, & Rist, 1999, p. 6). The purpose of internal evaluation is to mitigate subjective distortion and emotional attachment to organizational issues and present persuasive, empirical evidence about the operation and performance of programs. When used appropriately, internal evaluation can penetrate the Sturm und Drang that characterizes many organizational environments and insert a methodical, objective approach to problem solving. For internal evaluation to become an enduring success in an organization, evaluators have to demonstrate to the organization their ability to collect and present credible data that inform the decision-making process and contribute to goal achievement.

Central Themes

What we have learned during the short history of internal evaluation can serve as the foundation for future development of its practice. It will be stressed throughout this book that the keys to successful internal evaluation are explicit linkages of evaluation activities with management operations. Is it also important to recognize the significant reciprocal relationship between these two entities that must exist if evaluation is to become institutionalized in an organization. Managing and evaluating in organizations are complementary activities, inextricably linked and potentially mutually supportive. Optimizing evaluation's contribution to the decision-making process is possible only with unequivocal support from an organization's senior management team. This support will be forthcoming if internal evaluators can regularly demonstrate that the information they produce is useful, adds value to the organization's operations, and justifies the resources allocated to the evaluation process. In the absence of senior management's commitment to the evaluation process, internal evaluators can, nevertheless, identify individuals or components within the organization who appreciate the value of evaluation and independent analysis and provide information for their use. Over time, this approach can infuse the evaluation ethic into the organization.

The following central evaluation and management themes that will be discussed in this book summarize some of the major axioms I have discovered about internal evaluation. They stress the significant linkages between evaluation and the decision-making process that are crucial to evaluation success. These themes can be conveniently arranged in three categories: organizational conditions, decision making, and internal evaluation.

ORGANIZATIONAL CONDITIONS

1. Organizations are not homogeneous structures but collections of individuals united in a common purpose, yet separated by variations in values, beliefs, agendas, career aspirations, and program implementation and operation views. These individuals have parochial and emotional attachments to their own programs and skeptical attitudes toward the value of other organizational entities.
2. Organizations have both personal and technical dimensions; internal evaluators must be sensitive to both during evaluations.
3. Managing organizational change is difficult because of the inability to accurately predict downstream outcomes of decisions and the severe consequences for being wrong.
4. Fact-based information has a value in organizations.

DECISION MAKING

5. Decision making is the primary enabling mechanism in organizations, shaping and directing operations, administration, and goal achievement.

6. Decision making in organizations is complicated by the enormous volume of information available, the inability of decisionmakers to rapidly judge its quality, and the constraints on human capacity to gather and process data.

7. Organizational decision making can be improved through the production of independent evaluative data on major issues, policies, program performance, and problem areas.

8. Information asymmetry (an imbalance in information quality and availability—see Chapter 3) may result in suboptimal decision making.

9. Improved decision making leads to improved organizational performance.

INTERNAL EVALUATION

10. The primary purpose of internal evaluation and the expectation of management are that evaluation supports the decision-making process.

11. Internal evaluation can influence the organization's decision-making process, not substitute for it.

12. Internal evaluators can function as agents for positive change and organizational learning.

13. Internal evaluation is an independent activity yet is linked to organizational administration and operations.

14. Crucial to the success of internal evaluation is a reciprocal, trusting, and supportive relationship between evaluators and senior management, each recognizing the needs, roles, and responsibilities of the other.

15. Internal evaluators must operate independently and credibly if they are to become an influential part of an organization.

16. Internal evaluators must view the organization as a holistic entity and consider the effect of their recommendations in one area on other organizational components.

17. Successful internal evaluators will conduct their activities in an impartial manner, yet with empathy toward clients, reflecting evaluator concern and understanding of client interests.

These 17 central themes form the philosophical framework for the application of the internal evaluation process in organizations. Because of evaluation's generic analytical capability, it is a uniquely suited management instrument to employ across organizational boundaries, both vertically and horizontally. Evaluation's multifaceted applicability permits it to be used to help design new programs, develop performance indicators, assess performance, review program implementation status, analyze problems and identify needs, determine program effectiveness, detect organizational inefficiencies, and help organizations learn as they benefit from these evaluative activities. Evaluation has both ex ante and ex post dimensions, assisting in the design and development stages of new programs and retrospectively reviewing the performance of established programs and projects. The protean functionality of evaluation allows it to be combined with planning and budgeting operations, adding value by voicing an independent perspective, favoring no single organizational component but representing the whole organization.

Evaluation can also be a significant component in an organization's overall review and feedback systems. Properly integrated and coordinated with performance measurement, inspections, audits, quality assurance reviews, and other internal review mechanisms, evaluation both supplements and complements an organization's feedback loops, feeding data into management and communications systems and networks. Internal evaluation has no proprietary allegiances but regards the entire organization as a holistic system organized to accomplish a goal.

Preconditions for High Impact Evaluation in Organizations

When analyzing organizations to determine the likelihood that evaluation will be used and have a positive influence (high impact), five conditions appear to predict the ultimate success in institutionalizing the evaluation function. (Chapter 6 contains a detailed discussion of a high impact internal evaluation model.)

❖ *A supportive top management team:* Optimum internal evaluation practice is dependent on senior managers and executives in organizations who have an appreciation of the value of evaluation and support it as an independent contributor to improved decision making.

❖ *Availability of competent evaluators:* When experienced organizational personnel who have received education and training in applied research techniques are used as evaluators, the credibility of the evaluation process is enhanced.

❖ *An organizational culture of internal review:* Organizations with a history of internal review are more likely to accept evaluation as one additional tool to analyze the organization's operations. It is a hallmark of a healthy organization to continuously conduct rigorous self-assessments and take corrective action when needed.

❖ *Reliable data systems:* Organizational traditions of accurate data origination greatly facilitate the work of internal evaluators, who can then rely on existing data collection systems.

❖ *Unlimited access by evaluators to the organization's data and personnel:* Evaluators should have full and unrestricted access to the organization's data and be allowed to confidentially interview all personnel.

These are the ideal circumstances for initiating internal evaluation, yet they may not always be present in organizations. The absence of one or more of these preconditions, however, should not deter beginning an evaluation function. Organizations without these ideal preconditions may be able to initiate approaches that begin building the necessary environment to nurture evaluation. It is unlikely that most organizations will have the philosophical predisposition and infrastructure to initially support evaluative activities to the extent that an evaluation office will immediately encounter acceptance and positive results from evaluative output. It is more probable that evaluation credibility and benefits will have to be repeatedly demonstrated to be a value-added exercise before complete acceptance is assured.

Trends in Internal Evaluation

Several trends in internal evaluation have important implications for practitioners. Adjustments to working within organizations and reactions to external criticisms have begun to form discernible patterns that will significantly shape the future direction of internal evaluation practice. The continuation of these trends and the recognition of their efficacy by practicing internal evaluators will contribute to the paradigm reframing process taking place in the field of internal evaluation.

1. **Lengthy program evaluations will be replaced by shorter, management issue-oriented studies**
   Executives in organizations are demanding more timely responses to requests for information, requiring internal evaluators to devise new strategies and methodologies for expeditious resolution of problems and prompt data feedback.

2. **Increased client focus will drive the internal evaluation process**
   Awareness and acute sensitivity to the needs and expectations of the client will become a major emphasis of internal evaluations.

3. **Analysis, not compliance or accountability, will become the focus of evaluative efforts**
   The intrinsic accountability component of evaluation cannot be completely removed from the process, but emphasis on positive support can minimize the threat often perceived by clients. Solving problems without assessing blame can overcome some of the resistance encountered by internal evaluators.

4. **Cooperative relationships with program managers will become necessary**
   Full integration of internal evaluation in an organization will require acceptance by program managers. This condition will occur only if a trusting relationship is established between evaluators and managers and evaluation is viewed on balance by managers as more beneficial than harmful to them and their programs.

5. **More marketing efforts by evaluators will be required**
   Increased attention to the demand side of the evaluation equation will be essential to building internal evaluation capacity. Internal evaluators will increasingly become aware of evaluation as a product to be "sold" to the organization. As understanding

of the evaluation product increases, so too should acceptance and utilization. An ancillary duty of the internal evaluator will be to explain why and how evaluation can add value to achievement of the organization's goals and objectives.

6. **Additional tasks for evaluation staffs will be necessary for their survival**

In the modern, streamlined organization, all components will perform multiple tasks, and evaluators will be no exception. Planning, performance measurement, quality improvement, and myriad ad hoc tasks will supplement traditional evaluative efforts.

7. **Measuring and evaluating performance will become primary tasks for internal evaluators**

Increasing demands on organizations for demonstrated performance will involve evaluators in formulating performance indicators, assisting in performance measurement, and evaluating performance outcomes.

8. **External evaluation consultants will be used more frequently to train internal evaluators, add expertise to evaluative efforts, bring outside perspectives to the organization, and analyze and critique internal evaluation staff work**

External consultants can assist fledging internal evaluation offices (and also experienced evaluation staffs) by examining and critiquing their work, bringing fresh perspectives to issues, and contributing to credibility when an outside opinion is necessary.

9. **The notion of advocacy will become more accepted and recognized as an integral feature of internal evaluation**

The tradition of evaluator neutrality after completion of an evaluation will be seen as counterproductive in internal settings. Evaluators inside organizations will recognize that evaluators' input can improve the decision-making process when they become more involved in communicating evaluation results to organizational components. The commonly accepted impression that advocacy of evaluation findings and recommendations tarnishes evaluator credibility will continue to challenge internal evaluators to maintain their objectivity.

10. **A diversity of evaluation approaches will be applied within organizations**

Adapting scientific techniques to practical use and recognition of multiple avenues to problem solving represent a new pragmatics in the application of science to solve social problems. The extraordinary complexity and ambiguity of many modern organizational problems hinder resolution using a single approach. An integration of numerous analytical devices is needed to bring some semblance of order to the turbulence regularly encountered inside organizations. The dynamic and complex nature of the *evaluand* (that which is being evaluated) in organizations requires integrated assessment techniques and the ability to identify and analyze each individual situation and apply the proper analytical tools. No single evaluation approach can claim superiority over others, and professional internal evaluators will have to become familiar with the diversity of methodologies—their advantages, drawbacks, and appropriate application. In the evaluation community, proponents of qualitative, quantitative, empowerment, fourth-generation, internal, external, utilization-focused, developmental, advocacy, and participatory evaluation are seeking rapprochement and extending understanding and empathy for fellow practitioners. Each of these conceptions of evaluation can be applied in internal evaluation settings under the appropriate circumstances.

Evaluation Opportunities and Obstacles

Internal evaluation, being a nascent enterprise, presents evaluators working inside organizations with unique opportunities to develop the practice of internal evaluation that will consequently affect its acceptance and use. Throughout this book, it will be stressed that internal evaluators have not only the opportunity but also the responsibility for demonstrating the value of evaluation to organizations and aid in its institutionalization. Using evaluation technology to convert data into useful information to solve the organization's problems is the primary purpose of internal evaluation. By demonstrating the utility of evaluation and linking evaluation activities to other essential organizational functions, such as strategic planning and budgeting, the image of evaluation as a fundamental organizational function is begun.

At the same time, internal evaluators must recognize the significant obstacles that face institutionalizing evaluation in organizations and devise strategies to overcome them. Most organizations are uncomfortable with detailed scrutiny and criticism of their activities, even when the criticism is from within. Resistance, therefore, will continue to be a major impediment to the acceptance of the evaluation function. Evaluation will continue to be resisted with ideological, political, and managerial opposition threatening the independence and credibility of the internal evaluator. Occasionally, the technical incompetence of evaluators will be cited as justification for rejection of evaluation results. This argument can be overcome only with rigorous attention to evaluator selection, training, and professional behavior. Table 1.1 lists some of the most significant opportunities and obstacles that face internal evaluators consulting inside organizations.

Evaluation Opportunities

The evolution of quality information and knowledge as strategic enabling mechanisms in organizations, indispensable to product development and high-quality service delivery, creates opportunities for internal evaluators. Internal evaluation offers organizations the opportunity to incorporate into their management structure an independent, systemic review function that moves horizontally and vertically throughout the organization's structure collecting, processing, and disseminating information about program functions, policy issues, problem areas, and performance. Offering an alternative viewpoint for decisionmakers to compare with other available data, internal evaluations can provide decisionmakers with fact-based decision options and alternative courses of action that can clarify complex policy issues and problems.

TABLE 1.1	
Internal Evaluation Opportunities and Obstacles	
Opportunities	*Obstacles*
Produce usable knowledge inside organizations by converting data into information	Resistance to evaluation
Institutionalize the evaluation function in organizations	Ideological management opposition to concept of evaluation
Use evaluation technology to help solve management problems	Political interference in evaluation activities
Link internal evaluation with strategic planning and budgeting operations	Lack of evaluator independence
End the prevailing dogma that objectivity of internal evaluators is impossible	Lack of evaluator technical capabilities
Develop an expanded consulting role for internal evaluators	
Legitimize the concept of advocacy for internal evaluators	
Develop internal evaluation models that are applicable across organizations	

KNOWLEDGE PRODUCTION AND USE

As organizations increasingly become knowledge based, rapid and accurate data collection and interpretation will be essential for optimum functioning. Establishing a research or evaluation department is one approach to increasing the quality of information available to the organization. The combination of technology and information availability has revolutionized the management of modern organizations. It is now clear that the inexorable trend toward information as a coterminous product with an organization's goods or services will make information a valuable and desirable commodity in all organizations. The ability to leverage the power of information to organizational use can be enhanced by using internal evaluators to review operations, detecting inefficient and ineffective practices and determining areas where improvements are necessary.

An evaluation office inside an organization can perform many of the systematic research-and-review functions needed by high-tech, modern organizations. "The objectives of systemic research include study of environmental trends, long-term organizational functioning, the nature of organizational structure, the interrelationship of the subsystems within the total system, and the impact of the organization on its environment" (Katz & Kahn, 1978, p. 459). However, one of the major obstacles to implementing a systemic research function in an organization is a conceptual limitation by senior executives, who may not have a systemic perspective on managing the organization (Katz & Kahn, 1978). However, a designated evaluation office is not the only approach to successfully integrating evaluation into organizations. Many organizations are initiating evaluation activities using part-time evaluators scattered among organizational components, periodically reacting to evaluative situations as self-directed evaluation teams and then returning to their primary responsibilities. Some organizations employ one or more full-time evaluators, who both conduct and coordinate internal evaluations. Program managers may have evaluation responsibilities in addition to their program operation duties. (See Chapter 6 for alternative internal evaluation configurations.)

Communicating evaluation findings to organizations is one of the specialized tasks of internal evaluators. Normal communication channels in an organization are primarily designed to transmit routine information and are not readily capable of processing complex research data. The capacity for organizations to collect, assimilate, and use research data may be severely limited because of employees' specialization and the continuous commitment of employees to other tasks. Future advances in internal evaluation will be built on the foundation of knowledge production through information dissemination. The challenge of modern decision making is to replace capricious, intuitive, and emotional approaches to decision making with knowledge-based approaches. Partisan arguments supporting constituent positions in policy debates within organizations can be partially overcome by injecting fact-based information into the debate. Recognizing, within organizations, the dysfunctional nature of information asymmetry and the potential role that evaluators can play in correcting information imbalances among organizational constituents can minimize the emotional dimensions that often accompany issues and events. When supplemented with independent assessment data, emotion and experience can be significant contributors to decision making. Successful internal evaluators will be viewed as knowledge producers and information providers to level the playing field during consequential organization debates.

STRATEGIC EVALUATION
LINKAGES WITH ORGANIZATIONS

The fate of an internal evaluation function in an organization—its integration and sustainability—may very well depend on the ability to develop strategic linkages to the organization's management components. For successful integration to occur, evaluation must be sufficiently associated with other vital organizational functions so that its absence would be noticed and the lack of evaluative input into these processes would reduce their effectiveness. Associating the evaluation function with traditional organizational operations creates dependencies that, over time, will aid in sustaining the evaluation ethic through routine personnel changes and strategic operational alterations.

The obvious and most productive linkages are with budget formulation departments, strategic planning offices, and resource allocation groups. Independent feedback from the evaluation staff to these fundamental and universal organizational activities strengthens decision-making deliberations and acts as a counterbalance to the vested and parochial data presented by other organizational components. Through participation in meetings when budget, planning, and resource items are on the agenda and providing objective data to illuminate these discussions, internal evaluators can demonstrate the value of evaluative information and begin building an organizational dependence on high-caliber information. The Federal Bureau of Investigation (FBI) evaluation staff attended annual budget allocation request meetings and offered comments on operational and administrative functions when requested. By establishing this linkage with important and basic organizational functions, the evaluation function can begin to be understood as contributing to the organization and sustained as one of the essential components of the organizational structure.

Internal evaluators, however, are not limited to the budget, planning, and resource arenas when attempting to forge linkages. Reaching out to the operational components and demonstrating the value of evaluative information when these components present their requests and supporting arguments to central organizational entities establishes additional linkages. Through the creation of an informal, interconnecting network joining evaluation with the essential components in the organization, the evaluation function can build its reputation and develop support for its participation in the operations of the organization.

Evaluation Obstacles

Even though internal evaluation is growing rapidly throughout the world, and arguably is the most widely practiced form of evaluation, many challenges and constraints to its successful introduction into organizations remain unresolved. Unused evaluation findings are a major obstacle facing internal evaluators; avoiding this phenomenon, one of their primary tasks. The goal of internal evaluation is to have evaluation results used for positive organizational development, not ignored. "Intended use for intended users" is the mantra espoused by Patton (1988) to define evaluation utilization, and internal evaluators are no exception to this simple, straightforward interpretation of the primary objective of evaluative activity.

EVALUATION FANTASY VERSUS REALITY

An evaluation fantasy is that someday the intrinsic benefits of evaluation and the personal magnetism of evaluators combine to captivate senior management officials in organizations to view internal evaluation as a necessary, useful, and integral function in organizations. Lacking much evidence that this fantasy is probable anytime soon, internal evaluators have to face the reality that their craft has yet to gain universal acceptance and commence efforts to market the value of this technology.

The beneficial effects of internal evaluation may paradoxically suffer from the arrogance of its purveyors who, convinced of its intrinsic merit, captivated by its functionality, and convinced of its catholic application, fail to recognize the environment and viewpoint of the evaluation recipient, thereby developing a myopic intolerance toward the client. Evaluation is but one commodity in the cornucopia of management techniques available to program managers, and its acceptance will occur only when the trade-off between risk and benefit appears to favor the manager. Refocusing evaluators toward understanding their responsibility for utilization and away from blaming the evaluation user for lack of evaluation impact is an important step toward increasing internal evaluation utilization.

Two flawed assumptions by evaluators tend to hinder progress toward evaluation acceptance. The first assumption to be questioned and examined is that the efficacious nature of evaluation is self-evident and therefore readily apparent and acceptable to those persons being evaluated. A more common reaction to evaluation is that it threatens stability and presages change. A second flawed assumption is that evaluation has a predictable linear elegance that can be predicted with a calculable degree of certainty, that is, a problem can be identified, an evaluation initiated, findings enumerated, recommendations made and implemented, and the problem solved. This methodical and orderly approach to evaluation is desirable but unrealistic. Belief in its universal application may contribute to disappointment as evaluation is introduced into an organization.

The "curse" of evaluation is its capacity, when done correctly, to discover and suggest corrective action for inefficient and ineffective management policies and procedures. Educating the evaluation consumer can help minimize the intrinsic arrogance that attaches to this evaluation discovery process that is both its strength and vulnerability. Use of evaluation products is far from automatic and will depend, to a great extent, on the salesmanship of evaluators. Michael Patton, speaking at a plenary session of the 1987 American Evaluation Association (AEA) annual conference in Boston, challenged evaluators to become advocates for the evaluation profession, using sales techniques to market the value of evaluation (Patton, 1988).

INSTITUTIONALIZING
THE EVALUATION FUNCTION

A recurring theme throughout this book is that conducting high impact internal evaluations only partially fulfills the role of the internal evaluator. The ultimate objective is to build evaluation capacity in the organization to an acceptance level where evaluation is perceived as an indispensable component in the structural, administrative, and operational configuration of the organization. Institutionalization is accomplished when evaluation activity is legitimized as a meaningful pursuit and the results routinely used in the decision-making process. The initiation and institutionalization of internal evaluation in an organization is not a linear, straightforward process but an iterative endeavor, requiring patience and long-term commitment by evaluators. Love (1991) suggests that organizations go through stages in developing internal evaluation capacity, as they advance toward progressively greater capacity for self-evaluation. He posits six stages beginning with isolated ad hoc evaluations and moving to the assessment of strategic benefits and social costs of products or services. Along this pathway, evaluation becomes systematized and begins evaluating goals, effectiveness, and finally efficiency as the organization progresses from a focus on the operational level to the management control level and ultimately to the desirable strategic planning level. This developmental model of internal evaluation capability can be used as guidance for internal evaluators instituting an internal evaluation function and lessen the frustration they will undoubtedly encounter during the process.

To achieve or even approach the "ideal" internal evaluation condition, where organizations monitor their activities, initiate necessary changes, and incorporate evaluation results in their strategic planning process, requires a supportive group of senior managers along with a clear vision by evaluators on how they would function in this type of environment. The pursuit of the "self-evaluating" organization requires a radical departure from the traditional, hierarchical authority structure toward a consultative environment where extensive communication and deliberation occur among all facets of the organization but particularly between evaluators and executive management. Table 1.2 contains the essential questions that need to be addressed when an organization contemplates the creation of an internal evaluation office.

TABLE 1.2
Key Questions to Develop Internal Evaluation Capacity

1. Where in the organization will evaluators be located?

2. What will be the selection criteria for recruiting evaluators?

3. What training will be afforded the evaluators after they are selected?

4. How will the independence of the evaluation office be guaranteed?

5. How will the evaluation office relate to the rest of the organization?

6. How will the evaluation mission be defined?

7. Who will be the primary client for the evaluation product?

8. What is the intent and purpose of internal evaluation in the organization?

Focusing on these questions and their answers and involving both senior management and prospective leaders of the evaluation office in the discussions will create the proper atmosphere and understanding critical to the beginning of an evaluation enterprise in an organization. Two indispensable topics in these discussions are credibility and independence—attributes automatically imputed to external evaluators, but daily concerns for internal evaluators. Without these two characteristics, the effectiveness of internal evaluators is substantially reduced. Credibility is dependent on evaluator independence, competency, and impartial and objective behavior. The location of the evaluation office in the organization's hierarchy and the autonomy of the evaluators affect independence. These same questions are relevant for organizations contemplating the use of part-time evaluators but not setting up an independent evaluation office.

Evaluation Observations

Modern organizations will increasingly rely on information-based strategies to compete in the marketplace, and the ability to leverage the power of information and information technology for product and service development will favor some organizations over others. Internal evaluation is a conceptually simple management tool that can be used inside organizations to develop and leverage information to assist the decision-making process. Providing feedback to organizations on the efficiency and effectiveness of operations simultaneously provides performance, accountability, and learning data for use in decision making. By consulting inside organizations, evaluators can help harness information technology and use it to mine available organizational data, converting the data to useful information.

EVALUATION AND MANAGEMENT

Internal evaluation is arguably the fastest-growing and largest segment of the evaluation community, yet with a relative short history and little consensus on effective practice, it has not developed a recognizable image or consistent demand. Internal evaluation is about organizations: knowing their culture, learning their behavior, understanding their functions, questioning their assumptions, investigating their problems, researching their policy issues, detecting their flaws, and celebrating their accomplishments. Internal evaluation is, above all, a management function, and competent management involves evaluating. "It is important to realize that evaluation is useful only if it is, in fact, a tool of management. . . . Evaluation is needed principally in support of policy analysis and management discretion" (Horst, Nay, Scanlon, & Wholey, 1977, p. 109). Internal evaluation is also about decision making, more precisely, about supporting the decision-making process. In spite of the self-evident symbiosis between management and evaluation, evaluation inside organizations remains an enigma, useful and beneficial yet frequently misunderstood, often superficially supported, and suboptimally used. Before substantial progress can be made in the practice of internal evaluation, conceptual clarification is needed in four areas:

◇ Evaluation support of decision making
◇ Evaluators as internal consultants to organizations
◇ Demonstrating and marketing the value of internal evaluation
◇ Modifying evaluation theory and practice for use inside organizations

DECISION-MAKING SUPPORT

Support of the decision-making process, the raison d'être of internal evaluation, is often misunderstood as obsequious allegiance to individual decisionmakers or decisions themselves (particularly when evaluations are sometimes misused to justify decisions already made). Internal evaluation, however, is a management tool designed to furnish unbiased information that improves decisions, not a mechanism for decision justification. Nor is internal evaluation a substitute for decision making. It is simply a source of alternative information to alert and inform managers and executives to possible alternative views and options when they are confronted with complex organizational issues. "To be effective as a management tool, an internal evaluation unit must focus on the information needs, concerns, and priorities of senior management. Evaluators must adopt a management perspective in planning and executing evaluations" (Winberg, 1991, p. 167). Internal evaluators, working within the organizational structure, can enhance the decision-making *process* with independently collected and analyzed data furnished to decisionmakers for use in their deliberations.

EVALUATOR-CONSULTANTS

Internal evaluators in modern organizations will become more valuable to the organization if they see themselves and are seen by the organization as consultants with a broad range of practical, analytical skills, rather than simply as evaluators. The roles of consultant, advocate, problem solver, evaluator, performance monitor, planner, facilitator, and management analyst combine to form a composite characterization of the modern, professional internal evaluator. An internal evaluation office with a reservoir of competent analysts and a broad scope of proficiencies increases its value and service to an organization. Willingness to move beyond evaluative activities, to develop expanded competencies, and to seek imaginative avenues to serve the organization will be the hallmark of successful internal evaluators in modern, knowledge-based organizations.

EVALUATION MARKETING

The concept of marketing has applicability in the field of internal evaluation and may be a partial solution to the utilization issue. Chapter 9 will outline the responsibilities of evaluation office directors for marketing and discuss some of the available techniques. Marketing the evaluation product is a continuous process and is an obligation for all internal evaluators. The ubiquitous lament in the evaluation literature on the lack of utilization, centered on the failure of program managers to accept the value of evaluation, may be ill focused. It should by now be apparent to the majority of evaluators that the value of evaluation is not self-evident to the majority of clients, or where it is, the potential hardship in participating is not deemed worth the effort. (See Chapter 4 for the viewpoints of program managers on evaluation.) If evaluation is to be accepted within the workplace, it must not only demonstrate effectiveness but also be administered in a manner empathic to the concerns of program managers. To correct the ambiguous role of internal evaluation and clarify its value to the organization, internal evaluators must move beyond the traditional neutral posture of re-searchers. If internal evaluation is to become an indispensable compo-nent in the management of the modern organization, evaluators will have to become more visible in the organization and demonstrate, or market, the utility of evaluation and related activities.

One key approach to facilitate evaluation demand is to educate the consumers to understand the strengths and limitations of evaluation and to be able to articulate what they want from evaluation (Boyle, 1999). A popular television advertisement for discount clothing states that "an educated consumer is our best customer," stressing the point that knowledgeable customers will recognize the value in shopping for name-brand clothes at discount prices. This retail analogy has applica-tion for evaluators. Comprehension of the organization as a consumer of an evaluation product reframes the evaluation utilization issue and opens the door for recognition of the marketing and educational aspects of internal evaluation. Boyle (1999) reports that European Union offi-cials involved in overseeing evaluation activities attend four-day semi-nars created to increase their knowledge of evaluation, allowing them the opportunity to exchange views on evaluation. Educating the evaluation client about evaluation and the nature of change not only reduces the uncertainty surrounding the practice of evaluation but has the potential to increase the demand for evaluation products. Developing creative opportunities to communicate the value of evaluation to the organization's executives and managers is one facet of internal evaluation requiring evaluator attention if integration and full utilization are to be successful. Requesting a one- or two-hour time block at executive retreats to make educational presentations about evaluation is one approach to increased management understanding.

REFRAMING THE CONCEPT OF INTERNAL EVALUATION

Internal evaluation is not simply the application of traditional evaluation methodologies inside organizations but the adaptation, reconstruction, and reframing of evaluation methodologies to operate effectively inside organizations. Internal evaluation requires both a methodological and philosophical adaptation of standard evaluation techniques. Although the basic tenets of science and evaluation theory are applicable in any setting, the organizational culture will dictate modifications to accommodate unique internal environmental requirements. Rapid responses to short deadlines, service to the decision-making process, expansion of the role of evaluation, marketing the evaluation process, formulation of recommendations, and advocacy of evaluation findings are some of the adjustments that internal evaluators will have to make to move toward full integration of evaluation.

The organization as client, employer, career choice, work environment, and social outlet creates a unique set of dynamics for the internal evaluator, conditions not encountered to the same degree by contract evaluators outside organizations. Insider environments and the potential allegiances formed by these conditions require new models of evaluation, specifically crafted to function in the insider climate: models that maintain the robust dimensions of traditional science, yet are adapted for use within organizations to support the demands of dynamic and rapidly evolving circumstances.

Purpose and Genesis of the Book

Internal evaluation is widely practiced but poorly reported. Although a paradigmatic change is taking place in internal evaluation, little commentary on this major development has occurred. A profession depends on its literature to establish its knowledge base, promulgate its theoretical underpinnings, set boundaries for the field, and announce its developments and successes. As a profession matures, its literature constitutes what is known about the field and serves to authenticate the existence of the profession. Although a significant literature has been accumulated as the evaluation profession grows, unfortunately, there is a dearth of material on internal evaluation. I am aware of only two books, *Internal Evaluation: Building Organizations From Within* (Love, 1991) and *Developing Effective Internal Evaluation* (Love, 1983a), that are devoted entirely to internal evaluation.

The available literature suffers from a lack of discussion of the management of internal evaluation offices and the importance of the relationship between an evaluation office and the organization it serves. Nor has sufficient coverage been given to the variations of internal evaluation in organizations, such as single and part-time evaluation practitioners. This condition is lamentable but not unexpected. The intrinsic nature of internal evaluation contributes to the paucity of available information on its practice. Internal evaluation reports are intended primarily for consumption within the organization and are only infrequently circulated externally. Additionally, most organizational reward systems are not oriented to motivate internal evaluators to publish their experiences in professional journals, and in some cases may actually be structured to inhibit any public recognition of evaluation results. What has been written on this topic comes primarily from academics studying organizations, consultants working in internal environments, and internal evaluators attending graduate school.

Although the practice of internal evaluation is stressed as a pragmatic exercise, it is not atheoretical: Attention needs to be directed to how evaluation works inside organizations and why. Practice informs theory. Shadish, Cook, and Leviton (1991) believe that "the pragmatic concepts developed in practice probably constitute the most important basis for academic theories" (p. 35). For them, evaluation theory is better if it contains a complete, accurate, and realistic theory of practice. Such a theory lists the tasks that evaluators must do, the options for doing them, the resources required for each, the trade-off among them, and the justification for choosing one over another in particular situations. Practicing evaluators need a discussion to avoid doing evaluations that are incomplete, impractical, or technically inferior. (p. 64)

Scriven (1996) reinforces the importance of theory in practical evaluation applications when he argues, "One can no longer—and should no longer—design, do, monitor, or teach the skills of practical program evaluation without clarifying the underlying theoretical assumptions" (p. 394). Given these deficiencies in the literature, increased attention needs to be devoted to the practice, reporting, and theoretical framework of internal evaluation.

Audience for the Book

There is no universally accepted approach to the practice of internal evaluation. It is practiced by large and small dedicated units; part-time, self-directed evaluation teams; single practitioners; internal-external hybrid units; and program managers with part-time evaluation responsibilities. The book is relevant for all of these practitioners in internal settings. In addition to practitioners, organizational users of evaluation findings, program managers, executives, and evaluation students should find this book useful. Although primarily U.S. in orientation, international examples of evaluation and opinion are included, and the processes, techniques, philosophical basis, and experiences of U.S. evaluators should be useful for organizations in other countries. Core organizational elements are similar throughout the world, and the material in this book should be beneficial if adapted to the local circumstances, culture, political structures, and the idiosyncrasies of individual organizations. This book should be of particular value for those wishing to establish or manage an internal evaluation office. The evaluative techniques and problem-solving approaches are also relevant for those persons working in social service agencies who must conduct self-evaluations to satisfy reporting requirements for accountability and effectiveness. Evaluation students should also find the book useful as an aid to understanding the unique interface between evaluators and the organizations they serve and the crucial differences between the practice of internal and external evaluation. Love (1983b) states that the formal training of evaluators leaves them unprepared for working in the internal evaluation arena. This book may fill some of that void. It is hoped that this endeavor will stimulate other internal evaluators to write about their experiences and begin building a body of work about this important and rapidly developing segment of evaluation and fill the lacuna in the literature.

One important goal of this book is to reach and educate the user audience in organizations unfamiliar with evaluation and its benefits. Demands for performance and accountability data will obligate organizational leaders to become more familiar with assessment techniques and capabilities. The recent trend toward greater accountability for funding in the management of nonprofit organizations requires program managers to acquire evaluation expertise and assume leadership roles in internal evaluation (Minnett, 1997). Clients and stakeholders may have a better appreciation of the value of evaluative efforts if their understanding of evaluative processes can be increased. I suspect that a contributing factor in the underutilization of evaluation stems, in part, from a lack of understanding by the user community.

The lack of recognition of evaluation as a profession and useful organizational tool presents a constant challenge to those of us in the field to expand the understanding and use of evaluation. For many, the word *evaluator,* or *internal evaluator,* is not represented by any specific imagery unlike that conjured up when *doctor, engineer, lawyer,* or *nurse* are mentioned. Symbolic representations are critical determinants in the way we perceive professions. The myths, symbols, traditions, history, and practice that constitute the aura of a profession serve as the communication medium for the profession. Evaluation, although a relatively young profession, has a rich history, a substantial literature, a growing number of practitioners, and a legacy of contribution to the development of public programs. Nevertheless, evaluation tends to suffer from an identity crisis, possibly from a failure to effectively communicate who we are and what we do. It is hoped that this book will contribute to the advancement of the evaluation profession by describing one segment of its practice.

Internal evaluation is useful in all types of organizations, and this book is not specifically focused on private sector, nonprofit, or public organizations. Most organizations are neither completely private nor public but have some mix of private or public authority influencing their behavior (Bozeman & Bretschneider, 1994). Although most of my experience has been with federal government agencies, I believe that the practice of internal evaluation described in this book has application in all types of organizations and at all levels of government. The public-private distinction is a much studied area among organizational theorists, with a growing recognition that the distinctions between the two sectors are becoming blurred (Robertson & Seneviratne, 1995) and a strong tradition that rejects the belief that public organizations differ fundamentally from private ones (Rainey, 1991). A review by Rainey (1991) of major studies analyzing organizations for the purpose of developing taxonomies and typologies produced little evidence of a strict division between private and public organizations. Robertson and Seneviratne (1995) applied meta-analysis techniques to a study of 16 public and 31 private organizations to determine if there was a difference in outcomes of planned change. They found that "change efforts [in public organizations] certainly appear to be equally efficacious as those in private organizations across a range of variable categories defined at a fairly general level" (p. 555).

Although goals, end results, resources, and constraints are variables that differ among public and private organizations, no conclusive demarcation is evident in their fundamental operations. Because internal evaluation is a generic, analytical approach, not discipline dependent, it has substantial applicability in public, private, and not-for-profit arenas, and the information in this book should be of interest to evaluators in all types of organizations.

Organization of the Book

Internal evaluation is a management activity (Love, 1991) that takes place in organizations, and the chapters that follow are sequenced to examine and understand the organizational context where internal evaluation is practiced before exploring the specific practice of successful internal evaluation. Chapters 2, 3, 4, and 5 define and build an understanding of the organizational context of internal evaluation and the nexus between organizational change and internal evaluation. Chapters 6, 7, 8, and 9 discuss the art and craft of evaluation practice inside organizations. Chapter 10 synthesizes the major themes of the book, incorporating the essential elements necessary to practice high impact internal evaluation, and suggests strategies for evaluation institutionalization.

Chapter 2 defines internal evaluation, reviews past and current practices, and discusses the emergence of a new internal evaluation paradigm. Chapter 3 establishes the framework for internal evaluation, discussing the importance of understanding the organizational context where evaluation is practiced, the relevant processes and behaviors, organizational theories, and the organization's capacity for learning. Also reviewed are the value, use, availability, and nature of acquisition of information in organizations and how culture, individuals, conditions, and decision-making processes affect it. Chapter 4 examines conflict between evaluators and program managers, the phenomenon of change in organizations, mechanisms to cause change, the effect of change on behavior, and ways to overcome resistance to change.

Chapter 5 begins the discussion of internal evaluation in organizations, defining and explicating five models of internal evaluation and suggesting one model that is particularly relevant for internal evaluators. Because internal evaluators are subject to criticism that their commitment to objectivity is impaired because they are employees of the host organization, one section of Chapter 5 is devoted to the importance of establishing that objective observations are capable of being performed in internal settings. House (1986) in an article in *Evaluation Practice* suggested that career concerns, identification with administrators, and evaluation routinization may affect the objectivity of internal evaluations, concluding that "internal evaluation is not necessarily a worse situation; it is a different situation. And what we need are new ideas for dealing with it." He suggested more serious, scholarly attention to the new demands and opportunities presented by this transformation from external evaluations to internal evaluations. These concerns of House and their solutions are reviewed as well as a discussion of the relevant "independence" issue.

Another important component of the practice of internal evaluation is the concept of advocacy and its relationship to ensuring use of evaluation results. Traditionally, the notion of advocacy has been heretical, burdened by the acceptance of neutrality as a professional ethic dominating the practice of evaluation. More recently, however, the conception of advocacy in its variety of nuances has gained currency. The concept of advocacy evaluation; its major features, pros, cons, and consequences; and its indispensability to internal evaluation practice are studied. Evaluation office identity and evaluator power are discussed as well as the limitations of internal evaluation offices. Ethical dilemmas confronting internal evaluators are presented, and a practical code of ethics for internal evaluators is offered.

Chapter 6 begins the discussion of the consulting approach to internal evaluation, locating the office, selecting a methodological approach, establishing an evaluation agenda, and identifying relevant issues to study. A model for conducting high impact internal evaluations is presented, and evaluation use and methods for increasing use are reviewed. Chapter 7 begins the methodological section of the book with a look at the mechanics of designing and conducting high impact evaluations. The importance of understanding the evaluation question, matching appropriate evaluation designs to questions, and the theory of program operation are covered as well as the procedures for methodically approaching evaluation in internal settings. Techniques for rapid responses to evaluation questions are also discussed.

Because evaluation has limited impact without wide circulation and debate of the evaluation findings, Chapter 8 is devoted to the indispensable aspect of reporting the results in a manner that will positively affect the organization. Converting evaluative activities to organizational action using written reports, briefings, and recommendations is discussed. Chapter 9 reviews the essential components in the management of an internal evaluation office, the influence of the office director's management style on the practice of internal evaluation, and the integration of evaluation with the organization. Administrative tools and techniques are discussed. Because evaluation offices should not be immune from the performance reviews that others undergo, methods for determining the impact of evaluation activities are presented. Chapter 10 concludes the book with a synthesis of the significant points in the book; observations on successful, high impact approaches to internal evaluation practice; and suggestions on techniques to help institutionalize internal evaluation in organizations.

Definitions

Because of the short history of internal evaluation and the lack of documentation of its practice, it is important to build consensus on terminology. This section will outline the meanings of common internal evaluation terms that will be used in this book. The term *internal evaluation* is normally used to define the location of the evaluators working inside organizations and to distinguish them from external evaluators. Although evaluation has been practiced professionally for decades, with some writers tracing its origins to biblical times, internal evaluation is a recent trend in the evaluation community and contextually different from the type of evaluation practiced by external contractors. The primary difference between internal and external evaluators is the contractual arrangements that define the nature and length of the relationship with the organization. Also integral to distinguishing internal from external evaluators are the internal evaluator's commitment to the organization, cultural awareness, decision-making support, and rapid-response capability. Throughout this book, the term internal evaluation refers to in-house staff conducting evaluations within organizations and furnishing evaluative information primarily for internal consumption. *Internal evaluators* are employees of their organizations and have career commitments to the organization, continuous contact with program operations and personnel, and a greater understanding and appreciation of the organizational culture and personalities. Their vantage point in the organization aids in developing an institutional memory and in analyzing the dynamics surrounding issues.

External evaluators are commonly defined as contractors from outside the organization who conduct specific ad hoc evaluations specified in their contracts. They are primarily associated with universities, research institutes, and private consulting or evaluation firms. The many evaluations of the U.S. General Accounting Office (GAO), conducted in the executive branch of the U.S. government and reported to the

Congress, are considered external evaluations. Occasionally in the literature, the terms *insider* and *outsider* will be encountered, referring to organizational researchers who are located either within or external to the organization. Throughout this book, the predominant terms referring to location of evaluators will be *internal* or *external;* however, when appropriate or more descriptive, the terms insider or outsider will be used.

The usual application of the term internal evaluation juxtaposes it with external evaluation, connoting the difference as absolute. In actuality, internal and external evaluation are defining terms anchoring opposite ends of a continuum with differences in degree more accurately describing the situation than concrete distinctions. Internal evaluation models include "stand alone" units specifically devoted full time to evaluative work, temporary evaluation teams assembled for self-evaluation efforts, single evaluators practicing full time, and hybrid arrangements mixing internal and external evaluators. Some internal evaluators employed in organizations fulfill their duties overseeing the work of external contractors. The National Science Foundation evaluation staff of three is an example of this variation. Scriven (1991) describes evaluators that come from the same institution but not the same program as partially external. The Offices of Inspectors General (OIG) are another model of internal evaluation, independent yet attached to their organization, with a responsibility to report findings to both the host agency and the Congress.

Evaluation will be used in this book in a commodious sense, encompassing all those activities performed by internal evaluators that have an evaluative purpose. This will include program reviews and problem-solving projects and management studies, as well as classic evaluations. (It should be noted that some of the internal evaluation work conducted in the OIG community in the federal government is labeled *inspections.*) In fact, much of the work performed by internal evaluators does not qualify as classic evaluation, where causal attribution is the goal, but can more properly be described as *management studies* supporting the decision-making process by seeking solutions to specific problems. The terms *evaluation* and *study* will be used interchangeably throughout the book to connote internal evaluation activities. The rationale for the all-inclusive approach in this book is to describe the totality of activities of internal evaluation personnel and develop the importance of the consultative relationship between evaluators and their organizations. The trend in internal evaluation is to use evaluation personnel in a variety of management tasks, not solely as evaluation specialists (Clifford & Sherman, 1983; Love, 1991; Sonnichsen, 1988). The term *program evaluation* is often seen as a description of evaluative activities. In this book, a *program* is defined as a discrete group of resources directed toward a common goal.

As the title indicates, the fundamental premise of this book is that internal evaluations and management studies can have a positive impact on organizations and influence the decision-making process. *High impact* is intended to describe those situations where top officials in the organization *regularly* use evaluation results for decision making on the organization's *major issues*. When this condition exists, *institutionalization* of evaluation has occurred. Major issues are those organizational questions that are relevant, require decisions by top agency or company officials, and significantly affect the administration or operations of the organization. It is important to emphasize the importance of evaluating major issues. An evaluation staff can be nominally established yet have limited influence in the organization if it continually receives and accepts trivial assignments that have minimal effect on operations or administration. The regularity of the evaluative function is also critical to institutionalization. Evaluation, to have a high impact, must be viewed within the organization as sufficiently important to be routinely employed as one approach to problem solving. A successful internal evaluation office producing high impact evaluations will have an influence on organizational performance with measurable results indicated by positive changes in organizational functions. Institutionalization also occurs when evaluation results are routinely used by the organization but produced by entities other than a separate evaluation office.

One of the core intellectual and pragmatic issues for debate among internal and external evaluators is the concept of evaluation support of decision making. This debate sometimes suffers from a misunderstanding of the term and conception of decision making. It will be argued throughout this book that the purpose and justification for internal evaluation is to support the decision-making *process*. Supporting the process, however, should not be interpreted as intrinsic support for either the individual decisionmaker or the decision itself (although there is nothing wrong if evaluation findings do agree with the decision or the position of the person making the decision). The value of evaluative support for the decision-making process is that it affords the organization independent, alternative views of problems and issues. Evaluation findings may or may not agree with the positions of individual decision-makers or of decisions already made. These points will be discussed in greater detail in Chapter 3, but the reader is reminded that the important distinction is that evaluation support for decision making is commitment to and support for the process within the organization, not for individuals or specific decisions.

Formative evaluations are usually conducted by internal evaluators to improve programs, whereas *summative evaluations* are generally conducted by external evaluators to determine the merits of continuing or discontinuing a program. However, evaluations conducted inside organizations may contain both formative and summative aspects.

CONCLUSION

Internal evaluation is growing in practice, developing its own methodologies and applications in organizations, and becoming a specialized subset in the evaluation community. Practiced by single evaluators in small organizations, part-time managers with evaluation responsibilities, and full-time staffs in evaluation offices, the benefits of the evaluation process are being recognized as useful to organizations as they confront the dilemma of performance demands, information overload, and reduced resources. The emerging new internal evaluation paradigm is results oriented. To accommodate the organizational environment, internal evaluators are adapting basic evaluation methods and experimenting and developing rapid data collection techniques to expeditiously respond to the needs of decisionmakers with short deadlines. Supporting the decision-making process is becoming recognized as the rational for the creation of an internal evaluation function with increased sensitivity to client interests and expectations. High impact internal evaluation seeks measurable evaluation results that have a positive influence on the organization.

Internal evaluators are augmenting their evaluation capabilities with a diverse portfolio of skills designed to increase their usefulness to the organization's clients. Multiple tasks demand that expertise be developed in management science, organizational change, and performance measurement. Internal evaluators viewing themselves as consultants to organizations increase their connection with the organization as they diagnose problems and determine areas where their skills can be applied. The nature of the relationship between internal evaluators and their host organizations is moving away from a neutral, detached posture to engagement and participation in the decision-making process. Competent evaluators operating inside organizations and supported by senior leadership have the capacity to promote increased use of evaluation as a problem-solving technique that aids the decision-making process.

This book was written to fill a void in the internal evaluation literature and to attempt to acquaint internal evaluator practitioners with theories and practices that have proven successful in the past. The book is also aimed at dispelling some of the mystique that surrounds the practice of internal evaluation and threatens the very clients that evaluation is designed to serve. It is intended as a guide to the practical and ethical practice of internal evaluation that results in a positive influence on the organization.

RECOMMENDED FOR FURTHER READING

Chelimsky, E., & Shadish, W. R. (1997). *Evaluation for the 21st century.* Thousand Oaks, CA: Sage.
   Looks at both the history and future of evaluation with an emphasis on international trends.

Love, A. J. (1983). *Developing effective internal evaluation* (New Directions for Program Evaluation, No. 20). San Francisco: Jossey-Bass.
   A good treatment of some of the basic issues in internal evaluation.

Love, A. J. (1991). *Internal evaluation: Building organizations from within.* Newbury Park, CA: Sage.

The first book on internal evaluation, it contains an excellent explanation of the relationship between internal evaluation and the organization.

Wye, C., & Sonnichsen, R. C. (1992). *Evaluation in the federal government: Changes, trends, and opportunities* (New Directions for Program Evaluation, No. 55). San Francisco: Jossey-Bass.
Reviews the use of evaluation in the U.S. federal government.

Chapter 2

Internal Evaluation History and the New Paradigm

KEY CHAPTER TOPICS

⬧ Internal evaluation history
⬧ New internal evaluation paradigm

A migration to a new paradigm of internal evaluation is taking place. To increase the utility and effectiveness of evaluation inside organizations, evaluators are engaging the organization in the evaluation process, moving away from the traditional evaluation model of neutral inquiry toward more active evaluator participation in interpreting and disseminating evaluation data to organizational clients. This relatively recent development in internal evaluation practice occurred as a reaction to the nonuse of many evaluations and recognition by internal evaluators that organizations are competitive market-places and evaluation is but one product in competition with other sources of information. This chapter will chronicle the history, growth, and current practice of internal evaluation and describe the characteristics of the new emerging paradigm.

Past, Present, and Future
Internal Evaluation Practice

The history and visibility of internal evaluation are somewhat obscure due to the insular nature of its practice inside organizations and lack of documentation in published reports or journal articles. Much of the available information on internal evaluation practice comes from federal government publications, particularly in the United States and Canada. As the profession matures, more practitioners are writing about their experiences.

GROWTH AND VISIBILITY
OF INTERNAL EVALUATION

The purpose, justification, acceptance, use, legitimacy, and value of internal evaluation have long been controversial and the subject of debate in the profession, with little consensus surrounding its practice or worth. Yet there is increasing evidence that internal evaluation is being used by organizations to improve the decision-making process and is having an impact on organizations (Boyle, 1993; Love, 1991; Patton, 1997; Sonnichsen, 1991; Wholey, 1989). This increased use of internal evaluators chronicles a transition from externally funded evaluations to internal evaluations (General Accounting Office [GAO], 1988; House, 1986; Love, 1983b; Patton, 1997) and has been predicted to be the next wave of evaluation activity in American society (Mathison, 1991). Love (1983b) attributes this trend to disillusionment with external evaluators, reduced funding for large-scale evaluations, and increased concern for the management of human service organizations. Patton (1997) believes this trend is due to the mandates added to legislation in the 1970s, more available training for evaluators, and the emergence of evaluation as a profession. Bellavita, Wholey, and Abramson (1986) see pressures for efficient and effective government in the political and fiscal environments increasing the demand for evaluator skills.

Although the trend to internal evaluation has been identified, its dimensions and impacts are not well documented. It can be reasonably argued that a significant portion of the worldwide evaluation community performs evaluative activities that logically fit under the internal evaluation umbrella. Love (1991) estimates that internal evaluation accounts for three-quarters of evaluation activities in North America. The growth in internal evaluation is not limited to North America. Elizabeth Sommerlad (1995) of the Tavistock Institute in London estimates that self-evaluation is practiced by a substantial number of the 300,000 nongovernmental, nonprofit organizations (NGOs) in Britain, whom she refers to as "practitioner evaluators." Lacking professional evaluation skills, these practitioners nevertheless reflect on their own practice, achievements, successes, difficulties, and failures, seeking insights that will allow incremental changes and enlightenment about how their activities contribute to social change. Indrebo (1997) reports that research data from a three-year study of school self-evaluation in primary and lower secondary schools in Norway suggest that school self-evaluation "seems to hold high potential for developing schools from within" (p. 18). Evidence from the study suggests that school self-evaluation contributes to development and change and increases teacher awareness of improved teaching through the process of critical inquiry. Hansson (1997) reports that internal evaluations "are a fast-growing type of evaluation activity in Denmark" (p. 184). According to Stame (1998), one of the evaluation trends occurring inside Italian national and local government departments is recognition of the need to strengthen internal evaluation capacity, and evaluation units are being created to improve evaluation demand and implementation. An informal survey in 1997 of my colleagues in the International Working Group on Evaluation (INTEVAL) reflects the growing practice of internal evaluation worldwide. The results of this survey are shown in Table 2.1.

Although they are a large and growing segment of a worldwide professional evaluation community, internal evaluators remain a somewhat invisible population. Conflict among their roles as internal evaluators, members of an organization, and members of a community of researchers and practitioners can limit internal evaluators' contact with professional associations (Mathison, 1991). Organizational control of finances may also make it difficult for internal evaluators to maintain contact with professional evaluation organizations (Newman & Brown, 1996). These arguments have merit, but I believe that establishing a professional and credible image as an internal evaluator requires membership and participation in professional organizations. By participating in conferences of evaluators such as the American Evaluation Associa-

TABLE 2.1
International Internal Evaluation Survey

Country	Estimated Percentage of Evaluators Who Are Internal	
Korea (central government)	95	
Canada (central government)	75	
France (central government)	75	
United Kingdom	50	
United States	50	
Ireland	30	(increasing)
Netherlands (central government)	30	
Norway	25	
Denmark	20-30	(increasing)
Spain	20	(increasing)

tion (AEA), internal evaluators have the opportunity to keep abreast of current developments in the field, share their experiences with other internal evaluators, and maintain their professional credentials. Sharing experiences and presenting papers will expand the knowledge base of internal evaluation.

ACCEPTANCE AND PRACTICE OF INTERNAL EVALUATION

Paradoxically, although the concept of evaluation as a helpful tool has been acknowledged by many, internal evaluation has been slow to be permanently accepted in organizations and recognized as a useful contributor to administration and operations. Resistance can be partially attributed to the judgmental nature of evaluation, which is often interpreted by managers as threatening the status quo. Program managers see evaluation as intrusive and burdensome with little empathy from evaluators for their viewpoints. A distinguished panel of public managers convened at the University of Southern California's Washington Public Affairs Center criticized the use of evaluation findings as serving the executive hierarchy in organizations with little input from, or interest in, the views of the program managers (Sonnichsen, 1989c). These program managers agreed on the potential benefit of evaluation but believed its failure to be accepted was directly attributable to its end use as a judgmental tool with little or no control exercised over the process by the affected personnel. (See their expanded remarks in Chapter 4.) Evaluators, working to secure a permanent niche in an organization, have an obligation to recognize how they may be viewed and to develop an understanding and appreciation of the roles of all organizational actors.

One of the major arenas for the practice of internal evaluation in the United States has been the federal government. During the past three decades, evaluation has been meaningfully represented in the executive branch at the federal level, but rather than steady growth and increased acceptance, its fate has suffered from ideological political shifts and accompanying budget limitations. Notwithstanding its checkered acceptance, internal evaluation has been practiced at most federal agencies at one time or another either centralized at agency headquarters or decentralized to the program level. As far back as 1987 and 1988, the GAO noted the increase in internal evaluations conducted in federal executive agencies with some alarm, citing the lack of long-term program evaluations available to Congress as input into the policy process (Sonnichsen, 1991). The Office of Management and Budget (OMB) contested the GAO position, arguing that the purpose of internal evaluation is to support agency decisionmakers, not to supply information for Congress and the public (GAO, 1987). The most recent 1998 GAO survey of 13 cabinet-level departments and 10 independent executive agencies in the federal government found that evaluations or studies in these agencies continued to primarily serve internal program purposes and not congressional oversight needs (GAO, 1998). The study selection criterion most often cited in the survey was "the interest of high-level agency officials in the program or subject area" (GAO, 1998, p. 15). The agencies reported that the primary role of evaluation was internally focused on program improvement with program managers and higher-level agency officials the primary audiences (GAO, 1998).

House (1986) saw a pernicious rationale behind the trend toward internal evaluations, linking it with the need for government agencies to justify their decisions. This criticism was not limited to the United States. In the United Kingdom, "there is a fear within the evaluation community that 'quick and dirty' work is on the rise and that this work may be used by government agents to provide their superiors with retrospective justifications of programme effectiveness" (Pettigrew, 1996, p. 6).

In 1987, GAO reported a reduction in evaluation activities at the federal level and attributed it to a reduction in congressional funding; increases in block-grant legislation; and the reduction of "set-asides," which encouraged evaluation of public programs. In its program evaluation transition paper prepared for the 1988 incoming political administration, GAO stated that program evaluation activities in federal executive agencies were in a "depleted state" and called for a renewed commitment to program evaluation (GAO, 1988). Federal executive agencies experienced a 52% reduction in evaluation staff between 1980 and 1988, from 419 to 200 (Chelimsky, 1992). In 1990, OMB established a small evaluation function in the newly formed Evaluation, Planning and Management by Objectives (MBO) branch, tasked with revitalizing evaluation in the executive branch, but in 1994 the entire branch was dissolved (J. S. Wholey, personal communication, September 1997). In 1998, GAO reported that the resources allocated to conducting systematic assessments of program results or evaluation studies "were small and unevenly distributed across the 23 agencies we surveyed" (GAO, 1998, p. 8).

An additional burden for internal evaluators to overcome is the legacy of the halcyon days of evaluation in the 1960s when President Lyndon Johnson's Great Society effort launched many longitudinal evaluations designed to determine the impact of federal social programs. During the Johnson administration, "evaluation research" emerged as a central component in the federal policy-making process. Congress began exercising oversight on the executive branch of government by including funds for evaluation in legislation. Although numerous longitudinal evaluations of government social program were initiated during the 1960s, the complex methodologies used and the extended time frames for completion rendered many of them unsuitable for use by political operatives accustomed to rapid responses to their questions. "Evaluation fell out of favor as the federal initiatives of the 1960s and 1970s proved disappointing and early attempts at evaluation were shown to be flawed or biased" (Richardson, 1992, p. 20). The residual effect of those underutilized evaluations was to diminish the efficacy of evaluation as a useful management tool in the eyes of many government executives. Internal evaluators also received criticisms for their misplaced emphasis on measuring inputs and not accomplishments.

> In an era in which the limited resources of the federal government are stretched to the breaking point, the most serious weakness in evaluation may be the instinct of the evaluator, *particularly the internal evaluator* [italics added], to apply input measures rather than to find out if the activity under examination is actually accomplishing anything. (Richardson, 1992, p. 17)

For the foreseeable future, internal evaluation appears to be inextricably tied to budget considerations. Failure to gain acceptance as a necessary component of the organization's administration creates a chronic vulnerability for internal evaluation when organizations change executive personnel, initiate cutbacks and downsizing procedures, and confront crises. The Program Review Group, an internal evaluation function begun in 1994 in the Environmental Protection Agency's Office of Air Quality Planning and Standards (OAQPS), was slightly over two years old when severe budget cuts forced the curtailment of evaluation efforts and redirection of evaluation resources to implementation activities to comply with provisions of the Clean Air Act. In 1994, the Federal Bureau of Investigation (FBI) reduced the number of personnel assigned to the Office of Planning, Evaluation, and Audits (OPEA) and reassigned special agent investigative personnel to field assignments as a response to criticism that excessive administrative positions at FBI headquarters were held by investigators. The Office of Program Analysis and Evaluation (OPA&E) in the Office of Community Planning and Development (CPD) in the U.S. Department of Housing and Urban Development (HUD) suffered during the 1980s from inconsistent support from assistant secretaries with short tenures (three assistant secretaries and one acting assistant secretary from 1981 to 1989) and a shift in ideologies of the Reagan administration (Rymph,

1989, 1992; Sonnichsen, 1991). From a staff of approximately 70 people in 1976, OPA&E declined to a low of 18 in 1984 with a slight increase in 1988 to 26 (Rymph, 1992; Sonnichsen, 1991). In 1991, in response to budget cuts, OPA&E was reorganized as a policy implementation coordination unit, specifically excluded from analytical activities or evaluation of policy (Rymph, 1992). These examples underscore the practice of internal evaluation as a fragile enterprise, continually pursuing recognition as an integral component in organizational structures, yet exposed and susceptible to the vagaries of shifting management and governance philosophies and the accompanying funding transpositions.

There is, however, a possibility that this trend may soon begin to reverse. The passage of the Government Performance and Results Act (GPRA) in 1993 has the potential to resurrect the practice of internal evaluation within the federal executive branch of the U.S. government. The act requires federal agencies, beginning March 31, 2000, to annually submit evaluations of program performance, reviewing the degree of success in achieving the performance goals of the previous fiscal year. Whether these required evaluations will be rigorously conducted by internal evaluation specialists is problematic at this time, but compliance with the spirit of the legislation requires good faith efforts at examining and evaluating program performance. Wholey (1997) believes evaluators will have an important role in the implementation of the GPRA:

> Current reform efforts will increase the demand for training, technical assistance, and technical support that evaluators can supply—in particular, for evaluability assessment, outcome monitoring, interrupted time series studies, and qualitative evaluations of the effectiveness of public programs and of the reform efforts themselves. These demands will present exciting political, bureaucratic, and technical challenges for evaluators. (p. 130)

Unfortunately, an initial survey of federal evaluation activities does not support an optimistic outlook. In September and October 1994, Wargo (1995) collected data from 14 executive branch evaluation offices that were the most active in fiscal year 1994, in an effort to determine the effect of President Clinton's reinvention of government plan begun in 1993. The basic goal of the president's plan was to use the National Performance Review (NPR) of 1993 and the GPRA to restructure and streamline government, focusing on the client customer. Wargo reported that only 29% (4 offices) disclosed an increase in evaluation activities directly attributable to the GPRA, with the remaining 71% (10 offices) experiencing either no change or a reduction in evaluation activity. Wargo concluded that the first year of government reinvention accelerated the general erosion of federal evaluation capacity that began in the 1980s and continued through the early 1990s. In 1997, GAO reported that the implementation of the GPRA "has achieved mixed results, which will lead to highly uneven government-wide implementation in the fall of 1997" (p. 5). However, on a more optimistic note, GAO (1997) also found that "significant performance improvements were possible—even in the short term—when an agency adopted a disciplined approach to setting results-oriented goals, measuring its performance, and using performance information to improve effectiveness" (p. 5).

The government of Canada has also been one of the major practitioners of internal evaluation, particularly during the 1980s when internal evaluations were monitored and supported by the Program Evaluation Branch in the Office of the Comptroller General of Canada. However, evaluation is losing its distinct identity as evaluation units are being merged with internal audit functions (Barrados & Divorski, 1996). Segsworth (1994) reports that "in the past year, the Program Evaluation Branch of the Office of the Comptroller General disappeared as a separate entity and it is now included as part of the Audit and Evaluation Branch" (p. 253). According to Segsworth, the program evaluation function in Canada is losing status as it is merged with internal audit functions, and the evaluation function is on the decline.

However, these evaluation activities at the federal level may not accurately reflect the activities of the vast number of evaluators working in state legislatures, school districts, nonprofit organizations, development banks, and philanthropic enterprises. Observations about the use of evaluation at the state and local levels are more optimistic. Worthen (1995) reports that although politics is not absent at the state and local levels, political processes at these levels "seem to permit more demonstrable—and rational—use of evaluation data than is true at the national level" (p. 34). Basing his observations largely on educational evaluation, he notes a healthy trend toward state and local educational evaluations producing useful information that is being used to modify programs under study. Local and state educational policymakers are free enough from political influences to allow evaluation to be used to gather information needed to guide education program development (Worthen, 1995).

USE OF EVALUATION FINDINGS

Although the ultimate use of evaluation findings by organizations may sometimes fail to satisfy evaluators, utility, nevertheless, remains the focus, intent, and standard of performance for internal evaluators. Patton (1997) has long championed utility as the hallmark for judging evaluation. Stressing usefulness and a client-oriented, pragmatic approach to evaluation activity, Patton offers a utilization-focused conceptual framework that particularly applies to the practice of internal evaluation. This concept is indispensable in organizations where resources have been specifically devoted to the evaluation function and are expected to contribute, in a measurable way, to the accomplishment of the organization's mission. This focus on utility is not meant to diminish the value of evaluation activity in organizations to develop evaluation theory and contribute to a better understanding of human endeavor, but to reinforce the reality that in organizations, evaluation remains a purposeful, directed, practical endeavor intended to enlighten policy, support and enhance decision making, and improve operations.

The expectation that evaluation will somehow influence organizations because of its intrinsic value is naive. Evaluation implies accountability—responsibility for program performance—and managers are reluctant to cede external review of their program stewardship to evaluators. The adversarial relationship between program managers and evaluation staffs that accompanies many evaluative efforts finds its origins in this notion of accountability—the expectation that evaluation will detect deficiencies and suggest corrective action—and is the justification for much of the managerial opposition to evaluation. Eventual transition from an ad hoc event to successful institutionalization, where evaluation is a regular occurrence considered material to the effective functioning of the organization, requires evaluators' understanding of this adversarial phenomenon and its implications for their evaluative efforts. The significance of understanding this relationship and the importance of developing innovative approaches to minimizing its negative effect on evaluations cannot be overemphasized and will be stressed throughout the book.

Even though evaluation as an efficacious management tool may be accepted conceptually, its integration into the organization's administrative processes and operations must be continuously pursued. Internal evaluation is essentially an exchange of information between evaluators and their organization, but to maximize the effectiveness of this interface, a relationship has to be established between these two parties with an understanding of how each partner in the relationship is expected to act and react. Institutionalization of evaluation in an organization is an iterative process, based on reciprocal trust between evaluators and the executive management of the organization and a mutual recognition of the competencies and needs of the evaluators as well as the users of the evaluation product. Merely conducting evaluations in organizations, however, is insufficient for complete integration. Internal evaluators must continually market their product and become involved in the decision-making process much like other organizational entities. (The important distinction to note here is that evaluators need to become involved in the decision-making process, not in the decision making itself.) The traditional scientific orthodoxy of neutrality during scientific inquiry is valid during data collection and analysis but becomes an impediment if maintained after the evaluation is concluded.

FUTURE OF INTERNAL EVALUATION

Consulting to organizations with recommendations to alter or abandon the status quo is both a challenging and rewarding experience for those fortunate enough to be employed as internal evaluators. Wildavsky (1979) offers a colorful and paradoxical portrait of the internal evaluator:

> Evaluators must become agents of change acting in favor of programs as yet unborn and clienteles still unknown. Prepared to impose change on others, evaluators must have stability to stick with their own work. They must hang on to their own organization while preparing to aban-

> don it. They must combine political feasibility with analytic purity. Only a brave individual would predict that these qualities can be found in one and the same person and organization. (p. 213)

Wildavsky's portrayal of the role of the internal evaluator emphasizes the contradictions and dilemmas encountered by internal evaluators and the courage and independence required of the successful practitioner. The challenge to influence organizations is actualized by contributing empirical data to the decision-making process; the reward materialized in seeing positive organizational change and improvement based on evaluation findings. Evaluators working in internal settings in organizations can influence organizations through the independent production of information to aid decisionmakers and improve organizational performance, using evaluation as a tool for detecting inefficient and ineffective practices and making recommendations for positive change. Viewing organizational activities through the analytic lens of evaluation is a useful approach to prevent complacency and to detect and solve problems before they become unmanageable.

Internal evaluation has a bright future. The economic transformation, not only in the United States but also around the world, is creating enormous pressures for organizations to exhibit measurable performance. The demand for accountability and requirement for high performance in organizations, combined with the increased understanding of the value of internal evaluation as a useful strategy to enhance performance, will have major, positive implications for the practice of internal evaluation. The value of accurate and unbiased information and its ability to affect decisions will also increase the demand for evaluative activity. To adequately respond to the organization's need for information, internal evaluators will have to reframe their approach and expand their repertoire beyond traditional evaluative activities.

Evaluation and Public Policy

Much of the business of executive branch government agencies is the implementation and administration of public policy and programs designed for improvement of existing social conditions. These public programs have been and can continue to be operated without any formal evaluation. However, absent an independent review process, government programs, with their multistakeholders' diverse and sometimes conflicting views, make performance judgments difficult. The complex legislative process originating these programs, the latitude in interpreting and shaping implementation strategies, and the expectations of programs recipients render nearly impossible any objective determination of the success and impact of the program by participants in the process. The political nature of the legislative process, where compromise is often the enabling mechanism to ensure bill passage, sometimes results in ambiguous legislative language that relinquishes interpretation to the implementing agency. Stakeholder bias will almost always cloud opinions because the original intent and expectations of the parties involved are for a successful resolution to the problem that the program was designed to address.

Legislators and public administrators are disinclined to be confronted with data indicating that all is not well with legislation they sponsored or programs they administer. Internal evaluators have the capacity to assist program administrators in the public policy arena by determining if programs have succeeded or failed in pursuit of their intended purpose. The purpose of evaluation is not to find fault but to suggest improvements where necessary and publicize high performance when it is encountered. Wholey (1983) suggests that "evaluators and other analysts should place priority on management-oriented activities designed to facilitate achievement of demonstrable improvement in government management, performance, and results" (p. 8).

An example of effective evaluative feedback to Congress occurred in 1989 when the Office of Evaluation and Inspections (OEI), Office of Inspector General, Department of Health and Human Services examined the financial arrangements between physicians and health care businesses (Sonnichsen, 1991; U.S. Department of Health and Human Services, 1989). This study examined conflicts of interest that may arise when physicians refer patients to clinics or laboratories that are owned by the referring doctor. The study discovered that 12% of the doctors in the Medicare program had financial interests in outside health care entities and that the patients of these physicians received 45% more laboratory services than the general Medicare population. OEI estimated that the higher use of services by patients of physicians owning clinical laboratories cost the Medicare program $28 million in 1987. The evaluation report was furnished to Congress and legislation was passed restricting Medicare payments to these laboratories.

Evaluation may become superfluous in highly politicized environments. The axiom that ideology is the enemy of analysis may prevent evaluation data from being debated in open forums, or worse, from being collected and disseminated. A potentially crippling impediment to the successful practice of internal evaluation is the introduction into an organization of a senior management team infused with either a political philosophy or management system that is unyielding to the value and use of empirical data and analysis. In these environments, evaluation will never be instituted and if found established, will either be neutralized through bureaucratic devices or disbanded outright.

Evaluation also has the potential for malevolent use. Nowhere is this more evident than in the Heritage Foundation's conservative, polemical book *Mandate for Leadership II* (Butler, Sanera, & Weinrad, 1984). Michael Sanera (1984), describing techniques for implementing a conservative political agenda, asserts that

> policy evaluation is a key instrument, uniquely suited to the purposes of conservative government, but it currently is underutilized. Properly employed, policy evaluations can be used for two purposes: to bring about policy change within government programs, and to combat the growth of government by demonstrating the wasteful and destructive nature of expansive government. (p. 541)

According to Sanera, policy evaluation can "underscore the general fraudulence of liberal assumptions and promises concerning the effects of affirmative government" (p. 543). Sanera believes that "the control over information is perhaps the single most important resource of the career bureaucracy" and many political executives fail to recognize this phenomenon, leaving information production in the hands of bureaucrats (p. 541). For Sanera, policy evaluation is a tool for conservative government seeking to halt government growth and institute reductions:

The political executive can use program evaluation as a principal way to find and objectively document performance gaps. Once documented, the political executive can use the evidence to initiate fundamental program changes. In other words, the political executive must ensure that the information-producing resources of his agency are gathering information which is useful for the development and implementation of his political agenda. (p. 542)

Internal government evaluators must remain alert, particularly as political administrations change, to the possibility that they may be used as tools for establishing a political ideology with total disregard for the collection of objective, factual data.

The Self-Evaluating Organization

In a seminal work on policy analysis, Wildavsky (1979) pondered why organizations do not evaluate their own activities and suggested that the ideal organization would be self-evaluating, leading to improved understanding and accomplishment of its objectives:

The ideal organization . . . would continuously monitor its own activities so as to determine how well it was meeting its objectives or even whether these objectives should continue to prevail. When evaluation suggested that a change in objectives or programs to achieve them was desirable, these proposals would be taken seriously by top decision-makers who would institute the necessary changes without vested interest in continuing current activities. Instead they would steadily pursue new alternatives to better serve desired outcomes. (p. 213)

Is this idyllic portrayal of an organization realistic, probable, or possible? Can organizations conduct introspective activities and then rationally act on their outcomes? Can individuals within an organization produce useful information that will be used in decision-making forums? Wildavsky's vision can be achieved, but it requires building a conceptual and structural framework for implementing a self-evaluating mechanism that demands commitment by both evaluators and organizational leadership.

In some organizations, the self-examining, introspective acts of reviewing, auditing, evaluating, and inspecting are highly regarded feedback mechanisms, with the results playing an important role in resource allocation, personnel actions, operational strategies, planning, marketing, and decision making. Social scientists, on the other hand, are openly skeptical that internal organizational review processes are sufficiently independent and objective for their results to accurately describe and guide program direction and performance. The social scientist external to the organization views with some cynicism organizational attempts at self-analysis, citing insufficient expertise in science, inadequate evaluation training and education, and empathic allegiance to the organization as material impairments to impartial internal evaluative functions. The remaining chapters of this book will be devoted to discussing the structural arrangements, organization and evaluator commitment, and management and evaluation techniques for meaningful, internal self-evaluation to occur.

An Emerging Paradigm

The concept of the self-evaluating organization obligates internal evaluators to reexamine traditional evaluation practices. Changes are beginning to take place in the practice of internal evaluation to customize techniques for increased usefulness to organizations. The evolution is replacing the neutral-investigator research model of evaluation with an applied science, interactive management-oriented model. The old model of internal evaluation isolated evaluators from the organization and ceded responsibility for interpretation and use of results to the organization. Internal evaluators believed that detachment from the organization was necessary to preserve their independence. They further believed that evaluation findings were self-evident and would be appropriately acted on by rational officials in the organization.

The concept of internal evaluation as an isolated research function in an organization fails to recognize the indispensable communication linkage between evaluators and users. If evaluation is to precipitate positive improvement in organizations, internal evaluators must extend their involvement beyond data collection and analysis and become the mechanism to channel evaluation results to the organization. Modern internal evaluators will have to become advocates of evaluation findings and recommendations if evaluation data are to be included in discussions and debates over organizational issues. Guiding appropriate decisionmakers through the interpretation of evaluation results, persuading them of the efficacy of recommended changes, and advocating positive change will become responsibilities of evaluators working within organizations. In 1988, I suggested what I believed was an effective approach for internal evaluators to increase utilization of their work and become recognized as contributors to the organization's mission:

> Internal evaluators have to view themselves as change agents and participants in policy formulation, migrating from the traditional position of neutrality to an activist role in the organizational decision-making process. The practice of *Advocacy Evaluation* positions internal evaluators to become active participants in developing and implementing organizational improvements. Operating under an advocacy philosophy, evaluation becomes a tool for change and a vehicle for evaluators to influence the organization. (Sonnichsen, 1988, p. 141)

Since that writing a decade ago, I am even more convinced that the proper role for evaluators working within modern, complex organizations is increasingly more holistic, involving not only advocacy but a philosophical orientation to the belief that evaluators can change and improve organizations by using their skills in a myriad of consultative modes. *Advocacy evaluation* (discussed in detail in Chapter 5) is a philosophical approach to the practice of internal evaluation. It is an activist orientation for evaluators to ensure that evaluation findings and recommendations receive the organization's attention.

In the 1970s and 1980s, the focus of evaluation moved into the organizational workplace without an explicit recognition of the contextual change in the environment. Traditional social science methodological practices were used in organizations with little regard for the new audiences, clients, and users of internal evaluation information.

The new paradigm began to emerge when it was discovered that assumptions about evaluation use were flawed, a neutral-investigator orientation was not effective in influencing organizations, and evaluation findings were either being ignored or underutilized. Evaluation practice has traditionally been dominated by the natural science paradigm of hypothetico-deductive methodology (Patton, 1997). This scientific tradition of experimentation and emphasis on quantitative measurement techniques has been one of the reasons for the reluctance of organizational decisionmakers to accept internal evaluation as a useful and value-added technique. A 1976 symposium on the use of evaluation by federal agencies, attended by both evaluators and policymakers, surfaced the complaint that the experimental research design, then dominant in evaluation practice, was neither relevant nor timely to the requirements of agency decisionmakers (Chelimsky, 1977). The traditional scientific process of formulating hypotheses, conducting experiments, making observations, and reporting results grounds the internal evaluation process in scientific methodology. The application of these scientific principles inside organizations, however, requires adjusting to the environment and adapting the scientific method to accommodate the information needs of the organization.

Wholey (1983) writes that "because the more 'researchy' evaluation designs often are unfeasible or too costly we suggested evaluation approaches more appropriate to the environments in which public managers operate" (p. 201). Complex data presentations are often not clearly understood, and the traditional neutrality of researchers precluded their participation in the data digestion process in organizations. The new paradigmatic approach to internal evaluation engages the organization as both partner and benefactor. A symbiotic relationship is formed, with evaluators receiving support from the organization while the organization benefits from independent assessment and empirical evidence about organizational activities. This new paradigm differs from the traditional approach by recognizing that evaluation's influence in an organization requires an active interchange between evaluation and the organization. The new paradigm employs the concept of advocacy evaluation, the commitment of evaluators to ensure that evaluation findings and recommendations are clearly understood by appropriate stakeholders and receive a fair hearing during debates. This emerging paradigm recognizes the contextual environment of organizations where internal evaluation is practiced, the needs of internal clients, the expanded role for internal evaluators, and the reciprocal relationship between evaluators and clients.

The defining characteristics of this emerging paradigm are the following:

- ◇ *Adaptation of evaluation principles:* The conversion of evaluation research tenets to effective application inside organizations
- ◇ *Activist evaluator orientation:* A recognition that internal evaluators must engage and involve the organization in evaluative activities
- ◇ *Decision-making support:* Recognition that the primary purpose of internal evaluation is to support and improve the decision-making process
- ◇ *Change agent evaluator:* Recognition that evaluation is a change mechanism
- ◇ *Product marketing:* Viewing internal evaluation as a product to be "sold" to the organization as a beneficial endeavor
- ◇ *Client focus:* Developing an empathy and understanding of client views, needs, and expectations
- ◇ *Information production:* Viewing internal evaluation as balanced information production and dissemination to prevent information asymmetry among participants debating organizational issues
- ◇ *Advocacy:* Active engagement with the organization in publicizing, clarifying, and supporting evaluation findings and recommended courses of action resulting from evaluative activities
- ◇ *Recommendations:* Issuing recommended courses of action based on evaluative activities and following up implementation efforts
- ◇ *Consulting:* Internal evaluators moving beyond the traditional evaluator role and functioning as consultants to the organization
- ◇ *Coalition building:* Recognizing evaluator responsibility for incorporating and justifying evaluation as a value-added function inside an organization

These 11 characteristics define the new internal evaluation paradigm and constitute the organizing framework for the book. The remaining chapters will be devoted to an explanation and expansion of these themes.

CONCLUSION

Modern technology and public disenchantment with government and corporate enterprises have combined to create new environments for public and private organizations, increasing pressures to perform. With constant change now affecting how organizations function, coping skills and problem-solving mechanisms will have to be developed to ensure effective performance and organizational survival. Internal evaluation is one available technique supporting the decision-making process by offering unbiased data on programs and issues affecting the organization. The rationale for promoting internal evaluation as a management tool is not that the skills for problem solving and program reviews are not available within the organizations but that these resources have usually not been identified, aggregated, and specifically charged with the responsibility for independent assessments, nor do they have the requisite autonomy to bring insightful and fresh perspectives to relevant issues.

Evidence exists that internal evaluation is being used and is having an impact on organizations. However, internal evaluation will not be portrayed in this book as a panacea to all organizational problems, but as one analytical approach that can assist in sorting through the parochial viewpoints, self-interests, and emotions that attach to many organizational issues. Stripped of its jargon and fixation on methodological subtleties, evaluation is simply designed to produce factual information for program improvement. It is recognized that evaluation is but one input in the decision-making process; nevertheless, it represents an independent, data-based, alternative voice for use in problem solving and support for decisionmakers.

Integration and acceptance of the evaluation function in the organization are preconditions for a high impact internal evaluation office. However, acceptance and use do not obviate the need for routine justification of the value of internal evaluation to the organization. The nature and volume of work assigned can be used to measure the performance of an internal evaluation office, but a more important gauge of the magnitude of influence of evaluation on the organization is the significant positive changes effected by evaluative effort.

In his 1979 seminal work on policy analysis, Wildavsky challenged organizations to become self-evaluating. The establishment of an internal evaluation office is one step in that direction. Evaluation personnel can assist organizations in the all-important tasks of introspection, examining and reviewing programs and performance and offering alternative approaches to routinized organizational rituals. However, it would be naive to anticipate that the establishment of an internal evaluation office will immediately affect an organization or that the evaluation office will be graciously accepted as an integral component in the organization. Internal evaluators must live with the consequence that their evaluative services are not intrinsically attractive. Installing evaluation in an organization is an iterative, long-range process. What can be expected is that where evaluation has been adopted, properly located in the organization's hierarchy, and operating independently with competent evaluators, it can influence the organizational decision-making process. This use of internal evaluator-consultants will amplify organizational capacity to cope with change and remain alert to perturbations in the internal and external environments that demand immediate attention. There is enormous potential benefit for those organizations that discover the advantages of using an internal evaluation staff.

RECOMMENDED FOR FURTHER READING

General Accounting Office. (1987). *Federal evaluation: Fewer units, reduced resources, different studies from 1980.* Washington, DC: Author.

General Accounting Office. (1998). *Program evaluation: Agencies challenged by new demand for information on program results.* Washington, DC: Author.
   GAO periodically reviews the status of internal evaluation units in the U.S. federal government. See the above GAO publications for historical data.

Chapter 3

Understanding the Internal Evaluation Context

KEY CHAPTER TOPICS

- ❖ Internal evaluation's role in organizations
- ❖ Internal versus external evaluation
- ❖ Theories of organizations
- ❖ Decision making in organizations
- ❖ Organizational learning
- ❖ Information asymmetry

Given the importance and complexity of the environment where internal evaluation is practiced, it seems prudent to examine the functioning of this environment so that internal evaluators will be equipped to successfully navigate in the turbulent world of organizations. Organizations are seldom tidy environments easily categorized. Without knowledge of the theory of organizations, management roles, organizational values and priorities, culture, the mechanics of the decision-making process, and the role of information, evaluators are limiting their potential effectiveness. Little evaluation research has focused on organizational context and culture; an under-

standing of these organizational phenomena prepares evalua-
tors to conduct more useful evaluations (Preskill, 1991). Ac-
cording to Attkisson, Brown, and Hargreaves (1978), program
evaluation has been victimized by its own limited concept of
organizational functioning. Studying and understanding how
organizations function are the first steps for the internal evalu-
ator before beginning the design and execution of an evaluation.

Many fine books exist on organizational theory and behav-
ior and how organizations function, and no attempt will be
made to duplicate that body of work. The goal of this chapter
is to expand the awareness of internal evaluators of the relevant
processes, behaviors, key components, and relationships that
exist in organizations that are important and particularly rele-
vant to the evaluation function. Learning about and under-
standing organizations is an endeavor combining experience
with study. Internal evaluators, with a basic knowledge of
organizations acquired through their insider location, can ob-
serve and thoughtfully reflect on the attributes and unique
features of their organizations and, armed with this information,
contribute to improved operations. This chapter begins by
discussing the role of internal evaluation in organizations and
how culture, organizational conditions, and behavior affect it.
The importance of understanding theories of organizations,
organizational learning capacity, and the decision-making pro-
cess is discussed next. The chapter concludes with a review of
the role and value of information in organizations.

Role of Internal Evaluation in Organizations

Complex organizational issues are characterized by multiple, discordant
views. Evaluators operating internally in organizations can assist the
decision-making process in this new, complicated, change-driven environment. Two dominant themes form the conceptual basis for this book
and serve as the intellectual framework for discussing the practice of
internal evaluation:

1. Organizations can benefit from an independent fact-gathering body, inside the organization, developing empirically based data to inform and improve the decision-making process.
2. Competent evaluators, properly positioned in the organization and with access to executive decisionmakers, can act in the capacity of consultants, collecting and reporting objective data, challenging the status quo, and offering an unemotional, unbiased, empirical perspective on issues.

The successful achievement of these goals by internal evaluators involves the paradox of simultaneous organizational commitment and detachment. Internal evaluators must have empathy and identify with the core organizational mission, yet retain the ability to assume the mantle of an objective observer while examining organizational phenomena.

The basic function of the internal evaluator is to support planing and management to maximize the amount of intelligence and analytical discipline involved in the decision-making process (Love, 1983b). Research by evaluators can help organizations avoid the negative impact of capricious events. Failure to maintain pace with the blinding speed of technological advances, societal evolution, and significant political events may contribute to loss of market share or the congressional budget ax.

EVALUATION CONTEXT

Because internal evaluation takes place in organizations, it is contextually bound, conceptually committed to the core mission of the organization, and regulated by the policies, rules, procedures, administrative constraints, operational parameters, and cultural norms of the organization.[1] Although internal evaluators conduct their activities within the common framework that many organizations share, each evaluation office must study and adapt to the idiosyncratic nature of its own organization. I would be reluctant to portray the Federal Bureau of Investigation (FBI) as the typical organization, yet evaluation has been successfully adapted to its organizational culture. Organizations have distinct purposes, personalities, historical backgrounds, and approaches to goal accomplishment. Events, traditions, patterns of behavior, and administrative processes that comprise the organization are particularly relevant to the evaluation function and must be understood by internal evaluators if they are to be successful. A survey by Mayne (1994) of the 15 most experienced heads of evaluation in the Canadian federal government found that internal evaluation significantly adapts to organizational realities. Love (1991) stresses the importance of understanding the organizational context for internal evaluators, and Broskowski and Driscoll (1978) highlight the theme that program evaluation must be planned and implemented within the context of organizational structures and management processes. They believe that evaluators must have management skills and comprehend organizational operations before they can be responsive to complex organizational issues.

The placement of evaluators internally in organization does not lessen the quality or independence of information produced but benefits the evaluators by providing them with unique opportunities to observe and understand the organizational context. Torres (1991) articulates the value in studying and knowing the inner workings of the organization:

> The continuing experience and feedback—in short, the institutional memory—of internal evaluators makes the opportunity to study, understand, and interpret multiple contexts (e.g., political, economic, historical, physical) even greater. First, an initial analysis of these influences helps the evaluator understand where potential pitfalls in evaluation implementation and use lie. Labeling and diagramming these contextual operatives aids in understanding the relationships among them. Additionally, the evaluator can identify individuals who figure prominently in the operation of these influences. Continual reference to and refinement of this mapping alerts us to political undercurrents and unclear decision-making hierarchies in the implementation of evaluation activities, and so forth. Additionally, knowledge and understanding of these influences can help set realistic expectations about the pace and scope of change within the organization. As a result, evaluators may experience less frustration and exasperation.
>
> Second, for the evaluator, understanding the overall context including all major organizational goals and operational areas is central to (a) understanding organizational leaders, (b) developing evaluative systems which assess programs in terms of those goals, and (c) helping evaluators discern possible resolutions to conflicts among various constituents. Too often evaluators expend their resources on developing narrowly focused, but technically sophisticated assessment systems.
>
> Finally, evaluators can check their impressions of the context with organizational members periodically. Such checking not only aids in

developing the scheme but also gives members an opportunity to reflect on their own environment and clarify it for themselves. This documentation can provide valuable information about the operation of the organization to its constituents. As they come to understand issues within an overall contextual scheme, more traditional and specific evaluation findings are likely to have greater meaning. (p. 192)

INTERNAL EVALUATORS VERSUS EXTERNAL EVALUATORS

Organizations choosing to evaluate their activities have the option of instituting an internal evaluation function or hiring external evaluators and conducting evaluations on a contract basis. The two key issues to resolve when selecting an evaluation configuration are determination of the evaluation purpose and the primary use of findings. In other words, the client and the audience are the two decisive factors to consider before choosing one version of evaluation over another. If the organization is the primary client and the organization's hierarchy and program managers the principal audience, then internal evaluators should be the preference. However, if circumstances dictate that independent program performance needs to be continually assessed for use by externally funding organizations and summative rather than formative information is required, external evaluators may offer a greater perception of independence. Table 3.1 compares the advantages and disadvantages of internal versus external evaluators.

Organizations choosing internal evaluators or opting to contract out to external evaluators should maintain a flexible position on this issue. Both have pluses and minuses, and individual situations should dictate the choice. Placing internal evaluators inside the organization and supplementing them with external evaluators in appropriate situations may offer the greatest flexibility in responding to the needs of most organizations.

ROLE OF EVALUATION IN ORGANIZATIONAL ASSESSMENT

Demands for accountability and results dominate the management literature and influence management styles in organizations. Awareness

TABLE 3.1
Advantages and Disadvantages
of Internal and External Evaluators

INTERNAL EVALUATORS

Advantages
- Commitment to the organization
- Knowledge of the organization's personnel and operations
- Quick response to evaluation requests
- Greater perceived credibility by organizational components
- Function as an institutional memory
- Frequent client contact
- Support of the decision-making process
- Access to data
- Lower costs
- Greater ability to observe the organization's operations
- Flexibility to assume other than evaluation tasks on short notice
- Greater ability to monitor recommendation implementation
- Potential to educate organization regarding value of evaluation
- Serve as change agents
- Continuity of evaluation effort

Disadvantages
- Possible lack of power in the organization
- Possible lack of independence
- Ethical dilemmas
- Burden of additional tasks
- Perceived organizational bias
- May lack technical evaluation expertise

EXTERNAL EVALUATORS

Advantages
- May possess superior evaluation skills
- Perceived as more independent
- Bring fresh perspective to organizational issues
- Greater objectivity
- Less susceptible to co-optation
- Can objectively assess organization-wide programs that may include
  the internal evaluators as participants

Disadvantages
- Lack knowledge of the organization
- Limited access to organizational data
- More expensive

of what is happening in an organization is of paramount concern to modern managers. Effective management requires continuous feedback of reliable data on the operation and administration of the organization's activities. A comprehensive management oversight and assessment program will routinely review all organizational programs, activities, assets, personnel behavior, and resources. Essential elements of a complete assessment program should include, but are not limited to, ongoing performance measurement, inspections, operational and financial audits, evaluations, management controls reviews, quality assessments, and personnel integrity investigations. These analytical functions are not mutually exclusive, but overlap and complement each other. Properly implemented, they present a seamless, independent perspective to senior management on activities and problems in the organization.

Internal evaluation should be an integral component in this analytical review process, not a separate and distinct entity. Successful institutionalization of evaluation in an organization will require an understanding of the existence of other review functions, their purpose and goals, and the coordination of internal evaluation activities to both supplement and complement these other functions. The FBI combines inspections, financial audits, evaluations, strategic planning, and personnel integrity investigations in a single division and requires all senior managers to spend time in that division because of its value in executive development. Evaluations and investigations are both contained in the Office of Inspector General in the Department of Health and Human Services. Fair and objective oversight reviews within an organization can enhance productivity, detect problems in their incipient stages, and increase efficiency and effectiveness.

Organizational Diagnosis

Diagnosing organizations and gaining a comprehensive knowledge of their administration and operations are ongoing tasks for internal evaluators. "Familiarity with the organizational context, including norms and extraorganizational constraints that guide individuals' behavior, is helpful during all phases of an evaluation (design, data collection and analysis, and use)" (Torres, Preskill, & Piontek, 1996, p. 52). For internal evaluators, diagnosing organizations is not an academic exercise but a pragmatic endeavor designed primarily to identify the decision-making processes and power and authority positions.

ORGANIZATIONAL CULTURE

Organizational culture affects the entire spectrum of the internal evaluation process from data collection to reflection on findings to acceptance of recommended changes. Culture is the overwhelmingly essential variable determining whether an organization will even accept, tolerate, or use internal evaluation. The FBI has a long history of inspecting all field offices and headquarters divisions on a regular basis. These intensive, biennial reviews of all aspects of individual and group performance condition personnel to accept (but not necessarily welcome) the concept of work oversight. This culturally embedded phenomenon helped achieve acceptance of evaluation when it was initiated in the early 1970s. Radin (1987), commenting on the FBI culture, described the FBI as an example of a Weberian hierarchical organization that historically operated with a centralized management staff and employees who experienced a high level of socialization and identification with the agency. In my experience, scientific organizations are the least likely to welcome evaluation because scientists believe that only they completely understand their complex programs and they resent any intrusion into their domains.

Culture is a complex, accrued, and continually developing characteristic of organizations. It is the social character of a company or agency that shapes both internal and external relationships. And it is important for internal evaluators because it affects

the decision-making process,

the acceptance of review and self-evaluation processes,

organizational openness to change,

the value of information in the decision-making process,

organizational reaction to criticism,

an organization's ability to learn,

data availability and dependability, and

the cooperation of individuals with researchers.

Internal evaluators have an advantage, due to their vantage point within the organization, to monitor, analyze, and reflect on the organizational culture and its effect on their evaluative activities. Culture defines an organization and is a significant determinant affecting the success of an internal evaluation function. The most significant implication of culture for internal evaluators is its affect on the decision-making process. In traditional, stabilized, hierarchically aligned organizations with clearly established, centralized lines of authority, internal evaluators achieve their power (and thus the ability to influence the organization) through the support of senior officials and "champions" who provide legitimacy for the evaluation process. In matrix-type or consensus-managed organizations where executives share authority and responsibility, internal evaluators are required to build coalitions and consensus among executives to achieve legitimacy.

ORGANIZATIONAL CONDITIONS

The most significant and relevant activities in organizations usually attain the status of programs, and program managers are the primary interfaces for evaluators. These encounters set the stage for evaluation activities. Although each organization has specific adaptations based on purpose, there are certain conditions that internal evaluators will encounter in most organizations. I believe that the following axioms are important for evaluators working within organizations to understand:

1. **Program managers are reluctant to point out flaws in their programs to their superiors**

   It is contrary to human nature to be completely accurate and truthful when describing to a superior the activities in a program for which you are responsible. The picture portrayed will contain embellishments, distortions, omissions, and probably an overly optimistic outlook of the program's potential. Little incentive exists for complete honesty. Careers, income, reputation, advancement, ego, and self-esteem are at stake. In a study of upward communications by Read (1962) reported by Katz and Kahn (1978), subordinates with strong upward-mobility aspirations were less accurate than those who were less ambitious. "Full and objective reporting might be penalized by the supervisor or regarded as espionage by peers" (Katz & Kahn, 1978, p. 447). Therefore, the description of a program or project may bear little resemblance to the actual workings of the program or project. Program managers rationalize this approach to program description by assuming that any current deficiencies in the program will be identified and corrected before noticed by executive personnel. Positive news is always better received than detailed descriptions of unsolved problems!

2. **Few programs function at a sustained superior level**
Programs are complex entities and seldom reach optimum potential. There are deadlines, production schedules, personnel problems, quotas, resource constraints, and human inefficiencies. The corollary to this axiom is that evaluators can almost always find some deficiencies within a program.

3. **Objectivity about a program is inversely proportional to the distance of the observer from the program**
The closer one is to the program, the greater the attachment and commitment and the lesser the objectivity. As the distance from the program increases, the commitment and attachment diminishes and the potential for objectivity improves. (This axiom is particularly important to consider when deciding where to locate internal evaluators in the hierarchy of an organization. Placing them near senior management and away from program operations increases the potential for objectivity.)

4. **It is difficult, if not impossible, to separate the deficiencies in a program from the stewardship of the program**
Leadership and management of a program are inexorably tied to program administration and operation, and credit and blame attach equally to the person in charge.

5. **Careers depend, in large part, on performance of programs over which managers and executives have authority and responsibility**

   Perceived positive performance is the goal, if not the reality, that program personnel strive to portray. This axiom is the basis for a significant portion of the resistance evaluators encounter when attempting to evaluate a program.

6. **Authority and responsibility are not always allocated in appropriate amounts to program managers**

   This creates dysfunctional imbalances where managers who have insufficient authority to make proper decisions are, nevertheless, held responsible for a program's success or failure.

7. **Programs, once initiated, develop survival mechanisms designed to ensure their continued existence**

   There are limited organizational incentives to periodically review, in a summative manner, a program for which you are personally responsible and recommend its discontinuance. On the contrary, prestige, power, self-esteem, and reputation dictate that even marginally effective programs be maintained. It is the rare organization that rewards failure or the individual who focuses attention on it.

The above conditions exist in most organizations. They are listed here to illustrate some of the prevalent, complex inner workings of organizations so that evaluators can be better equipped to practice and integrate evaluation. Obviously, this list does not include all the conditions and situations in organizations, but it does present some of the particularly relevant dynamics that evaluators are likely to encounter.

CLARIFYING PROGRAM OPERATION

In my experience, and I suspect this is common, many program administrators succumb to the "in-box, out-box" syndrome. Seldom questioning either the former office holder or their own actions, they simply rely on their intuition or their predecessors' instructions on job functions and continue to move paperwork from their in-box to their out-box. This robotic adherence to routinized program functions per-petuates original program operations and precludes any imaginative or creative endeavors at discovering improvements. It is a conformable posture for incumbent managers reluctant to initiate changes that might embarrass the previous occupant of the position, who may now be their superior. Program administrators often have their sights set on promo-tions, and maintaining the status quo precludes being labeled a "boat rocker." Internal evaluators can question program assumptions and clarify goals and activities unencumbered by emotional attachment to the program.

A corollary to the secure in-box, out-box management syndrome is the "sunk-cost" management approach to decision making. In this scenario, the newly appointed manager of an expensive program as-sumes that past and recurring costly funding outlays legitimize the program operation and that it would be foolish to question underlying assumptions or theories. Anesthetized by previous funding decisions, the incumbent manager feels compelled to proceed with the program or project, spending available funds without any attempts to discover if originally intended expectations are being met. A classic example of sunk-cost management (Box 3.1) occurred in the FBI's Fingerprint Identification Division.

The in-box, out-box and sunk-cost management approaches are but two examples of inattentive and ineffectual management styles that highlight the importance of examining and questioning program theo-ries of operation. During the life span of the automated fingerprint project, many managers and executives had opportunities to conduct the same review conducted by the evaluators, yet none chose to do so because they believed that the significant commitment of funds pre-cluded halting an expensive project and admitting failure. Here, internal evaluators, with neither preconceived notions nor involvement in the project, were able to objectively challenge the underlying assumptions, question the viability of the project, and recommend termination.

Theories of Organizations

Theoretical organizational constructs are meaningful for internal evaluators because their understanding offers insights into the organi-

---

Box 3.1   ॐ

Approximately 35,000 fingerprint cards are submitted daily to the FBI for identification. Their processing is labor intensive, requiring several finger-print examiners to review each card until final identification is determined. In an attempt to speed the process of identifying and matching newly submitted fingerprint cards, a moving "beltway" was designed to replace manual procedures and automatically move the fingerprint cards along a path where examiners could more efficiently perform the requisite identi-fication and processing functions. The beltway was expected to reduce the turnaround time for processing fingerprint cards submitted by police de-partments and other agencies. After several years of design and a $40 million investment in the development and building of the beltway, the efficacy of the beltway concept was questioned by the Office of Manage-ment and Budget (OMB) during annual FBI budget hearings. After OMB questioned FBI Director William Sessions on the value of continued funding for this project, Sessions asked the Office of Planning, Evaluation, and Audits (OPEA) to review the beltway project. Studying the reality of the beltway versus its expectations revealed that the operating concept was faulty, the project was behind in development, and it could not resolve the dilemma it was designed to alleviate. Yet three executives in charge of the operation had continued it, essentially because of the millions of dollars that had already been spent. OPEA's recommendation for discontinuing the project was approved.

---

zation's reaction to the development and use of evaluative information. Oman (1989) believes models of organizations have decision-making implications important for evaluators to understand:

> The classic bureaucratic model suggests a concentration of power at the peak of the organizational hierarchy. In organizations that conform to this pattern, the evaluator is less concerned about the involvement and support of organizational actors at lower levels. If the top decisionmaker can be convinced of the merits of a study recommendation, lower-level organizational actors will follow. If an evaluation is being conducted in an organization that conforms to [an] action-theory model, however, decision-making power may be dispersed over several levels. When an organization conforms to this model, it is essential that the evaluator gain the support of decisionmakers at various levels. It may be necessary

to make the evaluation process participative and involve all the individuals concerned. (p. 77)

The traditional Weberian hierarchical model of bureaucratic organization survives in many permutations and is the point of departure for most organizational theorists seeking to explain the inner workings of organizations. Weber's "rational," rule-based bureaucracy model, with its dominating hierarchy, rigid lines of authority, and clear role definition, remains the essential structure of most organizations today. The FBI is but one of many federal government organizations that are highly centralized, operating out of Washington, D.C., that conform to the Weberian model. Even though the traditional "bureaucratic" model of organizations is still prevalent, new technologies, diverse markets, and increased competition have forced changes in organizational structures to speed the decision-making process and allow rapid coordination across functional division lines (Rainey, 1991). Some organizations are now aligned along functions, products, or hybrid combinations of these. To stimulate creativity and innovation, structures without hierarchy, referred to as parallel structures, collateral systems, entrepreneurial teams, "skunk works," and so on, are being created (Blake & Mouton, 1988). These institutional arrangements have important implications for internal evaluators because they affect power alignments, decision-making authorities, determination of client(s), and the ultimate distribution of evaluation reports.

SYSTEMS THINKING

Viewing organizations as systems is an analytical process. It can help internal evaluators conduct inquiries into programs and problems by compelling them to focus on the interconnectedness of organizational entities and the consequences of their actions in one area on another. Systems thinking is a disciplinary framework for dealing with complexity, for seeing patterns of change and interrelationships, for seeing all the component elements of the "whole" rather than static "snapshots" (Senge, 1990; Vaill, 1996). Vaill (1996) coined the expression "permanent white water" to describe the "complex, turbulent, changing environment in which we are all trying to operate" (p. 4). "A systems approach at least helps an investigator understand that the problem is to discover the underlying connections and interdependencies" (Vaill, 1996, p. 108). Open systems theory and sociotechnical theory are two relevant organizational theories that view organizations as sets of systems with both social and technological dimensions. The relevance of these two theories is to sensitize internal evaluators to understand that organizations are combinations of interconnected systems and evaluative-induced changes in one system often affect others. Additionally, internal evaluators need to comprehend the technical and human dimensions of all systems during evaluations.

OPEN SYSTEMS THEORY

Viewing organizations as networks of systems with both social and technological aspects is one convenient approach to the study of organizations that incorporates all organizational phenomena, stressing the interconnectedness of each part to the whole. The systems approach espoused by Katz and Kahn (1978), although more a descriptive than theoretical approach to analyzing organizations, has increasingly been used as a framework for categorizing information about organizations (Rainey, 1991). Organizations viewed as systems have inputs, some transformational kind of activity conducted around these inputs, and an output or result of the inputs and activities.

A similar but alternative perspective is taken by Nadler and Tushman (1992), who believe that organizations can be understood as an arrangement of components (task, individuals, organizational arrangements, informal organization) that "fit" together in varying degrees of congruence. More effective organizations (defined as behavior that leads to higher levels of goal attainment, utilization of resources, and adaptation) are those with greater degrees of congruence. Viewing organizations from a systems perspective permits internal evaluators to construct explanations of organizations without being misled or biased by mission statements, organizational goals and objectives, or the multiple agendas that exist in most organizations. It is difficult to separate organizations into discrete components, and evaluating one entity invariably has consequences for other groups.

SOCIOTECHNICAL THEORY

Because organizations are groups of people organized around a common goal, they can be viewed as having both a *technical* (technology, systems, equipment, and material) and a *social* (human interaction, communication, motivation, and psychological) dimension. All organizations have some form of these two elements and a relationship between them. These two dimensions are inseparable, interdependent, and aligned in organizations so that each dimension has important consequences for the other (Morgan, 1986). Sociotechnical systems theory examines the vital interface between people and technology, recognizing that to produce either a product or a service in an organization both the social system and the technical system need to operate jointly (Huse & Cummings, 1985). This duality in organizational configuration has important consequences for internal evaluators who must understand that evaluating a technical organizational problem has human consequences and vice versa. Farley (1991) suggests that the sociotechnical theory of organizations offers a framework for evaluation in business and industry that overcomes the inadequacies of the rational organizational framework. For her, current philosophical, political, social, and economic trends may be forcing a "paradigmatic revolution" in organizational research and practice, requiring evaluators to reconsider the theoretical contexts between evaluators and corporate entities and corporate audiences.

The sociotechnical approach to understanding how organizations function provides a set of assumptions relevant to current corporate operating environments that have several important implications for evaluators (Farley, 1991):

- ❖ The sociotechnical framework frees evaluators from compartmentalized lines of inquiry, allowing them to let the context define the analysis rather than vice versa.
- ❖ The sociotechnical framework demands that evaluation be openly normative as well as practical.
- ❖ Treatment of the corporation as an open system means that evaluation has both a substantive and an instrumental role to play.

❖ The sociotechnical organization has multiple interests, pluralistic authority and accountability for decision making, and nontraditional labor-management distinctions, requiring evaluators to be responsive to multiple interests, not just management alone.

For evaluators working in organizations, it is essential to understand the relationships between the technical and social dimensions and how evaluative activities of one dimension inevitable affect the other.

Combining the open systems perspective of organizations with the sociotechnical approach to studying organizations offers internal evaluators an analytical lens to view and study organizations that accounts for technology, organizational arrangements, and the needs and concerns of employees. This explanatory approach to interpreting organizational actions ensures that internal evaluators do not overlook either the technological/structural components in an organization or the human/social aspect when conducting evaluations and making recommendations for change. By remaining alert to the complex interactions and interdependencies among people, technology, and their organizational arrangements, internal evaluators are better equipped and more sensitive to the potential consequences of their evaluative efforts and more professional in their approach to serving the organization.

Organizational Learning

Considerable effort is expended by organizations seeking factual answers and effective solutions to complex issues. I vividly recall my frustration in attending endless numbers of meetings scheduled to address recurring problems that were replicas of predicaments that had been previously addressed. Promotions, lateral transfers, preference transfers, retirements, and geographical personnel moves all contribute to the "reinventing the wheel" syndrome, thereby minimizing the learning experience by separating the decisionmaker from the results of the decision. "Herein lies the core *learning dilemma* that confronts organizations: *we learn best from experience but we never directly experience the consequences of many of our most important decisions* [italics in the original]" (Senge, 1990, p. 23). Certainly, personnel turnover, political and ideological shifts, and environmental permutations contribute to the changing nature of problems, but organizations are, nevertheless, generally ineffective at identifying and addressing the root causes of problems when they occur, thereby reinforcing the inevitability of being faced with similar problems in the future.

To overcome deficiencies in data collection, analysis, storage, conversion to knowledge, and application to problem solving, organizations need to develop the ability to "learn." The nature of the acquisition and use of information in organizations will reflect its capacity for learning. Argyris (1982) views organizations as poor learners that fail to examine the underlying causes of problems. He defines *organizational learning* as a process of detecting and correcting error, the mismatch between intentions and actual consequences. Discovering error constitutes the first step toward learning. Learning occurs when organizational problems are detected, analyzed, and lasting solutions formulated. The organizational learning process is an iterative process of applying assimilated knowledge to solve organizational problems as well as reflecting on the nature and causes of the problems.

The term *organizational learning* may erroneously convey an anthropomorphic conception that the organization has some abstract, theoretical capacity that allows it to mysteriously acquire and apply knowledge, thereby learning. Organizational learning is simply the metaphor used to transmit the idea of knowledge acquisition and use, but the actual learning process is the cumulative acquisition of data by people and their collective application and use of this information. Organizations learn through individual learning, but individual learning does not guarantee organizational learning (Senge, 1990). Rist (1994) also asserts the indispensability of the human factor in the learning process:

> Organizational learning happens among individuals. It is not a hypothetical or mystical event that has no grounding in the lives and experiences of human beings. It is not supernatural. It is linked to the biographies of the individuals within an organization, to the culture of the organization, to the styles of decision making, and to the means of communication (both formal and informal) within the organization. In sum, organizational learning takes place within the context of shared understandings, experiences, routines, values, and acceptable behaviors. (p. 189)

Argyris (1982) differentiates learning in an organization as single or double loop. Single-loop learning occurs when an organization can achieve its objectives through uncovering and correcting errors. Double-loop learning occurs when the underlying policies, norms, and objectives of the organization are questioned. Double-loop learning is difficult because it demands that organizations function in a continual questioning mode with contesting views of operations.

Collection and dissemination of evaluative information by an internal evaluation staff precipitates a sequence of events that illustrates one model of organizational learning and the use of information to improve performance.

Figure 3.1 depicts a five-step sequence of the flow of information generated by an internal evaluation staff and introduced into the organizational decision-making process through the advocacy process. After the inquiry phase is completed and evaluation findings publicized through the advocacy process, internal communication mechanisms channel the information to appropriate entities, where it is studied, discussed, debated, modified, and combined with other available data to inform the decision-making process. At this point, the organization is in the learning mode, deciding on the appropriate course and magnitude of possible actions. On completion of the learning phase, changes are recommended and implemented, program direction is altered, and performance affected. Although the flow of events in Figure 3.1 is depicted as linear, there is substantial overlap and feedback among the phases, each phase informing and affecting the other in a cybernetic loop. Table 3.2 expands the details of this sequence of events, setting forth the specific actions taking place in each of the five phases.

Internal evaluators can aid organizations in developing their capacity to learn by examining and questioning organizational activities and goals and surfacing alternative viewpoints. The contribution of internal evaluators to the organizational learning process is twofold: (1) Internal evaluators can point out the probable consequences of decision options, and (2) internal evaluators have an institutional memory that provides a historical perspective of past decisions. Preskill (1994) believes that "the evaluator's role in supporting the development of a learning culture is to *assess and communicate upper management's commitment* [italics in the original] to organizational learning and the benefits that individuals and the organization may experience as a result of this transforma-

Figure 3.1. Organizational Learning Sequence

tion" (p. 293). Internal evaluators will play a pivotal role working directly with the organization in examining the learning architecture of an organization, the framing mechanisms, memory, knowledge, and learning processes that connect these structures and through which these structures interact (Jenlink, 1994).

Three evaluation researchers studying the effectiveness of Norwegian international development assistance discovered that evaluation generates organizational learning in two modes: via involvement and via communication (Forss, Cracknell, & Samset, 1994). *Involvement* is characterized by program officers' acquiring new knowledge by taking part in evaluations; *communication* is defined as the acquisition of new knowledge in a passive mode by reading or listening. Both modes lead to organizational learning, and organizations wishing to maximize their learning capacity should pursue strategies to allow the two modes to supplement each other. These evaluators found that traditional evaluation, built on learning thorough involvement, was effective in learning about efficiency yet did not help innovation nor help organizations learn to question their basic assumptions.

The practice of internal evaluation can serve as the basis for organizational learning, detecting and solving problems, acting as a self-

TABLE 3.2
The Process of Information Use in Organizations

Inquiry
    Evaluation
    Management studies
    Problem analysis
    Database analysis

Advocacy
    Report published
    Recommendations issued
    Evaluators active in organizational discussions

Organizational learning
    Organization becomes aware of new data
    Organization reflects on new data
    Debate on value and use of information occurs

Organizational change
    Recommendations are approved
    Recommended changes are implemented

Improved performance
    Program direction is modified or redirected
    Consequences of changes are assessed

---

correcting mechanism by stimulating debate and reflection among organizational actors, and seeking alternative solutions to persistent problems. A learning organization is "an organization that is continually expanding its capacity to create its future" (Senge, 1990, p. 14). Internal evaluators can facilitate organizational learning if they approach their evaluative efforts with an understanding of how organizations acquire and use information to learn.

The Decision-Making Process in Organizations

The defining reality of organizations is that goal achievement is built on a foundation of intelligent decision making. It logically follows, then, that improving the quality of decision making increases the probability of goal attainment. Ninety-nine percent of American Evaluation Association (AEA) Evaluation Use Topical Interest Group (TIG) respondents to a 1996 survey on evaluation utilization agreed that one of the major purposes of evaluation was to provide information for decision making (Preskill & Caracelli, 1997).[2] However, simply producing and presenting research data to decisionmakers does not guarantee its use.

> In the original scheme of things, the individual policymaker was viewed as a rational actor who needed more and better information to make more and better decisions. The decisionmaker was portrayed as a thoughtful person who could be convinced by evidence and who would make sound judgments based on the merits of available knowledge. This knowledge directly shaped decisionmaking, which led directly to action. The relation of information to action was presumed to be linear and straightforward. . . . As the years have passed and the research into knowledge utilization has grown considerably, the evidence now suggests that this linear assumption is naive—it is naive for any given individual and it is naive for an organization. The incorporation of information into the knowledge base of an individual or an organization is selective, sporadic, and temporal. (Leeuw & Sonnichsen, 1994, p. 1)

DECISION MAKING AND EVALUATION

Although the context for the successful practice of internal evaluation is important, even more consequential is the critical recognition of the synthesis of the decision-making process with the internal evaluation process if evaluative efforts are to influence the organization. Historically, this linkage has not been well understood by internal evaluators.

> Within the field of program evaluation, whose mission is decision-focused assessment, initial attempts to link data and decisions were largely unsuccessful, in part because of the primary emphasis on "good science" and in part because of simplistic and generally undeveloped ideas and observations about the process of decision making. Subsequent work has highlighted the need to pay much more systematic attention to the traditionally "nonscientific," pragmatic aspects of the decision-making process, that is, to the more technological aspects of linking data to decisions. (Fishman, 1991, p. 359)

According to Attkisson et al. (1978), evaluation has failed to become an influential force in management and policy making because it has failed to deal with the complexity of the organizational decision-making process. This observation is still valid today. In 1976, Herbert A. Simon, in the Introduction to the third edition of his seminal work *Administrative Behavior,* states that this book "was written on the assumption that the decision-making processes hold the key to the understanding of organizational phenomena" (p. xl). For Simon, organizations are complex networks of decision-making processes that influence the behavior of employees. He proposes that the anatomy of an organization can be found in the distribution and allocation of decision-making functions.

Decisions in organizations are usually not the sole product of an individual, but reflect the influence of the organization. In every organization, distinct authority levels are established, lines of communications put in place, and rules and procedures enacted, setting the operating parameters for the organization. Some organizations delegate the authority for making decisions to decentralized organizational locations with a requirement that results of decisions be channeled to a headquarters entity. Other organizations operate in a centralized mode, where most of the important decisions are made at the upper levels of management and the results transmitted downward. In many organizations, memoranda are the vehicles for setting forth individual and group viewpoints and recommendations for action. Advisory boards, committees, and ad hoc study groups are all examples of organizational structures designed to aid the decision-making process.

Executives and managers will never have sufficient time or information to make the perfect decision, yet they are, nevertheless, required by their positions to make decisions. The change-oriented society in which we now live only exacerbates the difficulty of the decision-making process. Toffler (1981) observes that the transforming modern organization is undergoing an identity crisis that only intensifies the decision-making pressures: "For the very speed of change introduces a new element into management, forcing executives, already nervous in an unfamiliar environment, to make more and more decisions at a faster and faster pace. Response times are honed to a minimum" (p. 229). Simon (1976) calls decisions made under these conditions "satisficing," a course of action that is satisfactory given the information that is available and the limits to human capacity to acquire and process information.

DECISION-MAKING ENVIRONMENT

The interest and capacity of organizations for acquiring, processing, and using information varies with the mission, tradition, and incumbent leadership of each individual organization. However, there are common issues that apply to most organizations, and internal evaluators should become familiar with how they affect internal evaluation activities. Following are eight principles I have learned are common to many public and private organizations that affect the practice of internal evaluation and the use of evaluative information and research.

1. Decisionmakers will make decisions with or without sufficient information

Decision making is one of the core functions in organizations. Achievement of the organization's goals requires initiation of programs and adaptations as they are implemented. Confronting decisionmakers are uncertainty, ambiguity, special interests, and short time lines. Rarely do senior management officials have all the relevant data surrounding an issue. They are limited by time, their own cognitive processes, their awareness of the universe of information available on a particular issue, and the traditional decision-making framework in the organization. Having internal evaluators examine available alternatives and their consequences can reduce the risk of making the wrong decision.

2. Decisionmakers urgently need information

Seldom do executives have sufficient time and opportunity to examine in detail all the available information pertaining to the issue at hand and ponder the consequences of their actions. Deadline constraints, personal impatience, the need to appear decisive, and competitive pressures combine to expedite the decision-making process. Internal evaluators can quickly gather, analyze, and present relevant data in a usable format that strengthens the decision-making process.

3. Evaluations usually involve complex issues with complex solutions

Simple problems are routinely handled without extensive discussion or research, but complex issues present executives with the dilemma of which alternative to choose. Internal evaluators have a role in reviewing complex problem areas and can aid the decision-making process by researching the issues, conducting analysis, and presenting options and possible consequences. Evaluators, however, are usually confronted with the perennial time-versus-methodology conundrum: How much quality data can be collected and presented within the decision time frame? Short time frames clash with the use of elegant methodologies, and evaluators are often forced to compromise optimal methodological approaches to problem solving with expediency. Extensive research is not always needed to satisfy organizational decisionmakers. Intellectual fascination with *solving the problem* instead of *advising the decisionmaker* is one of the causes of overinvestment in research efforts (Downs, 1977).

Reviewing the approaches to complex problem solving requires balancing methodological perfection with pragmatic considerations. Knowing that decisions will be made with or without information, as mentioned above, is the impetus that forms the basis for the internal research approach. A prompt response to a request for information may affect data quality, but a little information that informs the decision is better than none at all. Patton (1986) prefers rough measures of relevant issues rather than precise measures of trivial issues.

4. Decisionmakers are generally more comfortable with in-house information

Credible information produced within organizations by permanent staff members apparently has greater receptivity than data from outside the organization. Rist (1994) reports that government organizations appear more receptive to information produced internally than to information produced externally. As reported by Rossi and Freeman (1989), a study in the Netherlands of internal and external evaluations suggests that internal evaluations may have a greater impact on organizational decisions (van de Vall & Bolas, 1981). They suggest that this occurs "partly in a higher rate of communication between inside researchers and policymakers, accompanied by greater consensus, and partly in a balance between standards of epistemological and implemental validity" (Rossi & Freeman, 1989, p. 451). Relationships established over time by evaluators working in organizations build confidence and may positively affect the acceptance of internally generated evaluation findings.

5. **Decisionmakers want answers to "What works?"**

In the pragmatic organizational arena, the theory of why things work is less important than what will work. Theory has its place in understanding organizations and the behavior of individuals, but the pragmatic, daily demands on managers and executives precludes in-depth theorizing on most organizational issues. The implication for internal evaluators of this is to conduct studies that are narrowly focused and adhere to the specific question being asked by management, and not be led astray by interesting, nonrelevant, research issues encountered during the study. The ability to employ truncated evaluation research methodologies that maintain data integrity yet are responsive to management inquiries characterizes a professionally mature internal evaluation office.

6. **Information must be presented in an understandable format. Know the audience!**

Not all of us process and digest information in the same way. Some individuals are comfortable with quantitative data, whereas others abhor confronting numerical data. Some prefer to read evaluation reports, whereas others, who find reading reports tedious, are more receptive to oral presentations. Charts and graphs appeal to some; others favor written narrative. Additional discussions of presenting evaluation data will occur in Chapter 8, but the important point here is the necessity for evaluators to diligently try to determine the preferable format for presenting evaluation findings by studying the intended audience. This is important whether the audience is one executive, a group of executives, or a group of employees. Within the

confines of the data, every effort should be made to accommodate the preferences of the audience when presenting evaluation
results. The last three FBI directors each had a different preference for receiving evaluation data: One favored written narra-
tives, one wanted data presented in graphic form, and one
preferred oral presentations by the evaluators.

7. **Information sometimes acts as a "referee"**
Executives can use unbiased, unemotional information presented by evaluators to solve conflicts between individuals and
competing organizational entities. Parochial interests, competition for resources, and individual agendas can obscure the germane issues in a conflict. Evaluators can elucidate an issue by
presenting alternative approaches, unencumbered by attachment
or allegiance to the program or issue in question. Defining issues
in unambiguous terms and offering options for solutions increase
the potential that conflicting parties can resolve their differences, or lacking agreement, result in a better informed decision
by a superior.

8. **Decisionmakers may have program responsibility but
insufficient decision-making authority**
It is essential to identify power and authority networks to avoid
presenting evaluation results to individuals without the capacity
to act on recommendations.

All organizations develop their own style of management and
decision making. Embedded in this process are the important mechanics
of communication. How do organizational entities communicate with
each other? What is the "chain of command"? What happens when a
decision needs to be made? What approach is used to solve problems?
How is authority distributed in the organization? Who are the power
brokers in the organizations? Are there persons in the organization who
do not have positions of authority who can still assert their influence
on major decisions? Is decision making an ad hoc function or the result
of a systematized approach? How can evaluators penetrate the decision-
making process with their findings? In every organization, these questions have answers that evaluators need to study and understand before

beginning their evaluative work. Operating inside organizations enables internal evaluators to accumulate valuable knowledge on personalities, behavior, decision-making procedures, formal and informal power distribution and authority networks, and idiosyncratic cultural artifacts that affect operations. Compiling an institutional memory of organizational activities and behavior facilitates the internal evaluation and consulting process. It is the decision-making process that is the primary benefactor of evaluative activities: Learning its intricacies and nuances will help internal evaluators achieve their goal of evaluation as a routine organizational activity.

Information as a Valued Organizational Commodity

If decision making is the engine that causes motion in organizations, then information is the fuel. The importance of information to modern organizations cannot be overstated, yet knowledge accretion and utilization in organizations are a haphazard process. The need for and use of information can be unsystematic, situational, and driven by events and crises that, once concluded, are soon forgotten. Problem-solving strategies and methodologies used during these events are rarely recorded and institutionalized. This random approach to organizational problem solving is a suboptimal use of knowledge-producing resources. Organizations can benefit from systematic strategies that facilitate knowledge acquisition.

INFORMATION AS KNOWLEDGE AND POWER

Information is the medium of exchange among organizational entities. "Communication—the exchange of information and the transmission of meaning—is the very essence of a social system or an organization" (Katz & Kahn, 1978, p. 428). Information is used, misused, manipulated, ignored, and sometimes discarded after use, yet it remains a necessary ingredient for the proper functioning of an organization. Information is an organization's primary source of nourishment, so vital that when unavailable, people make it up and rumors proliferate (Wheatley, 1992). When conflict arises, information takes on increased value as the disputing parties support their positions with their interpretations of the available data. Defense of a position on an issue and arguing a successful outcome may hinge on the quality of information available.

In organizations, information has both value and power. Only knowledge-based organizations will thrive (Peters, 1992). According to Drucker (1989), within two decades, the typical large organization will have no more than half the levels of management and no more than a third of the number of managers. He believes that large organizations will have little choice but to become information based. However, one of the paradoxes confronting managers in this information era is that even though there is an abundance of information, its utility quickly dissolves and it is constantly being replaced by new information that has to be learned, interpreted, and applied.

"We are drowning in information but starved for knowledge" (Naisbitt, 1982, p. 24). This aphorism accurately depicts the predicament of many organizations that are voracious collectors of data but ineffectual consumers, failing to effectively exploit the value in the data and profit from the collection expenditure. The "information pollution" (uncontrolled and unorganized information) described by Naisbitt (1982) is a common situation in today's organizations with immense data collection capability unsupported by concomitant analytical and interpretive competence. The technology to retrieve and store data far outstrips the capacity of most organizations for effective and efficient use of the data. Skilled evaluators, familiar with analytical techniques and database construction, can assist organizations, not only in analyzing raw data but in devising parsimonious strategies for selecting and retrieving essential data while curtailing the practice of amassing unwieldy and useless data. Even when collected and stored, raw data have minimal functionality. To become useful to an organization, raw data must be converted to information, integrated into the knowledge bank of the organization, and appropriately applied to relevant issues. Sensemaking of databases and the conversion of data to information are the contributions of an internal evaluation staff. One of the ancillary tasks of the Office of Program Analysis and Evaluation at the Department of Housing and Urban Development was the maintenance and analysis of the division's databases. At the Food and Drug Administration, many program managers are inundated with data but have neither the time nor the techniques to isolate and analyze significant variables (Barkdoll & Sporn, 1989). Helping program managers discover new perspectives and insights using available program data exemplifies the Office of Planning and Evaluation's approach to the evaluation process (Barkdoll & Sporn, 1989).

Credibility, quality, and timeliness are the hallmarks of useful information in organizations. One of the important pathways for information in organizations is upward from the operational and administrative components to the executive hierarchy. Information proceeding up this pathway, however, passes through many management layers that tend to filter and modify negative news. Each filtration level has incentives to present favorable information but limited rationale for highlighting program deficiencies. Rewriting, rewording, and reorienting upward-bound memoranda occupy considerable time at each stop on the way as the original content is manipulated to reflect each individual's imprint. These tendentious modifications revise the appearance of the original information to the extent that often when it reaches its final destination, it is biased, inaccurate, and nonrepresentative. Katz and Kahn (1978) note dryly that "the upward flow of communication in organizations is not noted for spontaneous and full expression" (p. 447). The resulting positive slant of vertical communication in organizations depicting favorable conditions may obscure program reality and undermine informed decision-making efforts by senior executives.

Packaging, flow, and use of information vary, not only with the management style of the organization's hierarchy, tradition, and organizational culture but also with popular management fads. The management theory landscape is littered with monuments of alliterative aphorisms, representing failed management systems, attesting to the futility of attempting to impose generic management precepts across diverse organizations: management by objectives (MBO), the planning and program budgeting system (PPBS), zero-based budgeting (ZBB), the performance management and recognition system (PMRS), and quality of work-life (QWL) are but a few of the management concepts originally thought to revolutionize the way organizations could be efficiently administered. Each of these management approaches affects the type of data collected and the way information is used in organizations.

Nevertheless, information is always a necessary and useful commodity in organizations: Management fads alter only its appearance, not its value.

INFORMATION ASYMMETRY

Some form of hierarchical decision making takes place in all organizations, and access to information plays a key role in the outcome of many decisions. It would be naive to assume that the information playing field is always level with the parties involved having equal access to all relevant information. Senior officials are regularly confronted with competing constituencies on major policies, procedures, programs, and problems, each faction justifying its position with information that, through purposeful omission or ignorance, may distort actual program conditions. This results in an incomplete analysis and presentation of the problem. Organizations are competitive environments with routine disputes over selection and assignment of high-quality personnel, equipment procurement, resource allocation, policy development, and program implementation. As the stakes in contestable issues increase, the propensity to slant the available information increases, the bias and emotional attachment to the argument increases, and the objectivity of the information furnished to decisionmakers diminishes. Gaining the advantage in important organizational arguments is often accomplished by exaggerating the positive aspects of the issue while minimizing or suppressing the deficiencies or imperfections surrounding the issue. Critical organizational issues can be obfuscated with technical jargon, specious reasoning, or deliberate suppression or misrepresentation of the facts. Some information used to support arguments may even be unintentionally fallible; nevertheless, its potentially damaging role in the decision-making process diminishes the quality of the eventual outcome.

In the ideal organization, information would be widely distributed and equally shared among relevant parties during decision-making discussions, disputes, policy development, resource allocation, and problem-solving exercises. This equal and universal access to information would benefit the organization by increasing the quality of decision making, leading to improved operations and more effective goal achievement. Although some information about specific issues may be generally available to the relevant parties, imperfections in information distribution leads to suboptimal decision making and an uneven distribution of influence in the organization. "The distribution of information in the [organizational] structure determines who knows what, and consequently, the likelihood of policies and decisions encountering opposition, and the ability of other organizational participants to undertake a serious challenge to present practice" (Pfeffer, 1978, p. 90). The cost (risk) of sharing information in an organization may be so high (job loss, project failure, career impedance, or tarnishing of individual reputations) that it hinders the free flow and availability of information to pertinent parties. Imperfect information distribution or information asymmetry limits the potential for optimizing the decision-making process.

Recently, in the field of economics, an *information paradigm* has been developed, providing insights into market performance by examining the role that information plays—the absence of perfect information and the cost of acquiring information (Stiglitz, 1994). I believe these same principles have application for evaluators in organizations to explain the flow, use, cost of acquisition, and differential availability of information. The imperfections and imbalances in information availability within organizations are analogous to imperfect information affecting market economies. The concept of information asymmetry is appropriate to analyze and explain many of the communications problems inside organizations.

Asymmetries of information limit the information available to the decisionmaker and shift the advantage to the individual or group of individuals with greater information access and knowledge. Better-informed positions have superior leverage in discussions and disputes, handicapping those less informed. This information manipulation results in incomplete and prejudicial positions being presented by the parties involved in a decision, leaving the decisionmaker at a disadvantage. Lacking complete and accurate information to refute participants' competing claims, decisionmakers are left to rely on their experience and intuition to resolve disputes.

Internal evaluators cannot miraculously transform asymmetrical information conditions in organizations to perfect knowledge environments, but they can contribute to leveling the playing field through independent assessment and dissemination of unbiased information to all relevant parties. Internal evaluators, by removing the emotion and parochial bias from discussions and neutralizing advantages gained through disingenuous data manipulation, can focus discussions on relevant data and ensure all participants have equal access to essential information.

CONCLUSION

Evaluation has failed to become a mainstream event, fully integrated into the administrative apparatus of organizations for at least three valid reasons: (1) It encounters resistance because of its judgmental nature; (2) evaluators enjoy no preferential status among organizational components but compete with other organizational components for resources; and (3) organizations do not always function in a rational way, and there is no guarantee that evaluation findings will be used or exert an influence. By recognizing and addressing these impediments, evaluators gain a comprehensive understanding of how organizations work, which is imperative to the successful integration of evaluation into organizations.

The discovery of how organizations work is a combination of study, experience, and learning. Organizations are practical places where individuals work together in groups to produce goods and services. Organizational leaders are more interested in what works and less interested in the underlying theory of why it works. However, there is a theoretical aspect to organizations, and evaluators can become more effective with an understanding of the relevant theoretical underpinnings of the organization. Understanding how and why organizations work is a precondition for initiating positive change. Organizational reality can be understood by using empirical observation supplemented with theory.

Decision making, information usage, and culture are not exhaustive of all the conditions found in modern organizations, but they are the salient functions that most often have a direct influence on the practice of internal evaluation. Nor are organizational theories, systems thinking, information asymmetry, and learning the only variables to explain differences within and among organizations. However, evaluators who are familiar with these organizational conditions and explanatory concepts will be better equipped to conduct evaluations and integrate evaluation into organizations.

RECOMMENDED FOR FURTHER READING

Evaluation and Program Planning, Volume 14, Number 3.
Contains a special section of six articles on various aspects of internal evaluation.

Rainey, H. G. (1991). *Understanding and managing public organizations.* San Francisco: Jossey-Bass.
An excellent treatment of how organizations function. Although oriented to public organizations, it is also relevant to other organizational configurations.

Senge, P. (1990). *The fifth discipline: The art and practice of the learning organization.* New York: Doubleday.
Makes a compelling case for using systems thinking to analyze organizational situations.

Torres, R. T., Preskill, H. S., & Piontek, M. E. (1996). *Evaluation strategies for communicating and reporting: Enhancing learning in organizations.* Thousand Oaks, CA: Sage.
Discusses the role of evaluation in organization learning.

Vaill, P. B. (1996). *Learning as a way of being: Strategies for survival in a world of permanent white water.* San Francisco: Jossey-Bass.
Examines individual learning and systems thinking and their application in organizations.

Notes

1. Conceptual commitment to the core mission of the organization refers to the probability that internal evaluators have a commitment, by virtue of their employment in the organization, to the overarching values of the organization. The implication of this phenomenon is that it would be difficult for internal evaluators to question the rationale

for the very existence of the organization. If this became necessary, external evaluators would be better positioned to independently assess the value of the organization's mission.

2. The response rate was 54% ($n = 282$). Respondents identified themselves as 36% external evaluators, 34% internal evaluators, or 31% as both internal and external evaluators.

Chapter 4

❦

Evaluation, Conflict, and the Change Process in Organizations

KEY CHAPTER TOPICS

* Program managers' views of internal evaluation
* Organizational change
* How to cause change in organizations

Evaluation offices think they're program offices and want to run the program. You don't want to evaluate it, you want to tell programs what to do and yet not be held accountable. They [evaluators] absorb resources but don't produce anything. They are not responsible. Ultimately, no staff officer is ever held accountable for what a program office does. Evaluators are competitors for program direction and resources. . . . The thing that gets me is the workload that staff offices generate for line operations. As the line manager, I cannot see any relevance to the mission we have. (quoted in Sonnichsen, 1989c, p. 19)

This passionate indictment of internal evaluators was expressed by members of a distinguished panel of federal government program managers assembled at the University of Southern California's (USC) Washington Public Affairs Center (WPAC), in Washington, D.C. in 1987. This insightful inventory of complaints about evaluators vividly communicates the antagonism and contempt that program managers hold for evaluators. It epitomizes one of the intriguing paradoxes of evaluation: its ability to aggravate those whom it is designed to help. According to Derlien (1990), a German professor and evaluation colleague:

> It is almost an anthropological proposition that people do not like to be supervised and resist having their activities monitored, because they basically fear negative sanctions in general and threats to their careers in particular resulting from the documentation of failures. In addition, external controls—by definition—change the existing balance of power between organizational systems and therefore are resisted for political reasons. (p. 161)

These program managers' comments should serve as a wake-up call for internal evaluators, alerting them to opposing viewpoints on the efficacy of the evaluation process. Evaluators working inside organizations need to understand the nature of conflict and change in addition to their evaluation and management skills if they are to maximize their effectiveness. The necessity for knowledge and skills beyond evaluation captures the essential purpose of this book, that is, to acquaint and prepare evaluators working inside organizations with the background, understanding, and tools necessary for the successful practice of internal evaluation. This chapter will examine the nature of conflict and change in organizations and how conflict and change are precipitated by evaluative activities and will introduce strategies for overcoming organizational resistance and dealing with conflict.

Evaluator-Manager
Conflict in Organizations

The judgmental nature of evaluation activity tends to generate conflict between evaluators and program managers, yet internal evaluators need their support if evaluation is to be institutionalized. Internal evaluators can minimize some of the hostility the arises during evaluation by studying the nature and cause of these conflicts and developing an empathy toward the viewpoint of the program manager.

PROGRAM MANAGER VIEWPOINTS

The WPAC program manager panel criticized the use of evaluation findings as serving the executive hierarchy in organizations with little input or interest in the views of program managers (Sonnichsen, 1989c). The program managers viewed evaluation as yielding limited benefits to them yet having significant potential to alter their programs, damage their reputations, and affect their careers. Program managers are particularly sensitive to their roles as providers of services or products. They are judged by the quantity and quality of their outputs and held accountable for efficient and effective use of resources. They viewed evaluation as an imposition, conducted by evaluators not held accountable for the organization's productivity, yet standing in judgment of their program performance. They saw evaluators as a "burden" to their programs and were indignant that they had to divert resources to respond to evaluators' demands for data and in some cases even redirect program funds to pay for the evaluation. Resentment of evaluation is further reinforced when program managers are required to furnish program data that are then used to demonstrate deficiencies in the program. WPAC panel members wanted increased input into the data collection process and a voice in the eventual use of the data.

Program managers on the panel took umbrage at superficial analysis of quantitative program data. They believed that statistical program data did not always accurately portray the complete impact of the program, focusing more on outputs than outcomes. Lacking difficult-to-obtain program impact data, oversight bodies tend to focus on easily obtained output numbers. Exclusive concentration on quantitative data, however, either by evaluators or evaluation clients, precludes in-depth program reviews. The unintended result is that program performance may be misrepresented. Program manager resentment is further evidenced by these comments on data collection and use:

> We need good data, but we should be very involved in the definition of what those data needs are, and they should not be imposed on us. You feel you are not always measured against what you think are the relevant objectives of your program. (quoted in Sonnichsen, 1989c, p. 20)

PROGRAM MANAGER CHALLENGES

It is obvious from the above comments that evaluators and program managers view the management of programs from distinctly different viewpoints. Evaluators see evaluation as an elegant management tool, a rational, scientific approach to enlightened management, designed to detect inefficiencies in programs and offer improvements. Program managers see evaluation as intrusive, threatening to highlight flaws and deficiencies in their programs and, by inference, question their managerial skills. An evaluation report is typically a widely available document and generally suggests improvements and changes, which can appear threatening (Chelimsky, 1985). Most programs are "moving targets" rather than static entities, a condition not always well understood by evaluators. Unfortunately for evaluators, the conditions within organizations are not laboratory settings but vibrant clusters of activity, turmoil, and constant movement. Programs are always in various states of implementation, adjustment, and reaction to internal and external stimuli.

Program managers deal with complex and sometimes ambiguous program designs, confront and attempt to satisfy multiple constituencies, and manage fluctuating implementation conditions. The perplexing predicament confronting most program managers is how to resolve the conflict between expected high program performance and the reality of underfunding, insufficient resources, ambiguous goals, faulty program theory, and militant and conflicting stakeholder views on implementation and expected results. Managers in the public sector may face additional role ambiguity because of the complexity of implementing programs without complete authority and control.

Weiss (1975) points out that managers of social programs in particular are reacting to legislative and bureaucratic politics, and therefore their views will vary from those of the social scientist/evaluator. She accurately describes the myriad functions required of program managers:

> Bureaucrats, or in our terms program administrators and operators, are not irrational; they have a different model of rationality in mind. They are concerned not just with today's progress in achieving program goals but with building long-term support for the program. This may require

attention to factors and to people who can be helpful in later events and future contests. Administrators also must build and maintain the organization—recruit staff with needed qualifications, train them to the appropriate functions, arrange effective inter-staff relations and communications, keep people happy and working enthusiastically, [and] expand the influence and mission of the agency. There are budgetary interests, too, the need to maintain, increase, or maximize appropriations for agency functioning. Clients have to be attracted, a favorable public image developed, and a complex system managed and operated. Accomplishing the goals for which the program was set up is not unimportant, but it is not the only, the largest, or usually the most immediate of the concerns on the administrator's docket. (Weiss, 1975, p. 15)

LESSONS FOR EVALUATORS

The sentiments of program managers generated at the symposium have instructive value for internal evaluators. Once program managers' concerns are recognized as naturally occurring phenomena in organizations, evaluators can begin developing an understanding and empathy, which can be used as a foundation for collaborative evaluations. Internal evaluation often deals with emotional issues, and both evaluators and program personnel are susceptible to viewing evaluation as a sporting event with winners and losers. During research conducted with program managers at the Food and Drug Administration, Barkdoll (1982) determined that the program managers he interviewed "appeared comfortable with categorizing much of the evaluation team's behavior into two roles: critic and supportive consultant" (p. 148). My experience at the Federal Bureau of Investigation (FBI) was that program managers almost universally resented evaluation of their programs, becoming defensive of their "turf" and challenging most evaluation findings. The interpersonal skills of the evaluators play an important part in dealing with program managers and personnel during these conflicts, and it is helpful to develop a sense of the viewpoint of the program manager.

The burden for transforming the evaluation encounter into a productive endeavor lies with the evaluation team. A misunderstanding of each other's domains, interests, objectives, goals, and rationale for evaluations often causes evaluator-program conflict. I recall one of my evaluation staff assuring me that he was regularly briefing the head of the FBI Training Division during an evaluation of its program. Needless to say, I was astonished when I visited the site and encountered an irate program manager, who informed me that he did not understand what was happening in his own division. After some inquiry, I learned that the evaluator interpreted his casual conversations with the program manager as "briefings," whereas the program manager was expecting formal and detailed synopses of the evaluation progress. A lack of communication and understanding by the evaluator generated more animosity than was necessary during the evaluation.

Evaluators can gain the trust and respect of program managers through a genuine display of empathy, open communications, and a balanced assessment of the program's strengths and weaknesses. The message of the WPAC panel members can be easily distilled into a question of fairness. What program managers want during evaluations is

more involvement in the evaluation process,

honesty in conveying the purpose and the uses of evaluation,

a balanced perspective on programs by portraying successes as well as deficiencies, and

recognition that program managers are evaluation clients. (Sonnichsen, 1989c, p. 24)

Some program managers' concerns can be alleviated if evaluators confine their reporting of program deficiencies to major problem areas and communicate trivial, but helpful, observations of program deficiencies orally to the program personnel as they are discovered. It seldom serves any beneficial purpose to tabulate a litany of unimportant details in a final report, but it almost always drives an annoying wedge between evaluators and program managers. Resolving contentious issues with program personnel in a professional manner as they are detected during the evaluation promotes respect, accomplishes program improvement, and assuages some of the distress felt by program managers.

Reactions from program managers to evaluation efforts are always serious but can sometimes be amusing to the evaluators. The "blowfish response," named after the blowfish who expands its size to intimidate and repulse its enemies, was coined by my evaluation staff in the FBI after receipt of a rebuttal to an evaluation report on the management of information resources that exceeded the length of the original report.

The response argued in excessive and redundant detail for the preservation of the status quo and against recommended changes. Although the blowfish response could be considered a lame attempt at evaluation humor, it epitomizes the frustration of many program managers who have the misfortune to have their programs evaluated and changes recommended.

EVALUATOR RESPONSIBILITY TO CLIENTS

Evaluation clients, as well as evaluators, have expectations. Many clients see the commissioning of an evaluation as a high-risk undertaking. Gunn (1987) puts the feelings of many evaluation clients in proper perspective when he describes the contemplation of an evaluation as a "terrifying vision." Determining clients' wants, needs, fears, and expectations and accommodating them without breaching the integrity of the evaluation are essential for evaluators focused on utility. Braskamp, Brandenburg, and Ory (1987) summarize some of the recurrent themes they have encountered working with a variety of clients in education and industry:

> Clients want an evaluator who has had experience with similar projects in similar settings. They want evaluators (both internal and external) to maintain an objective viewpoint while demonstrating an understanding of their client's organizational work environments and a sensitivity to the client's need for information. Recommendations for action are also expected from evaluators. Whereas upper-level administrators want evaluators to collect and present information in a standard manner, for ease of interpretation, individuals in smaller units of organizations often want evaluators to detect uniqueness and distinctiveness. Clients want short, concise reports that they can clearly understand. Evaluation reports must be free of unfamiliar language and jargon. Reports must include information that is perceived as credible by the client, that is, information from trustworthy sources. Finally, evaluators must complete their reports on time. (p. 73)

Braskamp et al. (1987) found that when working as internal evaluators, the client expectation issue is more complex than for external evaluators because internal evaluators simultaneously report to several clients. Long-term success conducting internal evaluations depends on evaluator acceptance by several audiences and their ability to meet multiple expectations.

For fair and effective evaluations to take place, internal evaluators must recognize the managerial responsibility and total complexity of programs and their stages of implementation, resource availability, and factors affecting implementation. Empathy and understanding of the program or business is essential to the success of internal evaluation. Many internal evaluators focusing solely on program goals and outcomes may unfairly misrepresent the value of programs not fully developed. Businesses and industry programs can either be in start-up modes or mature enterprises, requiring different methodological designs. Business clients for evaluation want evaluators to be seen as experts, understand the client's product or service, and demonstrate the positive benefits that might accrue to the client as a result of the evaluation (Tate & Cummings, 1991).

Change in Organizations

At a conference in Virginia Beach, Virginia, on November 15, 1990, the FBI director and his senior executives heard futurist David Pearce Snyder, commenting on the realities facing America in the 1990s, assert:

> Today's organizational structures and management systems, originally designed to facilitate planning and decision making in a relatively stable, information-sparse operating environment, will have to be redesigned to facilitate planning and decision making in a dynamically changing, information-rich operating environment. If this is not done, investments in new technology and human resources development will be largely wasted!

Snyder's prediction is a wake-up call for the leadership in organizations to the indispensability of detection and analysis of change, as unpredictable internal and external events create the need for continual systems scrutiny and the initiation of appropriate adaptations and changes.

It is not too much of a stretch to conclude that evaluation and change are synonyms. Although some might debate that not all evaluations precipitate change (in fact this is the utilization lament), I would argue that the majority of evaluations (particularly internal evaluations) cause some changes in the behavior of program personnel, even if major program renovations are not forthcoming. Just the announcement and beginning of most evaluations cause, at a minimum, some minor behavioral alterations among program personnel and adjustments in program administration.

One of the basic assumptions of this book is that change is not an episodic event in organizations but a normal, everyday occurrence, and both public and private organizations' survival will depend on the development of a capability to detect, analyze, and respond to constant change. Public disenchantment with government programs, decreased funding levels, and demands for greater accountability create pressures on government agencies to perform more effectively with fewer personnel and lower costs. Responding to these pressures, both public and private organizations are reengineering, merging, demerging, downsizing, rightsizing, outsourcing, privatizing, partnering, unbundling, and reinventing themselves. The inconsistent and sometimes contradictory nature of this organizational behavior accentuates the quandary of modern organizations as they grasp at the bewildering array of management techniques to cope with change.

The transformation of organizations is being accompanied by similar dramatic developments in the information available to run these new modern organizations. The titanic developments in computer technology have made available a heretofore unimaginable volume of data to be processed by organizations. Equivocal information will habitually confront decisionmakers and impede attempts at traditional approaches to problem solving. Ambiguity will increasingly characterize the decision-making environment in modern organizations. Colorful and fascinating metaphors from the inventive imagination of organizational writers have been offered to describe the environment of the modern organization: chaotic (Peters, 1987), unstable (Schon, 1971), vulnerable (Drucker, 1986), permanent white water (Vaill, 1996), and fuzzy (Treadwell, 1995). Instability, disorder, confusion, and endemic change are the threads running through these descriptors that define the new reality of modern organizations.

Traditionally, however, organizations have been uncomfortable with change, seeking stability in routinized organizational activities with predictable patterns of behavior developing around operations and administration. "The core paradox [in organizations], then, that all leaders at all levels must contend with, is fostering (creating) internal stability in order to encourage the pursuit of constant change" (Peters, 1987, p. 395). Organizations have been depicted as having great difficulty in learning from past experiences and seldom question the underlying basis of their own problems (Argyris, 1982). Over time, an accretion of rules, regulations, policies, and acceptable behaviors act to constrain creativity and reward routine, methodical, standardized approaches to organizational activities and decision making.

Organizations operating in this traditional manner may become myopic and fail to conduct the internal and external scanning and analysis that are critical to survival in a change-driven environment. Decisionmakers may succumb to reliance on tradition and intuition with limited attention given to securing empirical data or fresh perspectives on problems. The staggering economic, social, legal, political, and technological complexities of running the modern organization invalidate many traditional management reactions to crisis. To prevent organizational impotence, decisionmakers will need to begin rigorously examining the basis for their actions and reasoning processes. The accelerating rate of change will require successful organizations of the future to develop coping skills to deal with constant economic, political, social, and market fluctuations.

What does all of this have to do with evaluation? Change and reacting to change are inevitable and essential features of modern organizations. Successful, modern organizations will be those that develop independent, objective review and monitoring mechanisms that feed back critical performance information to the organization's hierarchy. Early detection of external change stimuli and alert sensing of internal organizational disturbances will benefit modern organizations. Organizations will be required to "learn" from their activities by detecting and examining the root causes of problems, thereby avoiding repetitious commitment to solving recurring problems.

How to Cause Change in Organizations

Internal evaluators are often the initiators of change, recognizing areas for improvement through their evaluative and consultative activities.

Even large-scale change can be instigated by a small group of evaluators. Change agent is one of the fundamental roles of internal evaluators, examining organizational operations and making appropriate recommendations for improvement. An excellent example of evaluators acting as explicit change agents occurred in the FBI in 1974 (Sonnichsen, 1991). At that time, FBI Director Clarence Kelley asked the FBI's internal evaluation staff to initiate a comprehensive review of the FBI's approach to investigations. The evaluative effort took place over a period of five years and resulted in significantly reorienting FBI philosophy toward criminal investigations. Dubbed "Quality over Quantity," the evaluation determined that the traditional measures of FBI performance, emphasizing quantitative statistical accomplishments, were having the unintended consequence of directing resources to criminal activities productive in accomplishment data instead of complex criminal enterprises where quantitative accomplishment data were sparse, but impact on significant illegal criminal organizations was possible. The evaluation recommended a complete restructuring of the FBI approach to investigative activities, emphasizing the quality or potential impact of a case instead of the quantity of cases under investigation. A pilot project in five field offices confirmed the efficacy of the recommended changes, and Director Kelley approved the changes for all 56 field offices. The evaluation changed the emphasis in criminal investigations and resulted in the successful pursuit of criminal cartels in organized crime, drugs, and public corruption. In this evaluation, the internal evaluators combined organizational knowledge, analytical evaluation skills, fresh insight, and independent review to examine the traditional assumptions that guided criminal investigations. Conducted by only a few evaluators supported by the FBI director, it was an evaluation that significantly reoriented the FBI approach to investigative activities. It was a classic example of internal evaluators successfully using the evaluative process to cause change.

To become an effective change agent requires internal evaluators to possess a knowledge and understanding of their role, responsibilities, and behavior that contribute to successful change. The following eight beliefs, attributes, and skills characterize some of the philosophical attitudes and process mechanisms that affect evaluators involved in organizational change.

1. Believe you can cause change

In *Exit, Voice and Loyalty,* Hirschman (1970) depicts individuals in organizations as having essentially three choices if they disagree with the organization. They can leave the organization (exit), attempt to change the organization's policy they oppose (voice), or remain silent (loyalty). Fundamental to any change in an organization is an honest belief by the individuals advancing the proposal for change that the change is attainable and that they have the capacity to initiate it. Kiefer and Stroh (1984) characterize organizations that believe they can control their own destiny as *metanoic,* from the Greek word *metanoia,* meaning "a fundamental shift of mind." Kiefer and Stroh describe metanoic organizations as those where the individuals recognize that they are the organization and have the capacity to create the future and shape their own destiny. Evaluators desiring to cause positive change must first possess a fundamental belief that they can cause change through their evaluative activities.

2. Be a critical thinker[1]

Thinking critically involves recognizing the assumptions underlying our beliefs and behaviors, judging the rationality of justifications for our ideas and actions, and testing the accuracy and rationality of these justifications (Brookfield, 1987). According to Brookfield, becoming a critical thinker requires identifying and challenging assumptions, recognizing the contextual influence on our thoughts and actions, imagining and exploring alternative ways to accomplish tasks, and skeptical reflection on assumptions underlying our beliefs and actions.

Identifying and challenging assumptions takes place when people probe their habitual ways of thinking and acting (and those of others around them) for their underlying assumptions—those taken-for-granted values, common-sense ideas, and stereotypical notions about human nature and social organization that underlie our actions. (p. 15)

Reflective skepticism is not outright cynicism, nor is it a contemptuous dismissal of all things new. It is, rather, the belief that claims for the universal validity and applicability of an idea or practice must be subject to a careful testing against each individual's experiences. It is being wary of uncritically accepting an innovation, change, or new perspective simply because it is new. It is not to be equated with resistance to change. It is, rather, a readiness to test the validity of claims made by others for any presumed givens, final solutions, and ultimate truths against one's own experience of the world. As such, it is a major affective outcome of critical thinking. (Brookfield, 1987, p. 22)

These critical-thinking attributes, described by Brookfield, should not only constitute the basic philosophical approach for internal evaluators but also serve as guidelines for program managers to reflect on the management of their programs.

Internal evaluators can use the concept of critical thinking to analytically examine the assumptive basis of programs and issues within organizations. Continuing previously launched programs without critical examination of the original assumptions and implementation processes is one of the pitfalls of managers, and one where independent assessment by evaluators can be of assistance. Skepticism is a remarkable and valuable trait for evaluators. The often-encountered mantra "We've always done it that way" represents the myopic response of many managers when challenged by an evaluator to explain program processes. No program should be allowed to assume the mantle of immortality. Skepticism allows evaluators to look behind traditional work patterns and methods, analyzing and challenging assumptions and justifications for procedures and operations and examining alternative approaches to accomplish tasks.

3. Be credible

Credibility is a defining characteristic for internal evaluators because it establishes the level of confidence and trust that the organization perceives in the evaluation staff. Torres (1991) defines credibility as "the extent to which the evaluator is perceived as (a) competent in applied research skills and the content area of the program, (b) discreet in handling sensitive information, and (c) able to communicate and influence other parties in the organization" (p. 193). Evaluators not recognized as credible by the organization will have a difficult, if not impossible, time conducting evaluations. Credibility is developed over time and is both an individual attribute imputed to each evaluator and a collective characteristic of the evaluation office and its leadership. Research I conducted in 1991, attempting to identify indicators to assess the impact of internal evaluation offices in federal agencies, discovered credibility to be most frequently cited by both evaluators and program managers as the essential ingredient contributing to the effectiveness of an evaluation office (Sonnichsen, 1991). An aggregate definition from those interviewed established credibility as the skillful, objective, unbiased, and independent evaluation of organizational activities. Credibility was commonly cited, not only as one of the positive contributing factors for successful evaluations but also as a negative factor by those program managers who believed that when evaluations were unsuccessful, evaluator credibility was lacking.

Credibility is an essential, defining characteristic that attaches to an internal evaluation staff and reflects a trust, not only in the competency of technical research, management, and evaluation skills but also in the fairness of evaluators and their leadership. My research showed that for findings and recommendations to be accepted and used, the clients and stakeholders must be convinced that the results of the evaluation were arrived at through independent, unbiased, and competency-based judgment. Any tendentious rhetoric used to describe a program will immediately be detected and negatively affect the reputation of the evaluation office. Evaluation office reputation is a fragile commodity and under constant scrutiny by users of the evaluation product. Credibility is the badge of honor for internal evaluators. Without being viewed as credible by other organizational components, an evaluation office has severely impaired its ability to influence the organization.

4. Be independent and impartial

Credibility has its roots in independence and impartiality. Impartiality, the sum total of objectivity and independence, is the goal of internal evaluators, although perfect attainment is probably impossible. Acceptance of evaluation in an organization is de-

pendent on the evaluators' ability to demonstrate independence
and fairness when dealing with organizational entities.

5. **Understand the organizational decision-making process**
   Chapter 3 discussed the centrality of the decision-making process to organizational functioning and how the organization's
   structure and personnel behavior affect the process. However,
   each organization has its own distinct process for arriving at
   decisions, and it becomes imperative for evaluators to accustom
   themselves to their own environment and determine how to
   integrate evaluation data into the decision-making process. It is
   not unusual for major decisions to be the topic of discussion at
   numerous meetings before implementation. Evaluators should
   attempt to gain invitations to important meetings that affect
   their work so they may become aware of important issues, the
   internal dynamics surrounding issues, the politics involved, and
   the time frame for making decisions. It is important for an
   evaluation staff to pattern their evaluative work to be congruent
   with the decision-making processes in the organization. This
   requires awareness of the major issues in the organization, how
   and when decisions are made, and fitting the evaluation process
   into the mainstream administrative processes.

6. **Understand how to collect, analyze, and present data**
   Evaluator competency is essential for an internal evaluation staff.
   The knowledge and abilities of the internal evaluation staff and
   the perception of evaluator competence in the organization have
   an important effect, not only on the use of evaluation by the
   organization but on the utilization of evaluation results by the
   organization. Knowledge of evaluation methodologies, possession of computer and management skills, interpersonal traits of
   tact and diplomacy, and writing and speaking proficiencies are
   some of the capabilities necessary to be viewed as competent
   evaluators. Striving for educational diversity when recruiting
   internal evaluators can also expand the capabilities of the evaluation staff.

7. Be program knowledgeable

It is obviously impossible for an internal evaluation staff to become experts on all organizational programs and operations. However, it is advantageous for evaluators to develop some expertise in the key programs that support the core mission of the organization. The optimum means to attain this knowledge base is to recruit evaluators with subject matter knowledge from within the programs. Delegating certain members of the evaluation staff to develop program content familiarity and maintain currency with program issues will increase evaluator credibility in those areas where program knowledge is lacking.

8. Attempt to gain access to decisionmakers, either top management or "champions"

Access to decision-making individuals is critical to the utilization effort for internal evaluators. Top managers and executives who become accustomed to input from an evaluation staff before making major decisions are the key to the influence the evaluation staff will have on an organization. It is the evaluation office leader's responsibility to cultivate trust with the major actors in an organization and market the value of evaluative information. In some cases after the completion of an evaluation, it may be necessary to locate and cultivate "champions," those persons who believe in the evaluation findings and recommended courses of action. Champions can diffuse the resistance among their peers and hasten acceptance of the recommended courses of action. Widespread acceptance of new ideas or change in organizations is an iterative process, and publishing the results of the evaluation is only the beginning. Organizations have low thresholds for change and must be convinced of the value of any recommended alteration in the traditional way of doing things.

Evaluators, and particularly evaluation office leaders, must actively market change and aid its acceptance. For a new idea to become systematically potent, it must gain widespread acceptance, and that requires discussion, debate, and "hitting the briefing trail" (Nicoll, 1984). Much of the burden of "selling" a new idea falls on the shoulders of the evaluators. Advocacy evaluation, the involvement of evaluators in organizational discussions and debate after the completion of an independent assessment of an issue, is crucial to the acceptance and eventual implementation of the recommendations flowing from internal evaluations. (Advocacy evaluation will be fully discussed in Chapter 5.)

Stability Versus Change

All but incidental changes in organizations create uncertainty, cause upheaval among those affected, and generate resistance. Discord in organizations is routine, as individuals express opinions, power struggles take place, personalities clash, decisions are made, and agendas prevail or collapse. Evaluations are the source of much of this dissonance. However benign a suggested change may appear to evaluators, it generally encounters resistance and generates conflict. Wildavsky (1979) even suggests that *evaluation* and *organization* may be contradictory terms.

STABILITY IN ORGANIZATIONS

Paradoxically, organizations strive to maintain stability while struggling to accommodate change. The dominant paradigm of American organizations assumes the need for hierarchical control and organizational stability (Ledford, Mohrman, Mohrman, & Lawler, 1989). "Stability is accomplished by a complex set of constraints that include formal rules nested in a hierarchy, where each level is more costly to change that the previous one" (North, 1990, p. 83). Successful organizations develop internal stability with interlinked structures and systems that are familiar to employees, who feel comfortable within the system (Tushman, Newman, & Nadler, 1988). Individuals have been trained to do their jobs, structures and procedures have been put in place to accomplish the organization's mission, power and authority have been allocated, and funds have been spent to advertise and publicize the services and products of the organization.

However, an organizational culture that resists change may no longer be an option for companies and government agencies wishing to succeed. An alternative view of the functioning of organizations is offered by Peters (1987), who suggests that change must become the norm in organizations, not a cause for alarm, with leaders learning to love and become obsessive about change. For Peters, surviving companies will be those that respond to challenges and treat chaos and change as opportunities.

RESISTANCE TO CHANGE

It is always difficult, at the outset of a major organizational change, to accurately predict the eventually outcomes and their effect on each and every individual in the organization. Therefore, even those who might eventually benefit from the change are resentful, unsure, and skeptical, initially displaying resistance.

> Resistance to change is neither capricious nor mysterious. It almost always arises from threats to traditional norms and ways of doing things. Often these norms are woven into the fabric of established power relationships. The norm is entrenched because the distribution of authority and control is entrenched. (Senge, 1990, p. 88)

Logical explanations of the rationale and predicted consequences of impending change are crucial to acceptance by employees and a burden for evaluators communicating during the change process. Restricting access to change information only feeds rumor mills, builds mistrust, and initiates destructive behavior among employees.

> When [an] organization is willing to give public voice to the information—to listen to different interpretations and to process them together—the information becomes amplified. In this process of shared reflection, a small finding can grow as it feeds back on itself, building in significance with each new perception or interpretation. . . . [This] simple process of iteration eventually reveals the complexity hidden within the issue. From this level of understanding, creative responses emerge and significant change becomes possible. (Wheatley, 1992, p. 115)

The importance of adequate communication between evaluators and program managers during the change process was illustrated during an evaluation of probationary FBI special agent training undertaken by the FBI evaluation staff. Procedures for assessing the development of new special agents after they complete training at the FBI Training Academy and are assigned to field offices were evaluated. This evaluation determined that unrealistic time frames for assessment of their skill development and a poorly designed feedback report to the academy contributed to misrepresenting the effect of both the training and special agent development in the field (Sonnichsen, 1989c). An accurate appraisal of investigative skills was impossible during the short time frame allocated for assessment, and the feedback report was interpreted differently by the academy and the field offices. The academy viewed the report as a vehicle for assessing the quality and adequacy of its training, whereas field offices saw the report as an indicator of the special agents' abilities developed in the field.

Presented with the evaluation data, the program managers at the academy completely revised the probationary agents' training program, extending time frames for observation, restructuring the report itself, and reorienting the purpose of monitoring new agent performance to serve both field office and training academy needs. The success of this evaluation grew out of a collaborative evaluation environment beginning with locating the evaluators at the training academy adjacent to the program manager's office. He was briefed after each site visit and early in the evaluation conditioned to the reality that major changes would be necessary in the program to correct deficiencies. Securing his cooperation during regular interactions during the evaluation ensured that recommendations would be understood and implemented.

EVALUATOR RESPONSIBILITY DURING CHANGE

Evaluators, recognizing that resistance to change is normal, can respond with open communication and a cooperative spirit with the affected entities. Opposition issues need to be identified as well as hostile leaders who object to the proposed changes. Assuaging employees' concerns and convincing them of the benefits of the change is an important first step in the change process. It is unlikely that all resistance will be overcome before changes are implemented, but the goal for evaluators is to contain the resistance to a level where it does not threaten the implementation of the proposed changes.

CONCLUSION

Empathy and understanding of program managers' viewpoints is essential for evaluators working inside organizations. Managerial responsibilities for production and performance present unique perspectives of program operations, a view not always shared by evaluators. Conditioning internal evaluators to recognize the burden to programs and their managers that evaluation often represents is crucial to minimizing the conflict between program managers and internal evaluators.

As organizations confront the challenges of change, internal evaluators can be helpful if they are attuned to how evaluation can be used to assist organizations in detecting, reacting, and implementing positive modifications and transitions as the organization progresses. Change and the ensuing conflict and resistance encountered can be minimized if evaluators have a thorough understanding of the process of change and its effect on both organizations and individuals. Conflict among the organization's components is normal, and the introduction of evaluation can create discord among evaluators and program personnel and resentment toward evaluation as a management tool. But cooperation is attainable if evaluators recognize and address the negative behavioral effects generated by evaluation.

Employing evaluation as a change mechanism in organizations is a deliberate process requiring commitment by internal evaluators and conscious, premeditated behaviors and actions to ensure its success. Understanding how change occurs in organizations is a prerequisite for internal evaluators working as change agents.

RECOMMENDED FOR FURTHER READING

Adams, J. D. (1984). *Transforming work*. Alexandria, VA: Miles River Press.
    An excellent treatment of alternative views on changing organizations.

Brookfield, S. D. (1987). *Developing critical thinkers: Challenging adults to explore alternative was of thinking and acting.* San Francisco: Jossey-Bass.
Explores the value and techniques for challenging basic assumptions about our work environments and ourselves. It is an excellent book for internal evaluators to develop their analytical skills.

Mohrman, A. M., Mohrman, S. A., Ledford, G. E., Jr., Cummings, T. G., & Lawler, E., III. (1989). *Large-scale organizational change.* San Francisco: Jossey-Bass.
Describes the phenomenon of large-scale organizational change and strategies for causing it to occur.

Note

1. This material on critical thinking is adapted from Stephen Brookfield's *Developing Critical Thinkers* (1987).

Chapter 5

Understanding
Internal Evaluation

KEY CHAPTER TOPICS

- ❖ Internal evaluation theories
- ❖ Internal evaluator objectivity
- ❖ Evaluation office identity
- ❖ Advocacy evaluation
- ❖ Evaluation power
- ❖ Ethical issues
- ❖ Code of ethics for internal evaluators

*T*he major premise of this book is that competent, skilled, internal evaluators supported by senior management can influence organizations and precipitate organizational learning by providing independent assessment of programs and issues, leading to reflection, implementation of change, and subsequent positive improvement in organizational performance. The following assumptions about organizations are incorporated in this notion of internal evaluation.

1. Instability and uncertainty will confront organizations for the foreseeable future.

2. Modern organizations are complex systems that must continuously adapt to changing technical, social, and economic conditions and developments to remain competitive and survive.

3. Organizations are networks of systems with both technical and social dimensions.

4. Managing sophisticated modern organizations is a demanding task, requiring complete attention to daily operations and administration, leaving little time for reflective observation.

5. Detecting and solving problems internally before they become insurmountable or are noticed by entities external to the organization is rational and prudent.

6. Acceptance of information by organizations to be used as the basis for change depends on the credibility of the source (internal or external).

7. Quality information is not always available and equally distributed among parties to a dispute (information asymmetry).

8. Organizations perceive internally generated information as more credible than externally obtained information.

9. Organizations can develop the capacity to "learn" and apply knowledge to solve problems.

These assumptions form the basic foundation for internal evaluators to help organizations cope with change, initiate improvements, reflect on issues, and improve performance.

Chapters 3 and 4 examined how organizations function and the nature of change in organizations. This chapter will review the characteristics of internal evaluation and suggest strategies for institutionalization.

The acceptance of internal evaluation in organizations is less an intellectual penetration of the organizational psyche with fascinating scientific logic than a pragmatic realization of the value of alternative solutions to problems, unencumbered by emotional and intuitive baggage. The institutionalization task is complicated because evaluation is neither historically nor intrinsically a formal organizational function (Sonnichsen, 1989a). Evaluation bears the burden of being judgmental, detecting deficiencies, challenging assumptions, critiquing performance, and suggesting changes.

Evaluation is generally not thought to be necessary to the proper functioning of an organization. Because most organizations are totally occupied with operational demands, little time or thought is given to evaluating the outcomes of programs and operations. Organizations can perform their functions, achieve their goals, satisfy the needs of their employees, and maintain customer satisfaction all without the assistance of an internal evaluation staff! Max Weber, the German sociologist who first explicated the nature of bureaucracies, nowhere cites a systematic review process as an integral component of organizations. This should not be unexpected. Organizations are consumed with mission accomplishment and little thought and no formal, structural accommodation is given to the more philosophical aspect of organizations. Why are we doing what we do? Are we accomplishing our intended purpose? What is our future? Are we prepared to be competitive in the future? Will there be a market for our product? Evaluators, therefore, lacking a historical tradition, spontaneous demand, or intrinsic organizational need for evaluative activities, bear the burden of creating a market for their commodity (evaluation) that is often perceived in the organization as unwanted, unnecessary, and threatening.

This chapter begins by examining the theoretical models of internal evaluation, reviews the arguments for and against internal evaluator objectivity, and then presents the concept of advocacy evaluation. The chapter concludes with a discussion of the identity of an internal evaluation office, evaluator power, evaluator ethics, and the limitations of internal evaluation.

Internal Evaluation Theories

Because the practice of internal evaluation is a relatively new phenomenon, there is no established consensus for its conduct. Three theories (exchange, supply and demand, and decision making) have been used to explain the relationship between internal evaluation and the clients and organizations they serve. Action research has also been advanced as a problem-solving technique for use by evaluators within organizations. I believe expectancy theory is instructive as a fourth theoretical approach to understanding the complex relationship between individuals in organizations and evaluative efforts. Expectancy theory offers penetrating insights into the motivational behavior of individuals in organizations and their attitudes toward use or rejection of evaluative efforts. The common, defining attribute addressed by these theories (that is important for internal evaluators) is the distance between evaluator and client and the amount of communication and involvement of the client in the evaluation. The greater the interchange between two parties to an evaluation the greater potential there is for successful outcomes. The following discussion highlights the basic themes of exchange, supply and demand, and decision-making theories and concludes with a comparison of the three theories and the value of expectancy theory as an explanatory basis for successful internal evaluation.

EXCHANGE THEORY

Love (1991), in his book *Internal Evaluation: Building Organizations From Within,* stresses the importance of the relationship between internal evaluators and managers and the necessity for evaluators to focus on managers' needs. He offers exchange theory as a conceptual approach to understand this dynamic relationship. Exchange theory is based on the belief that individuals will exchange something when they perceive that the benefits of the exchange outweigh its costs. The implication of exchange theory for internal evaluators is that this approach requires evaluators to identify managers' information needs and respond to those needs with evaluation data. Internal evaluators must recognize that information is the organizational medium of exchange and that information can be marketed as a value-added effort supporting program managers. Internal evaluators can build relationships with managers where the costs of cooperation with the internal evaluation staff are outweighed by the benefits of the information furnished. For Love, this approach to internal evaluation practice is flexible, dynamic, and situationally responsive, emphasizing the helpful nature of evaluation by providing an ongoing service to managers.

SUPPLY AND DEMAND THEORY

A basic maxim in economic theory is that markets will create their own supply and demand and become efficient and effective when the supply of goods and/or services is in equilibrium with the demand. Mayne (1994) applies this approach to internal evaluation in organizations, arguing that evaluation will be used when the supply of evaluation information meets the demand for that kind of information. He points out that many of the evaluations produced are conducted with the demand-push explanation, where the supply of good evaluation creates the demand for the information, resulting in utilization. He believes that it is naive to expect organizational decision making to conform to the production of evaluation information. The demand-pull approach to explaining utilization suggests that if organizations are clear about their need for evaluation information, then evaluations will be produced to fill that need.

Mayne (1994) explains that the "market" in organizations is the decision-making regime and the "price" is the value placed by the organization on evaluations that are produced. Organizations will only consider and place a value on information when it is useful and timely. When the value and the need for information are equal, utilization will take place and continue until the marginal cost of the information exceeds the marginal value for further information. The goal for effective internal evaluation is a model that tries to balance supply and demand, where internal evaluators supply information to meet the demand and, at the same time, attempt to influence the demand. Influencing demand requires not only high-quality, useful evaluations but also a marketing effort by the evaluators of the added value of evaluative efforts. (See Chapter 9 for additional discussion on marketing evaluations.) According to Mayne, the supply and demand explanation for evaluation use is consistent with the federal Canadian experience with evaluation.

DECISION-MAKING THEORY

The predominant orientation of discussions in the literature about internal evaluation is its value in supporting the decision-making process. Love (1991) views internal evaluation as a management support system, helping managers cope with information overload and improving decision making under conditions of uncertainty. Clifford and Sherman (1983) describe the internal evaluation function as supporting "planning and management in such a manner as to maximize the amount of intelligence and analytical discipline involved in the decision-making process" (p. 23). Winberg (1991) believes that internal evaluators must adopt a management perspective in conducting evaluations. He feels that to be effective as a management tool, an internal evaluation staff must focus on the information needs, concerns, and priorities of senior management. Scriven (1993) makes the useful distinction in decision-making support between a "strong" version and a "weak" version. The strong decision support concept of evaluation is described as "evaluators . . . doing investigations designed to arrive at *evaluative conclusions to assist the decision maker* [italics in the original]" (p. 5). The weak decision support approach does not draw evaluative conclusions or critique program goals, but only gathers factual data, allowing decisionmakers to draw their own evaluative conclusions.

The decision-making model is the most common and dominant model of internal evaluation described and prescribed in the literature (Mathison, 1991). Mathison believes that the decision-making model has become predominant (1) because it is congruent with the almost universal view of organizations as bureaucratic institutions, and (2) because of the influence of business and industry on all organizational life. She describes the process of the decision-making model as follows:

1. A decision must be made and that decision presents itself as a dilemma.
2. The options that satisfy the decision dilemma are specified.
3. The effects (desirable and undesirable) are specified (including costs, benefits, and consequences) for each decision option.
4. The most desirable option is chosen by the decision maker(s) (Mathison, 1991, p. 161).

Mathison's decision-making model is instructive but it presumes decision making to be a rational and sequential process, which is seldom the case. Options, effects, and consequences are rarely clear, and the decisionmaker may not always choose the most desirable option. However, notwithstanding the irrationality of the decision-making process, internal evaluators can improve the process with the production and explanation of data supplementing the resources available to the decisionmaker.

The paradox of the decision-making model of internal evaluation is that although it is generally offered as the justification for internal evaluation, it is also the lightning rod for criticism that it favors the managerial and executive levels of organizations with decision-making data. (In some rare instances, an internal evaluation staff may be established for "window dressing" and their services diverted to menial tasks, but in an era of scarce resources that is a high price to pay for an evaluation facade.) At the risk of belaboring an obvious point, it seems incontrovertible that an organization would establish and staff an internal evaluation office that it did not intend to use (in some fashion) to support the organization and its decision-making processes. The decision-making domain of the organization is the appropriate venue for evaluation where it can support and improve the decision-making process. Support of the decision-making process does not, in and of itself, corrupt the independence of evaluation efforts, but there are certain inherent dangers that deserve mention.

Critics of internal evaluation underscore the potential erosion of evaluator independence and allegiance to the organization's administrators. One of the problems for internal evaluators is co-optation, where the organizational goals are internalized by the evaluation staff, who then become project advocates (Mathison, 1991). Internal evaluators deal with administrators on a regular basis, opening the potential for identifying with them personally, confusing the interests of the organization with those of the administrators, and becoming tools of the administrators (House, 1986). Internal evaluation may become like information management and lose some of the obligation to provide independent critique of programs (Mathison, 1991). Like most organizational functions, there are benefits and costs to performing internal evaluation. Internal evaluators need to strive to maintain a balance between serving the organization with objective production of information and being responsive to managers' requests and concerns. Independence does not signify indifference toward managerial concerns but a recognition by evaluators that evaluation can best serve and benefit organizations when evaluators maintain a reputation for credible and fair analysis.

EXPECTANCY THEORY

I am convinced that one of the more promising approaches to increasing the use of evaluation in organizations is for evaluators to find out what motivates managers to accept or reject evaluation as a useful tool. Because the core concept of evaluation (independent assessment and judgment) has minimal room for alteration (or it no longer is evaluation), increased use depends on either more successful marketing by evaluators, greater acceptance by managers, or a combination of both. I suspect that many of us tend to impute our own values and evaluation orientation to managers and evaluation clients and then fail to understand why these views are rejected. A lack of empathy, understanding, and knowledge of client motivation may contribute to the often contentious nature of the evaluator-client relationship. (Chapter 4 pointed out the disparate viewpoints of program managers and evaluators.)

Expectancy theory expands on the concepts of exchange theory by seeking to understand the motives for acceptance or rejection of the exchange activity. My conviction is that the traditional negative frame of reference, held by many managers toward evaluative activities (as evidenced by their comments in Chapter 4), can be modified by evaluators by studying the motives of managers who accept or reject evaluation. By minimizing the inherent intimidating nature of evaluation, clarifying the risk-reward probabilities involved when evaluations are conducted, and clarifying managers' motives for acceptance or rejection, managers may become more accommodating toward evaluative activities.

Expectancy theory is an explanatory framework for dealing with managers' disdain for evaluative activities. As defined by Rainey (1991):

> Expectancy theory holds that an individual considering an action sums up the values of all the outcomes that will result from the action, with each outcome weighted by the probability of its occurrence. The higher the probability of good outcomes and the lower the probability of bad ones, the stronger the motivation to perform the action. In other words, the theory draws on the classic utilitarian idea that people will do what they see *most likely* to result in the *most good* and the *least bad* [italics in the original]. (p. 136)

This approach requires increased interaction between evaluators and clients and greater communication during evaluations. If managers can be convinced that more good than harm will come from an evaluation, they may be persuaded to participate. "Expectancy is the belief a specific reinforcement will occur as a result of a particular behavior" (Marsella

& Yang, 1983, p. 659). Internal evaluators can decrease the dissonance experienced by managers and reinforce the advantages of evaluation with a better understanding of managers' aversion to program reviews. By reframing the evaluation process to accentuate the benefits, accurately depict the risk, and allow managerial input, internal evaluators may begin to erode the antipathy displayed by many program managers toward evaluation. Key to this transformation is the reputation of evaluators as fair and objective observers of programs and issues, yet empathic of the program manager's environment. Intensifying communication between internal evaluators and clients increases understanding of the purpose and process of evaluation and heightens the probability that evaluation results will be used. I am convinced that the combination of advocacy evaluation (discussed later in this chapter) and expectancy theory composes a practical philosophical and communication framework to guide internal evaluators in their relationships with the organization and with clients.

ACTION RESEARCH

Action research is one of the major approaches used by organizational development consultants initiating planned change in organizations, but it can also be applied to problem solving by internal evaluators. Approaching problem solving from an action research perspective moves evaluators away from the traditional research approach to problems and changes the relationship between evaluators and managers. In action research, the process of diagnosis, analysis, and implementing change is conducted with the full participation of the individuals in the program. It is less formal than evaluation but similar to formative evaluation, which seeks to improves programs. Action-oriented research generally requires long-term commitments and high levels of psychological intensity because researchers and the organization's members are jointly engaged in testing assumptions, generating new ideas, and reviewing alternative, innovative approaches (Cummings, Mohrman, Mohrman, & Ledford, 1985).

The fundamental distinction between evaluation and action research is the nature of the relationship between evaluator and client: Action researchers function in the capacity of facilitators, helping the organization identify and solve its own problems, whereas formative evaluators operate more formally as applied researchers. Occasionally, evaluators are asked to participate in action research endeavors because of their facilitation skills and objective perspective. Sometimes internal evaluators are called on to help solve a problem in an interactive manner with a specific organizational entity and an action research approach is more appropriate than evaluation. The distinction between formative evaluation and action research is blurred, but it is important for internal evaluators to be aware of the variations in research approaches because the methodology selected affects the conceptualization of the problem, the design of the intervention, and the eventual dissemination of the results of the research (Patton, 1990).

Observation, Objectivity, and Evaluation

The essential mechanism constituting the practice of internal evaluation is, like all science, the act of observing and commenting on organizational policies, procedures, operations, and administration. Legitimating internal inquiry requires and is dependent on objective observation and reporting. Anything less does not constitute science nor does it constitute a value-added evaluation effort. Evaluators who are perceived to be tools of the administration or open to manipulation by program managers or interest groups will not be seen as independent and impartial. The essential, epistemological issue is to establish whether internal evaluators can be sufficiently objective in their activities to be recognized as dispassionate, unbiased, neutral observers of the organizational scene. Scriven's (1997) notion of objectivity is "with basis and without bias" (p. 480). A fundamental requirement, therefore, for internal evaluators, is to establish that objective internal inquiry is possible and practiced. Chelimsky (1997) puts the importance of objective observation in proper perspective when she writes:

> The evaluator's role in the 21st century should include not only the assessment of what has been experienced and observed but also a constant questioning of his or her own objectivity and sensitivity in reporting on precisely what has been experienced and observed. (p. 25)

Neutrality and impartiality have long been the touchstone of science and professional evaluation. Yet a tautological proclamation that internal evaluators are objective because they are expected to be objective is unconvincing, depicts shallow reasoning, and represents an inadequate justification for the professional practice of internal evaluation. If internal evaluation is to be accepted in the evaluation community as a legitimate segment of the profession, then convincing philosophical and scientific arguments must be mobilized, not only to mollify critics but also to construct a plausible, epistemological foundation that legitimates the internal, impartial review process. The following discussion will present evidence suggesting that (1) absolute objectivity is improbable, inside or outside an organization; (2) both external and internal evaluators have impediments toward achieving perfect impartiality; and (3) there are motives, arrangements, professional standards, and organizational cultural artifacts that promote objectivity and minimize bias and subjectivity in internal settings.

The question to be answered to establish whether objectivity is plausible for internal evaluators is, Can internal evaluators render objective opinions when they

are employed by the organization;

depend on the organization for pay, benefits, and support;

ostensibly have some degree of allegiance to the basic principles of the organization's mission;

work in close association with other members of the organization; and

share, with other organizational entities, some responsibility for organizational performance?

PRINCIPAL CRITICISM

The principal criticism of internal evaluation is that internal evaluators can develop, by virtue of their location, contractual employment agreements and continuous, intimate association with the organization, an empathic identification with the organization and its administrators that taints their neutrality, objectivity, and ability to make unbiased observations. Total lack of bias and objectivity is the stuff of mythology as each of us, with our education, experience, values, and beliefs, leaves our imprint on our work. But our inability to attain this Sisyphean goal of objectivity does not make impartial evaluations impossible. Scriven (1997) writes of the challenge for the internal evaluator:

> Relatedly, the role of the internal evaluator is a very difficult one, because the program not only is the paymaster but also represents the social environment in which the evaluator has worked for some time. Still, the label is not an oxymoron; such a position is a great challenge for an evaluator, and the difficulties can be overcome to a remarkable degree. (p. 487)

Impartiality is the primary and most difficult criticism for internal evaluators to overcome. House (1986), comparing external to internal evaluation, depicts internal evaluators as tools of administrators, conducting evaluations to justify decisions, whereas external evaluators "conduct the evaluation in accord with . . . professional standards of evaluation, and ultimately let the chips fall where they may" (p. 63). He portrays internal evaluators as "bureaucrats" concerned about whether their careers "flourish or wither" and says that "it would be more than naive to believe they do not worry about the repercussions of their evaluations" (p. 64). House (1986) believes that the proximity of internal evaluators to their work materially affects their impartiality:

> Quite naturally, the evaluators deal with the administrators on a daily basis, try to meet the information needs of the administration, and identify with the administrators personally. It is only a short step to confusing the interests of the organization with those of the administrators. This is a serious error for the evaluator to make and can lead to all sorts of distortions in the evaluation process. (p. 64)

Mathison (1991) suggests that if internal evaluators adopt the decision-making model of evaluation, they will respond disproportionately to the needs of administrators and put organizational goals ahead of their professional obligations as evaluators. Kennedy (1983) sees the dynamics of organizations forcing internal evaluators to adapt their roles to the needs of the organization.

The implicit implications in these characterizations of internal evaluators are that attainment of objectivity is unrealizable. The act of crossing the organizational threshold is believed to somehow tarnish objectivity and render it inoperative. Criticisms such as these are not entirely unfounded, and examples can easily be found to support the allegations. In fact, it is a healthy sign in the evaluation community to be concerned about these issues and debate questions raised regarding the impartiality and institutional integrity of the internal evaluation process. Although House (1986) has been critical of internal evaluators, he nevertheless points out that there are opportunities in the growth of internal evaluation and "we should be paying serious scholarly attention to the new demands and opportunities of this transformation" (p. 64).

OBSERVATION AND EVALUATION

Objective observation for internal evaluators is of paramount importance and when lacking may be a crippling impediment to achieving influence in an organization. Embedding observation in scientific protocols is what begins the process of establishing it as objective. "Scientific observation is deliberate search, carried out with care and forethought, as contrasted with the casual and largely passive perception of everyday life" (Kaplan, 1964, p. 126). No matter how deliberate, detailed, and careful these observations are, however, they are difficult to establish as absolutely objective. "We like to imagine that we objectively observe whatever is present, but even what we see may be influenced by our expectations" (Krathwohl, 1985, p. 23). Put another way, "The conclusions to be drawn from a particular piece of data depended very much on the frameworks through which it was to be interpreted" (Morgan, 1983, p. 12). The interaction of subject and observer has profound implications for the determination of objectivity, and the ability of the internal evaluator to convince that an acceptable approximation of objectivity has been attained is the sine qua non for internal evaluators.

> Science is basically a process of interaction, or better still, of *engagement* [italics in the original]. Scientists engage a subject of study by interacting with it through means of a particular frame of reference, and what is observed and discovered in the object (i.e., its objectivity) is as much a

product of this interaction and the protocol and technique through which it is operationalized as it is of the object itself. (Morgan, 1983, p. 13)

In the 18th century, Kant drew our attention to the difficulty in being objective by suggesting that all reality is subject to the mind's interpretation. As summarized by Tarnas (1991), Kant concluded:

All human cognition of the world is channeled through the human mind's categories. The necessity and certainty of scientific knowledge derive from the mind, and are embedded in the mind's perception and understanding of the world. They do not derive from nature independent of the mind, which in fact can never be known in itself. What man knows is a world permeated by his knowledge, and causality and the necessary laws of science are built into the framework of his cognition. Observations alone do not give man certain laws; rather, those laws reflect the laws of man's mental organization. In the act of human cognition, the mind does not conform to things; rather, things conform to the mind. (p. 343)

Background knowledge, education, experience, values, and beliefs all contribute to confounding the issue of objectivity, making it difficult to approach the norm of absolute objectivity.

Observation cannot be a "neutral foundation," nor a "disinterested arbiter" of disputes, for the process of observation is influenced (unconsciously) by the theories or hypotheses that the observer holds before [italics in the original] the observations are made. (Phillips, 1987, p. 9)

Based on scholarly research, it would appear that the path to objective observation is strewn with formidable obstacles, not the least of which is the human mind as a filtering mechanism. Tarnas (1991) eloquently summarizes the difficulties faced by both scientists and internal evaluators:

Because scientific knowledge is a product of human interpretive structures that are themselves relative, variable, and creatively employed, and finally because the act of observation in some sense produces the objective reality science attempts to explicate, the truths of science are neither absolute nor unequivocally objective. (p. 359)

"INSIDERS" AND "OUTSIDERS"

Because the objectivity debate is one of degree—no researcher is totally free from impediments to absolute objectivity—are there circumstances, policies, structures, procedures, rules, or systemic biases that are fatal flaws to evaluative inquiry conducted by individuals permanently residing within an organization? Bartunek and Louis (1996), contrasting the physical and psychological distance or connectedness to phenomena being studied, reported on work by Evered and Louis (1981), who suggested

> that in "inquiry from the inside," the researcher is immersed in a setting and learns through being in the role of an actor in the real situation under study. This mode of inquiry is grounded in the epistemological assumption that knowledge comes from human experience and derives from an interpretive paradigm: By "being there," the actor comes to know. By contrast, in "inquiry from the outside," the researcher remains a detached onlooker, a non-participant in the social world under study. (p. 14)

Another view of the "insider/outsider" comes from a discussion of the sociology of knowledge by Merton (1972) and contrasts the interests and values of insiders and outsiders:

> Insider and Outsider scholars have significantly different foci of interest. . . . The Insiders, sharing the deepest concerns of the group or at the least being thoroughly aware of them, will so direct their inquires as to have them be relevant to those concerns. So, too, the Outsiders will inquire into problems relevant to the distinctive values and interests which they share with members of *their* [italics in the original] group. But these are bound to differ from those of the group under study if only because the Outsiders occupy different places in the social structure. (p. 16)

External evaluators are not impervious to organizational influences. "Although external evaluators have an air of objectivity, in truth many face the same pressures [as internal evaluators] to please their clients" (Torres, Preskill, & Piontek, 1996, p. 54). Evaluation consultant companies regularly rely on repeat evaluation jobs from contracting agencies for continuing business. Lengthy affiliation between evaluation consultants and agencies has the potential to contaminate objectivity much like the permanent employment status of internal evaluators is alleged to affect them. Many external evaluation contractors concentrate their resources in a particular sector, specializing in evaluating programs in health care, criminal justice, or education. It would be naive to presume that although these evaluations are externally contracted, the evaluators do not have normative viewpoints on the optimum performance of these programs. These viewpoints may influence their objectivity. Managers responsible for contracting for external evaluations have a vested interest in evaluation reports that, at the very least, do no harm and expectations that favorable findings will result. House (1997) reports that he has "come across a few instances in which government departments have told prospective evaluators what findings they want to appear in the final evaluation report and that they must include those if they want the contract" (p. 46). Scriven (1993) suggests that managers picking external evaluators may select for "friendliness" and also participate in writing the evaluation design, both of which bias toward favorable findings.

The notion that external researchers are objective and internal researchers are subjective is overly simplistic. It presumes that internal evaluators cannot escape parochial tendencies and distance themselves sufficiently from issues for a dispassionate review. It also presumes that external evaluators will always retain their scientific neutrality and never be influenced or charmed by the organization's programs and personnel or the expectation of additional evaluation contracts. We should refrain from assigning, a priori, objectivity dicta to either external or internal evaluators and judge evaluation results on their merits. Neither internal nor external evaluators have a defensible, monopolistic claim on objectivity. The organizational boundary should not demarcate objectivity, conferring objectivity to those external and subjectivity to those within. Rather, organizational borders should be seen as osmotic, permitting the objective condition to exist equally on either side wherever and whenever it can be demonstrated. Removing the borders as the operative key to determining objectivity allows objectivity to be decided situationally on merit, with observers other than evaluators serving as arbitrators.

INFORMED INVESTIGATORS

It would be presumptuous and arrogant to assert that internal evaluators are not influenced by the ambient organizational environment where they practice, but it would be equally irrational and unreasonable to unequivocally declare that these influences materially affect their impartiality. Internal evaluators are not unlike criminal investigators who, having a suspect in a crime, must nevertheless collect and present sufficient evidence to convince independent arbitrators (prosecuting attorneys, judges, and juries) beyond a reasonable doubt that the suspected perpetrator of the crime is in fact guilty. The preconceived opinions of criminal investigators must be temporarily suspended while they seek and assemble compelling factual evidence in their cases. Their education, investigative skills, prior experience, knowledge of criminal behavior, and judicial expertise do not hamper their investigative activities but are beneficial tools aiding them in their work. Like the "informed investigator" seeking known facts about a crime, so too, the objective internal evaluator is an "informed evaluator," knowledgeable about the organization and skilled in evaluative techniques, yet required to suspend biases, prejudices, and preconceived opinions while seeking accurate data. Total liberation from organizational influences is highly improbable and possibly not even desirable. An understanding of substantive evaluative issues, similar to the knowledge and skills of the criminal investigator, is more help than hindrance. Informed observation can be more efficient and effective than naive engagement with an issue if proper, professional objective standards are employed.

To avoid erroneously concluding that because absolute, objective observation is impossible none should be attempted, it is well to remember that all science, including evaluation, involves establishing an acceptable standard of precision at a level that is attainable given the circumstances and available knowledge at the time. "The role of social scientist concerned with achieving knowledge about society requires enough detachment and trained capacity to know how to assemble and assess the evidence without regard for what the analysis seems to imply about the worth of one's group" (Merton, 1972, p. 41). The distinction between objectivity and subjectivity is often obscure and eventually defined by the evaluation user. The subjective orientation that may affect insider observations is not always the sign of a defective product, and biases can be detected and corrected through the use of various mechanisms.

INCENTIVES TO MINIMIZE INSIDER BIAS

The intellectual struggle to remain unbiased while working in the capacity of an insider can be assisted by organizational arrangements, mechanisms, and conditions that minimize the potential for internal bias and establish an environment of objective ethos. In 1989 in *Evaluation Practice,* I enumerated eight incentives that motivated internal evaluators to act impartially during internal evaluations (Sonnichsen, 1989b). The following 12 factors are a further refinement of that argument:

✧ *Decision review process:* Evaluation findings and recommendations are normally reviewed by several layers of senior managers before final approval or rejection. Their divergent perspectives, scrutiny, and commentary, reflecting contrasting backgrounds, attitudes, values, and varying attachment to the evaluation issue, will likely uncover any examples of egregious bias. The counter-premise that these "objective arbitrators" are possibly susceptible to and possess similar unconscious and latent biases that infect the evaluators is offset by the heterogenetic makeup of personnel with their various perspectives.

✧ *Organizational mobility:* Owing to the internal rotational and promotional policies in many organizations, it is difficult to predict individuals' working environments or their supervisory hierarchy over an extended career. Developing a reputation for integrity in all assignments is a prudent course of action for organizational careerists. Career mobility also adds a safeguard, albeit indirectly, by limiting the formation of personal loyalties and other allegiances that may serve to distort the evaluation process, thus contributing to credibility and ethical performance.

✧ *Expert review:* Evaluation results are heavily scrutinized by program experts, who will likely detect the slightest departure from evenhandedness and will unhesitatingly publicize any perceived biases. Recognition of this expert review is a powerful motivator for the individual evaluator, fostering strict adherence to evaluation standards that can withstand even the most stringent review.

❖ *Organizational scrutiny:* Interested stakeholders in decision-making forums throughout the organization review the results of internal evaluations. The anticipation of public exposure, debate, and critical commentary on research and evaluation results minimizes any tendency toward bias.

❖ *Professional ethics and standards:* In 1994, the American Evaluation Association (AEA) promulgated "Guiding Principles for Evaluators" (AEA, 1995) and the Joint Committee on Standards for Educational Evaluation published the *Program Evaluation Standards.* Internal evaluators can use these principles and standards to guide them in conducting independent and objective evaluations.

❖ *Organizational ethics:* Many organizations pride themselves on reputations for ethical conduct that are embedded in their tradition and culture. Success within such an organization requires an evaluator's conformity to the organization's values of honesty and integrity.

❖ *Organizational location:* An evaluation office located sufficiently close to the head of the organization and possessing the necessary power base to influence the organization lessens the likelihood that internal evaluators will be asked to, or have any incentive to, manipulate data and/or findings.

❖ *Operating philosophy:* Internal evaluators with a change agent mentality may be less vulnerable to political manipulation because the staff has established an activist orientation. A quality of change agents is independence, which minimizes the attraction or need to manipulate evaluation data.

❖ *Accountability:* Internal evaluation components in public agencies are subject to both internal and external audits of their activities and outputs. This audit process serves as a deterrent to the manipulation of data or advancement of findings based on personal biases.

❖ *Conspiratorial difficulty:* Attempts to manipulate data to favor or disfavor a program or issue most likely involve more than one individual, either evaluators, program personnel, or both. For two or more individuals to successfully maneuver to accomplish this task and avoid detection by their colleagues is highly unlikely.

✧ *Professional training:* Trained researchers and evaluators are exposed to the basic tenets of neutral and unbiased inquiry during their education. Scientifically trained colleagues, grouped together in an evaluation office, reinforce this professional ethic.

✧ *Viewpoint diversity:* The diversity of viewpoints of internal evaluators tends to minimize the subjective distortion that may occur when examining organizational phenomena.

Not all of these 12 factors are present in their entirety in any organization or during any particular evaluation. Sufficient conditions, however, are present in most organizations to minimize the attraction of specious data manipulation by evaluators or attempts by program personnel to influence the evaluation outcome. These 12 factors, operating in the internal evaluation environment, function implicitly as well as explicitly to reinforce ethical behavior and contribute to the maintenance of evaluator impartiality.

POTENTIAL FOR INTERNAL EVALUATOR OBJECTIVITY

Based on the above discussion on objective observation, it appears that there are no unequivocally compelling arguments that would deny the potential for objectivity inside an organization and no intrinsic organizational impediments that preclude rendering an accurate assessment of organizational activities by insiders. Logically, therefore, I believe it is reasonable to assert that internal evaluators, employing their intellect, judgment, professional education, and training, can carefully review organizational issues and objectively collect and present evidence that is situationally responsive, contextually useful, and fact based. Although it cannot be guaranteed with absolute certainty that objectivity will become the hallmark of all internal evaluations under all circumstances, it is, nevertheless, a laudable and attainable goal and it seems reasonable to presume that many internal evaluations achieve that standard. We must, however, remember that all our incantations about the search for objectivity have limitations. Writing on the postmodern mind, Tarnas (1991) puts this quest in the proper perspective:

> All human knowledge is mediated by signs and symbols of uncertain provenance, constituted by historically and culturally variable predispositions, and influenced by often unconscious human interests. Hence the nature of truth and reality, in science no less than in philosophy, religion, or art, is radically ambiguous. The subject can never presume to transcend the manifold predispositions of his or her subjectivity. One can at best attempt a fusion of horizons, a never-complete rapprochement between subject and object. (p. 397)

During this discussion, I have attempted to establish the parameters of objectivity in internal organizational settings and the probability of its occurrence. The internal evaluator's role in the modern organization requires delicate balancing of the scientific cannons of independent observation and objectivity with the pragmatic requirements of organizations to produce useful, timely information for use in the decision making process. Objectivity's importance as the cornerstone of credibility and thus the foundation for successful insider inquiry is difficult to overstate. The ineluctable consequences of failing to achieve demonstrable objectivity during internal evaluations are the diminution of the value of evaluation to the organization and the validation of bias and subjectivity ascribed to internal evaluators.

Identity of the Internal Evaluation Office

A successful internal evaluation office is not an amorphous, ill-understood group of researchers toiling in obscurity, but a conspicuous, transparent, legitimized component of the organization. Any ambiguity in the identity of an internal evaluation office can have a corrosive effect on the institutionalization of the evaluation function. Successful evaluation offices have developed identifiable characteristics and a style of operation that is understood by the evaluators and perceived throughout the organization. The image of the internal evaluation office originates from a combination of the vision that the evaluation staff has of their purpose and role in the organization and the attitude and operational mandate from senior management. It is shaped by the relationships with other components in the organization. It results from the conception of the evaluation staff's organizational role and the myriad views and opinions of clients, peers, and superiors imputed to the evaluation staff. Figure 5.1 portrays the entities and relationships that form and affect this identity.

The behavior of internal evaluators and their leaders constitutes a significant portion of the office identity. Evaluation office identity is a function of relationships, leadership, credibility, independence, role definition, and evaluation ideology.

Relationships. Relationships are an outgrowth of the purpose of the evaluation office and the guidelines under which it was established. The executive leadership of the host organization helps shape the agenda of the evaluation office, which in turn affects the relationships that the evaluation office has with other organizational components. Internal evaluators have relationships with superiors, peers, clients, program managers, organizational executives and employees, relevant stakeholders, and parent organizational components. These dynamic relationships fluctuate with the organization's conditions, personalities, and events and mold the image of the internal evaluation office.

Leadership. Evaluation office directors exert considerable influence over the style and practice of internal evaluation due to the vague understanding of the nature of evaluation by most senior managers and the sometimes ambiguous mission assigned to the internal evaluation office. Chapter 9 will discuss leadership characteristics for evaluation directors in detail.

Credibility. Credibility, mentioned in Chapter 4 as one of the most important elements for internal evaluators acting as change agents, is a defining characteristic of an internal evaluation office. It is one of the attributes that legitimize the results of evaluations. The evaluators earn much of the credibility of an evaluation staff, but the perception of credibility among organizational components is external to the staff.

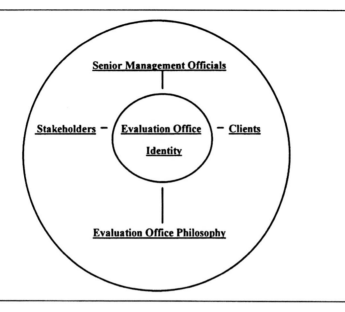

Figure 5.1. Evaluation Office Identity

Credibility is built on evaluation office attributes of independence, fairness, research capability, organizational commitment, and placement in the structure of the organization. It is a fragile component of internal evaluation office identity, subject to continuous renewal and potential loss.

Independence. Cited in Chapter 4 as fundamental to the role of evaluators as change agents, independence is also a vital component defining the identity of an evaluation office. The autonomy of the internal evaluation office legitimizes the practice of internal evaluation. Recognition of independence is the first step in establishing the office as a credible producer of information. It is an essential ingredient in authenticating the evaluation office as a bona fide component in the organization. Inability to project a reputation for independence vitiates the potency of an internal evaluation office. Organizational affiliation through employment and acceptance of core values does not preclude independent and skeptical review of those policies and activities supporting the core organizational mission. Assiduous commitment by evaluators and senior management to the agreements and structural artifacts establishing the role and parameters of evaluation will help sustain the independence of the evaluation office. The risks and problems associated with evaluator interaction with clients are not lethal to the conduct of objective evaluations.

Role definition. The purpose of internal evaluation and its expected use and value to the organization define the evaluator role. Evaluation information produced by the internal evaluation staff may be used for accountability, advocacy, and program improvement (Windle & Neigher, 1978). Acknowledging the legitimacy of these uses of evaluation has profound implications for evaluators within organizations (Love, 1983c). A mutual understanding, by evaluators and senior management, of the fundamental role of internal evaluators and the parameters of their activities will identify the office and establish its relationship with the organization.

Evaluation ideology. The philosophical and methodological premises on which internal evaluators base their application of internal evaluation constitute an evaluation ideology. This contributes to the evaluation office's identity. The selected approach to internal evaluation is a product of the agreement with the organization's leadership on the purpose of the evaluation office, but within those parameters exists a wide latitude. The management style and behavior of the evaluation office's leadership is instrumental in establishing this aspect of the evaluation office's identity.

Advocacy Evaluation

Advocacy evaluation is a philosophical and administrative approach to internal evaluation that seeks to increase the utility of internal evaluation information by emphasizing the role of evaluators as change agents. Advocacy evaluation is an overarching, philosophical, activist orientation that modifies the traditional neutral behavior of internal evaluators by increasing the evaluator's involvement with the organization (Sonnichsen, 1988, 1989a). The practice of advocacy evaluation was a major contributor to the success of the Federal Bureau of Investigation's (FBI) internal evaluation office. It is an appropriate role for internal evaluators seeking to have a high impact on organizations.

CONCEPTUAL FOUNDATION

Advocacy evaluation is partially a practical response to and resolution of the evaluation utilization dilemma. It has its conceptual basis in the competitive nature among organizational components. As both an evaluator and organizational executive, it was frustrating for me to observe the balkanization of factions in an organization over policy development, resource distribution, personnel assignment, change efforts, budgeting decisions, equipment procurement, and strategic planning. The rivalry and antagonism that could arise during organizational debates underscored the stakes involved among "turf"-conscious managers and executives. Emotional, parochial, and political arguments presented during discussions of major issues often ignored research data, simply because it was underrepresented at the table. If evaluative information is to have an influence, it must be represented during important debates on organizational administration and operations. In other words, it must have a sponsor or advocate inserting the evaluation findings and recommendations into the debates.

Justification for practicing advocacy in internal evaluation settings is conceptually anchored in the assumption that objectively derived information has a value in the competitive workplace and its failure to be used during deliberations contributes to suboptimal decision making. The advocacy role being recommended here has two dimensions: first, advocating that evaluation findings and recommendations have a value in organizational debates and should be considered as significant inputs into the organizational decision-making process; and second, the actual advocating of the recommended courses of action by the evaluators to ensure visibility of the outcomes of an independent assessment of a program or issue. This approach satisfies both instrumental and conceptual utilization tests by ensuring that evaluation results have the opportunity to influence the organization either by illuminating organizational debates with evaluative information; the actual acceptance, approval, and implementation of evaluation recommendations; or both. Evaluation study results can influence policy deliberations within organizations if the results are credibly and accurately represented and heard in discussion forums. Without an advocate, evaluation data are unlikely to achieve any significant influence. Advocacy evaluation is an excellent way to increase evaluation use, and its practice reflects evaluators' interest in the success of the organization. By improving organizational operations, evaluators can satisfy their own needs to contribute to the organization's excellence and success.

PRACTICE OF ADVOCACY EVALUATION

The practice of advocacy evaluation requires redefining the traditional role for internal evaluators. Traditionally, the research role has been neutral with neither interest in nor responsibility for the eventual use of research data. Bellavita (1986) conducted a nationwide survey to identify effective means of communicating research results and concluded that evaluators are reluctant to acknowledge their political role. He reported their preference for a policy analysis model of communication where evaluators complete their role when they submit their final report to the client. Bellavita concluded that evaluators adopt a neutral position because of their "ethos of objectivity," but cautions that this stance will risk having the evaluation results ignored by decisionmakers.

The objectivity born of neutrality must be maintained throughout the research phase for evaluation to maintain its credibility as an unbiased producer of information. The essence of the argument against advocating evaluation results and recommendations is the risk of contamination: the co-optation of evaluators through interaction with the client or program personnel. Interaction with personnel being evaluated has the potential to undermine objectivity and the search for truth (Scriven, 1997). However, advocacy and impartiality occur at different phases of the evaluation, and do not overlap. An impartial approach to research does not preclude internal evaluators from explaining, clarifying, and interpreting the results of evaluation and elucidating the empirical basis for the findings and recommendations.

The practice of advocacy evaluation does not align internal evaluators with any particular faction in the organization, but positions them to be an independent voice for positive change. Assertive positions by evaluators for program improvement or operational alterations are adopted only after the completion of an unbiased, valid, defensible evaluation of a program or issue. Advocating recommendations for positive change resulting from the evaluation places the internal evaluator in the role of an active participant in the deliberations over the results of the evaluation. Bellavita, Wholey, and Abramson (1986) describe the modern evaluator as a program advocate,

> not an advocate in the sense of an ideologue willing to manipulate data and to alter findings to secure next year's funding. The new evaluator is someone who believes in and is interested in helping programs and organizations succeed. At times the program advocate evaluator will play the traditional critic role: challenging basic program assumptions, reporting lackluster performance, or identifying inefficiencies. The difference, however, is that criticism is not the end of performance-oriented evaluation; rather, it is part of a larger process of program and organizational improvement, a process that receives as much of the evaluator's attention and talents as the criticism function. (p. 289)

To neglect to participate in the debate and discussion over evaluation results deprives the organization of an independent, knowledgeable program voice.

Few incentives exist for program personnel to identify and discuss deficiencies in their own programs, but the practice of advocacy evaluation can act to counterbalance biased program viewpoints. Most policy discussions in organizations confront decisionmakers with a variety of parochial inputs from the affected parties, factions, and interested stakeholders, each with varying degrees of rank, power, logic, and substance. Frequently, on major organizational matters, balkanization occurs, cleaving the organizations into uncompromising factions. In this emotionally charged atmosphere, evaluation data without an advocate may be ignored. Indifference and temerity by evaluators during internal policy debates may contribute to nonuse of evaluation data. The belief that evaluative data possess some intrinsic, transcendental, luminescent attractiveness ensuring their use ignores the competitive environment of the organization. Evaluative data fed into information processing systems of organizations, without sponsorship or advocacy, may be misinterpreted, indiscriminately dissected for partisan defense, totally ignored, or selectively discarded.

Practicing advocacy evaluation involves (1) the advocacy of evaluation as a useful analytical technique for supplying unbiased information to an organization; (2) the advocacy of debate within the organization over the findings and recommendations contained in the evaluation; and (3) the advocacy of the recommendations for positive change. These three supporting beliefs are not mutually exclusive, and the second and third are subsets of the first. The goals of advocacy evaluation are the following:

✧ Foster debate over findings
✧ Ensure that all relevant viewpoints are heard
✧ Increase the use of evaluation information
✧ Minimize information asymmetry
✧ Create positive change in organizations
✧ Convey to senior managers accurate information on program performance
✧ Contribute to organizational improvement
✧ Help integrate evaluation into organizations

A major component of the advocacy approach to internal evaluation is the formulation of recommendations when evaluation findings identify areas for potential improvement. The offering of recommendations at the completion of an evaluation and their eventual acceptance in the organization is not a straightforward, linear process but a complex procedure requiring input from all affected parties. Recommendations offered at the completion of an evaluation may be approved for implementation, modified, or ignored, but without an advocate, they will not be adequately represented during the policy-making process. Evaluators have an ethical responsibility to ensure that program realities are accurately presented during policy debates where resource and expenditure decisions are being formulated. Evaluator neutrality precludes effective representation of program performance.

Advocacy evaluation requires recognition by internal evaluators that they function in a dynamic, complex, political arena and their activism is an attempt to market evaluation information as a valuable commodity to aid decisionmakers. Attkisson, Brown, and Hargreaves (1978) believe that an inadequate conceptualization of organizational complexity blinds evaluators to their role and hinders evaluation use.

> Because evaluation is undertaken to support decision making about [human service] programs, it enters the political arena. In this adversary domain, evaluative findings must compete with a number of other perspectives, values, and influences. The more limited concept of evaluation as the sole source of feedback ignores these other influences on administrative decisions. As a consequence, evaluative results may not compete successfully with other types of information. Evaluators must recognize that their findings are one of many internal and external sources of information that administrative decisionmakers will utilize. (p. 64)

The conceptualization of advocacy evaluation requires separating the conduct of the evaluation from advocacy of the results. In the internal evaluation environment, there is an inherent tension between advocacy and credibility. The move from neutrality to activism on behalf of evaluation results requires appropriate timing and caution by the evaluators lest they be criticized for biased evaluations. The advocacy position can be adopted only at the completion of an evaluation after data have been collected, analyzed, and interpreted and recommendations formulated. Independence and objectivity are not lost if evaluators are vigilant in the timing of their movement to an advocacy role and initiate it only after the completion of an evaluation.

Occasionally, communicating evaluation results and advocating recommendations may raise ethical issues. Depending on the primary client and any restrictive agreements on dissemination of results made at the outset of the evaluation, evaluators may have to exercise caution when discussing program improvements.

> We . . . hold that the evaluator has what amounts to a responsibility to present findings and conclusions as vividly as possible to decisionmakers receiving the report. But it would seem to behoove the evaluator to proceed more circumspectly when it comes to amplifying the awareness of the *obligation* [italics in the original] to act beyond those for whom the report is intended. In no way would this impair full presentation of data and objective interpretation of the findings. What we are saying is that, at the same time we are advocating that the evaluator take a role

in stimulating motivation to take action on results, sensitive concern for
the ethics involved must be maintained. (Davis & Salasin, 1975, p. 638)

Advocacy evaluation is not a dogmatic commitment to the recommendations in an evaluation, but an awareness campaign, challenging
organizational inertia and initiating debate on the merits of the suggested changes. Vital to the advocacy approach is strict adherence to an
objective rendering of the results and a balanced and impartial commentary on the findings and recommendations. Internal evaluators will
achieve little success in their advocacy endeavor if they are perceived as
prejudiced, overbearing, or contemptuous of the opinions of others.
When advocating evaluation-based change, any deception, tendentious
argument, or interpretive sophistry by evaluators will be quickly exposed and undermine evaluator credibility.

Advocacy is a suitable role for internal evaluators seeking an inte-
grative approach to evaluation within organizations and an essential
component for evaluators functioning in a consultative role. Advocacy
recognizes the complexity of organizational issues, the intricacies of the
decision-making process, the difficulty in elucidating research results
and matching them to problems and issues, and the burden for evaluators acting as an independent voice. Its purpose is to enlighten and
persuade, and many variations exist in its practice. Three of the four
office directors I contacted for input on current internal evaluation
practices explained that advocacy and postevaluation involvement in
publicizing and explaining findings were a key to use of the results. The
model of internal evaluation at the Salesmanship Club Youth and Family
Centers in Dallas, Texas incorporates the combined notions of advocacy
and leadership, involving the internal evaluator during all phases of
agency projects: planning and development, implementation, assessment, and feedback to senior management (Minnett, 1997).

Advocacy, as defined here, is not an emotional, ideological, partisan
argument on behalf of programs. It has an empirical substance rooted
in the objective, evaluative determination of program functions and
outcomes. The advocacy espoused is advocacy of the evaluation findings
and recommendations and should not be confused with ideological
advocacy of a program or political agenda. Advocacy can be used inside
organizations to enhance utilization and improve program operation,
but it is not meant to further any particular program values.

Blending scientific tenets with a change agent perspective allows evaluators inside organizations to successfully practice internal evaluation. Neutrality is essential during the conduct of an evaluation but becomes an impediment once the organization's policy process begins. Internal evaluators with empirical program data, participating in discussions about programs and issues, can influence the organization and represent evaluation as a legitimate, value-added function of the organization. Otherwise, internal evaluation becomes relegated to the status of another management technique, with a diminished effect on the organization's policy.

Power Dimension of Internal Evaluation

Many evaluators eschew the power aspect of evaluation, denying its relevance. Scientific inquiry is a process of seeking truth, and the traditional academic approach to evaluation relies on rational responses to the presentation of empirical findings. However, as we discussed in Chapter 3, power is a characteristic of organizations and therefore affects evaluation and evaluators when they practice in internal settings. Pfeffer (1981) believes that power and its effects are always present in the organizational decision-making process.

Power tends to have a pejorative connotation because it implies domination; however, power is simply a fact of life in hierarchically structured organizations, defining roles, responsibilities, and authority levels. Power and decision making are closely related core issues in organizations because power determines who in the organization will make decisions (Rainey, 1991). In other words, power is one of the organizational dynamics that lubricates the organizational machinery. Some of the negative connotation of power in organizations may be traced to its close relationship with politics. Power and politics are often linked, with a resulting negative implication. However, power is a reality in organizations, sometimes abused, but always present, and evaluators need to understand its effect on their work. Toffler (1990) aptly describes the intrinsic, benign quality of power: "Power is inherent in all social systems and in all human relationships. It is not a thing but an aspect of any and all relationships among people. Hence it is inescapable and neutral, intrinsically neither good nor bad" (p. 473).

Gerald Barkdoll, at the University of Southern California, Washington Public Affairs Center, has adapted the following descriptions of seven types of power[1] for use in teaching graduate students the relationships between power and internal evaluation work:

- ❖ *Coercive power* is based primarily on fear of the evaluator's ability to cause public humiliation, exposure, ridicule, punishment, censorship, and loss of resources, privileges, and perks.
- ❖ *Connecting power* is based on the evaluator's connections with influential or powerful people. "Who the evaluator knows" is an important aspect of this form of power.
- ❖ *Expert power* is based on the evaluator's expertise, skill, and knowledge, which, through respect, influence others.
- ❖ *Information power* is based on the evaluator's possession of or ability to create information that is perceived as valuable to others.
- ❖ *Legitimate power* is based on the position held by the evaluator. The concept of legitimate power is associated with the concepts of bureaucracy and hierarchy. One measure of evaluator power can be determined by his or her position on the organization chart.
- ❖ *Personal power* is based on personal traits including charisma. The degree to which an evaluator (or an evaluation staff) is liked, admired, and identified with determines the extent of this form of power.
- ❖ *Reward power* is based on the evaluator's ability to provide rewards for clients and stakeholders.

Legitimate and connecting power are structural artifacts largely determined by the evaluation office's location in the organization. Location is important in institutionalizing internal evaluation: The higher the evaluation office is on the organization chart the greater the perception of power by employees. Information and expert power are the most important aspects of power for the internal evaluator. The ability to "create" a demand for information that is perceived as accurate and unbiased is esssential for an internal evaluation staff. Expert power is derived from the combined expertise of the evaluation staff and the perception among evaluation clients that the knowledge and skills possessed by the evaluation staff are useful and helpful to their programs. Coercive, or fear-based, power should be avoided by internal evaluators because it creates superior-subordinate relationships that are dysfunctional to the practice of internal evaluation. Personal and reward power are measures of the interpersonal skills of the evaluators and their ability to market the value of internal evaluation. This configuration of organizational power is useful as a reminder to internal evaluators that although power in organizations is intrinsically benign, its use is a reality of organizational life and affects the conduct and outcomes of internal evaluations.

Evaluators seldom explicitly exercise power. The ability of internal evaluators to influence their organization is nominally based on the perception but rarely the execution of power. The power actually exerted through the evaluation process is indirect and usually rendered by decisionmakers in the hierarchy of the organization as a result of evaluation information. *Empowerment* more properly describes the environment of internal evaluators. Their location in the organizational structure, their relationship with the organization's hierarchy, and their latitude in conducting evaluation activities are a conspicuous statement of the organization's commitment to evaluation. This empowerment of the evaluation staff is an *understanding* of how evaluations will be conducted and used, and it is a derivative form of power that assists internal evaluators in performance of their tasks.

Ethical Considerations

Ethical issues may be problems for some internal evaluators but not for others, their magnitude and prevalence partially dependent on the overall culture existing in the organization. Some organizations have explicit standards of behavior for members and ethical traditions that shape the conduct of employees. In other organizations, rules and regulations regarding behavior may be less rigid and left to individual interpretation. Honea (1992), researching the influence of context on ethical issues, interviewed nine evaluators in the public sector (most with some internal responsibilities) and found that organizational culture was an influence on evaluator behavior and ethical standards. Interestingly, an AEA survey of ethical problems in evaluation (Morris & Cohn, 1993) found that respondents whose evaluation work was predominantly internal were less likely than others to report ethical problems.[2]

The existence of this condition was reinforced by four internal evaluation office directors I interviewed for this book. Representing both public and private organizations, they commented that ethical issues were not a problem for them. One of the office directors explained that having explicit understandings with clients regarding the confidentiality of information obtained during evaluations precluded ethical problems. The nine evaluators interviewed by Honea (1992) were mostly internal to their agencies yet they reported rarely discussing ethical issues. She reports, "The interesting finding was the almost complete lack of any explicit discussion of ethics, values, and the ethical implications of study decisions as a part of the practice of evaluation and policy analysis activity" (p. 317). Honea identified three themes emerging from the data to explain the lack of ethical discussions among the evaluators she interviewed:

- ❖ *The objective scientist:* Objective and fair evaluations precluded unethical practices.
- ❖ *The assumption of ethics:* Ethical behavior is an expected component of a professional evaluation.
- ❖ *The team:* Conducting evaluations as a member of a team eliminates biases.

Notwithstanding the lack of reported ethical problems, internal evaluators have no option but to develop ethical standards to guide their behavior and support their credibility. For the internal evaluator, the most powerful source of credibility flows from ethical behavior, which implicitly incorporates the notion of fairness.

Professional evaluators are confronted every day with decisions about what projects to accept, what information to collect, and when and how to report the information, all of which have ethical implications and can become ethical dilemmas (Newman & Brown, 1996). Although ethical dilemmas can confront internal evaluators at any time during an evaluation, the more common problems can be organized into ethical issues involving (1) the reporting of results, (2) the relationships of internal evaluators with personnel they contact during evaluation activities, and (3) relationships with senior executives.

ETHICAL ISSUES AND REPORTING

The ability to report unadulterated and unaltered findings is primarily a function of the agreed-on role of the evaluation office. If reporting policies have been clearly established and procedures are in place to allow evaluation reports to proceed through the organization as originally written by the evaluation staff, then few pressures will be exerted on the evaluators to alter, embellish, or omit portions of their reports. The potential for deliberate misrepresentation and biased reporting of data by internal evaluators themselves is severely limited. Data manipulation requires a conspiracy among evaluators that is difficult, if not impossible, to achieve (Clifford & Sherman, 1983). Internal evaluation is a conspicuous enterprise, involving numerous components in an organization, and a purposeful misrepresentation of the data will likely be observed by either advocates or opponents of the issue in question. Many safeguards of ethical behavior such as codes of conduct and evaluation review procedures are intrinsic to organizations and hamper attempts to subvert an independent and objective evaluation.

ETHICAL ISSUES AND RESPONDENTS

Confidentiality when dealing with evaluation participants is the second major ethical dilemma confronting internal evaluators and notably more prevalent that challenges to impartial reporting. Unless explicitly expressed otherwise, confidentiality is normally assumed when interviewing respondents during an evaluation and should always be discussed during the preamble to an interview. "First and foremost, the researcher has an obligation to respect the rights, needs, values, and desires of the informant(s)" (Creswell, 1994, p. 165). Respondent names should be maintained only in evaluator workpapers and never included in draft or final reports unless explicit authority was obtained to do otherwise. In some cases, paraphrasing information gained from particular executives or personnel, who may be identified by their position or geographic location, poses a challenge for the evaluator to express the essence of a respondent's opinion without identifying the individual. Quoting a critical program opinion by "the head of a major West Coast office" may not be prudent and hinder subsequent visits to that site! Accurate but imaginative use of rhetoric can usually overcome these situations.

On occasion, evaluators may be asked by readers of an evaluation report to identify persons who made certain statements. The key to deflecting this type of inquiry is prior agreement between the evaluation staff and the organizational hierarchy on the issue of confidentiality. If the trust between respondents and evaluators is breached, the ability to solicit information from employees is seriously eroded and can irrevocably damage the credibility of the evaluation staff. It is important for evaluators to explicitly discuss, at the beginning of each evaluation, the issue of confidentiality and treatment of respondents. If there is any indication that confidentiality cannot be maintained during a particular evaluation, it is the responsibility of the evaluators to express this at the beginning of every interview. Cooperation of a respondent should be based on trust and informed consent. Interviewees should be not be put at risk replying to inquiries by an evaluator: They have a right to privacy and to remain anonymous. A clear understanding between the interviewees and the evaluators of the risks of participation should always exist in an atmosphere of mutual trust. Respondents have a right and evaluators a responsibility to clarify the confidentiality issue each time an interview is conducted. The burden for creating this arrangement lies with the internal evaluator.

Occasionally, internal evaluators will be confronted with information that may involve criminality, generally by a respondent who believes that someone in the organization is involved in fraudulent activities. More common are complaints of discrimination in personnel actions by management. In these instances, the evaluator has no choice but to pass on the information to the proper authorities, but this can usually be done in a way that protects the informant from retribution. Many organizations have personnel integrity departments that regularly investigate allegations of misfeasance, fraud, unethical behavior, and personnel discrimination. Confidentiality procedures built into these processes are usually sufficient to protect the identity of the original informant but it is incumbent on the internal evaluator to ensure respondent confidentiality and not develop a reputation for exposing the identity of personnel who believed their conversations with evaluators were private and protected.

ETHICAL ISSUES AND SENIOR EXECUTIVES

Two primary ethical dilemmas face internal evaluators when dealing with top executives in the organization: (1) On occasion, internal evaluators may be asked by senior executives to conduct an evaluative inquiry to justify a decision already formulated; and (2) evaluators may be asked to alter the results of an evaluation. The most effective rebuttal in both these instances is to have previously established ethical guidelines that govern the actions of both evaluators and executives and a reminder that any indication of collusion among the evaluation staff and executive leadership severely erodes the credibility of the evaluation enterprise and damages future endeavors.

ETHICAL GUIDANCE

The key to preventing ethical dilemmas for internal evaluators is preparation. Anticipation of possible ethical situations and a clear understanding of the proper means to manage the outcomes are paramount. "A solid grounding in the ethical principles and keen awareness of ethical theory can be highly useful in assisting evaluators in thinking about ethical issues and becoming ethical practitioners" (Newman & Brown, 1996, p. 53). House (1990) has suggested three principles of ethics for evaluators conducting qualitative field studies: "the principles of mutual respect, of noncoercion and nonmanipulation, and of support for democratic values and institutions" (p. 158). The first two principles—mutual respect and elimination of coercion and manipulation— incorporate most of the ethical elements that should guide the internal evaluator.

The American Evaluation Association (AEA, 1995) adopted "Guiding Principles for Evaluators" as a code of ethics for the evaluation profession. Five general principles were developed to guide the conduct of professional evaluators (Shadish, Newman, Scheirer, & Wye, 1995):

- ❖ *Systematic inquiry:* Evaluators conduct systematic, data-based inquiries about whatever is being evaluated.
- ❖ *Competence:* Evaluators provide competent performance to stakeholders.
- ❖ *Integrity/honesty:* Evaluators ensure the honesty and integrity of the entire evaluation process.
- ❖ *Respect for people:* Evaluators respect the security, dignity, and self-worth of the respondents, program participants, clients, and other stakeholders with whom they interact.
- ❖ *Responsibilities for general and public welfare:* Evaluators articulate and take into account the diversity of interests and values that may be related to the general and public welfare. (p. 22)

The ranking of these principles does not imply any priority, because their application will vary by circumstance and evaluator. Developed for use for the entire evaluation community, these guiding principles are equally applicable to internal evaluation settings.

The AEA "Guiding Principles" supplement the *Program Evaluation Standards,* developed by the Joint Committee on Standards for Educational Evaluation and approved by the American National Standards Institute. The *Standards* identify evaluation principles and guidance grouped under four headings:

- ❖ *Utility:* The utility standards are intended to ensure that an evaluation will serve the information needs of intended users.
- ❖ *Feasibility:* The feasibility standards are intended to ensure that an evaluation will be realistic, prudent, diplomatic, and frugal.
- ❖ *Propriety:* The propriety standards are intended to ensure that an evaluation will be conducted legally, ethically, and with due regard for the welfare of those involved in the evaluation, as well as those affected by its results.

❖ *Accuracy:* The accuracy standards are intended to ensure that an evaluation will reveal and convey technically adequate information about the features that determine worth or merit of the program being evaluated (Joint Committee on Standards for Educational Evaluation, 1994).

Sanders (1995) reviewed the "Guiding Principles" and the *Standards* and found "no conflicts or inconsistencies between the two . . . with both documents strongly emphasizing accuracy of results, inclusion of stakeholders in the evaluation process, regard for the welfare of evaluation participants, and a concern for service to stakeholders, the community, and society" (p. 48). The guidance embedded in the "Guiding Principles" and the *Standards* can be used to assist the internal evaluator in the ethical practice of evaluation.

CODE OF ETHICS FOR INTERNAL EVALUATORS

The above principles and standards have a generic application for internal evaluators, but a more specific set of guidelines may be more appropriate and functional for use by the internal evaluation community. The goal for internal evaluators is not only to avoid bias but to avoid the perception of bias. Adams (1985) believes that there is potential ethical conflict facing internal evaluators, who are in "an especially vulnerable position in balancing organizational loyalty and professional objectivity" (p. 54). The philosophical concept of internal evaluation ethics is uncomplicated: Instill integrity in the evaluation process, deal honestly with people, and ensure accurate data collection and reporting. Operating under a mantle of independence with these principles establishes a foundational framework for an internal evaluator code of ethics. Reducing these fundamental principles to a detailed, written code will both guide and obligate evaluators working inside organizations. I propose the following guidelines, which are relevant for internal settings and can be used to both direct the actions of internal evaluators and protect them from being misused by executive management.

1. **Independence**
    Internal evaluators should establish in writing an agreement with the organization's leadership that their evaluative inquiries will be conducted independently, without interference or influence by senior executives.

2. **Confidentiality**
    There should be a public understanding in the organization that all evaluator contact with personnel during the conducting of an evaluation will be confidential and that respondents will be treated fairly and will understand the purpose of the evaluation, their role in participating, and their guarantee of anonymity. Both parties should agree in writing to any exposure of a respondent's identity.

3. **Competency**
    Internal evaluators have the responsibility to decline any evaluative request for which they are unqualified. Complex methodological questions and technical evaluations can be contracted to external evaluators or consultants. Evaluator credibility suffers if internal evaluators do not understand the limits of their abilities and attempt analyses beyond their ken.

4. **Respect for clients**
    Upon initiation of any evaluative inquiry, internal evaluators need to explicitly clarify the purpose of the evaluation, the methodological process that will be employed, the role of the client and major stakeholders, the intended use of the results, and the methods for reporting and distributing findings and recommendations. Client expectations should be discussed and accommodated where possible. All clients should be treated with respect and dignity.

5. **Evaluator integrity**
    Many of the problems encountered by internal evaluators can be alleviated if the evaluators are viewed as honest and fair. Fairness can best be interpreted as balancing both the positive and nega-

tive sides of an issue and reporting findings accurately and in noninflammatory language.

6. Accuracy

Internal evaluators must strive to ensure that the data they collect are accurate and their reporting, analysis, and interpreting are precise and factual.

7. Administrative integrity

For professional appearance and resolution of disputes, all evaluative activity should be accurately recorded and maintained for a suitable length of time (see Chapter 9 for information on administration of documents). Third parties, interested stakeholders, clients, and oversight groups should be able to reconstruct the evaluation process by reviewing evaluator records (records may have to be redacted to maintain the confidentiality of respondents).

My intent in presenting this code of ethics is not to replace any existing evaluator ethical standards or principles, but to present guidelines specifically oriented toward use by evaluators working inside organizations. If internal evaluators maintain their autonomy in the organization and integrity in their interactions with superiors, respondents, and clients, ethical dilemmas can be avoided.

Limitations of Internal Evaluation

Evaluators should exercise caution when advocating internal evaluation as a solution to a problem. Internal evaluation is not a panacea for correcting and overcoming all organizational difficulties. It is a tool that can help organizations inform the decision-making process, but evaluation is not a substitute for astute leadership, intelligent decision making, adept marketing of quality products and services, competent employees, and efficient and effective service delivery.

APPROPRIATE APPLICATION

Even where internal evaluation is understood and valued, it may not always be the correct approach to reviewing issues and correcting problems. The realization that in some instances external evaluation, outside consultants, auditing, inspecting, quality assurance auditing, performance measurement or monitoring, organizational development consultants, or other management techniques may be more appropriate and effective is a sign of maturation for an internal consulting/ evaluation staff. Whenever eternal stakeholders will review evaluation findings and the perception of absolute independence is crucial, it may be more suitable to use external evaluators. External evaluators may also be more suitable for handling complex issues when internal expertise is not available. External consultants are also appropriate to periodically review the work of internal evaluators to ensure that methodologies are current and routinization has not set in. Internal and external evaluation should not be viewed as opposing approaches to inquiry and organizational decision-making support but variations of a research technique adapted to the circumstances, environment, and needs of the clients.

EVALUATION DEPENDENCY

The use and influence of internal evaluators ebbs and flows with conditions not always under their control, and internal evaluators are fundamentally dependent on organizational support for their existence. At this point in its history, internal evaluation has not gained sufficient recognition to be deemed essential to organizations and therefore suffers the vagaries of senior management predilections. Internal evaluation within the federal government is subject to the vagaries of political appointees who occupy their positions for relatively short periods of time.

Internal evaluation's dependency can be traced to two primary sources: (1) funding availability to provide staff resources to conduct internal evaluations, and (2) conceptual support from top management. Internal evaluators are always subject to budget formulation exercises similar to other organizational functions, with staff size depending on available funds and senior management's interest in evaluation. Top management's support for internal evaluation has an almost perfect correlation with the success of the evaluation staff. Any erosion or absence of this support threatens the survival of the evaluation process.

SELF-DESTRUCTIVE PRACTICES

Even though funding and top management's support are the primary determinants in the existence of an internal evaluation office, there are certain practices by evaluators that can be self-destructive. The following unsuccessful roles of internal evaluators identified by Love (1991) cause misunderstandings between evaluators and program managers and contribute to evaluation failure:

- ❖ *Spy:* Evaluators working for management collecting information on individual performance.
- ❖ *Hatchet man/dragon lady:* Evaluators collecting data to support a decision already made.
- ❖ *Number cruncher:* Evaluators functioning in isolation as statisticians and technicians without rapport or empathy with program personnel.
- ❖ *Organizational conscience:* Evaluators conducting accountability evaluations for use primarily by external funders or administrative bodies.
- ❖ *Organizational memory:* Evaluation obsession with collection and archiving of data from information systems with little regard to its relevance for use by program managers. (p. 9)

These roles are under the control of the evaluation staff, and internal evaluators need to be cautious when working to ensure their activities are not a cause for alienation by the program managers.

UNINTENDED CONSEQUENCES

Not all the outcomes of evaluations are predictable or desirable. Unintended consequences may sometimes offset the benefits of an evaluative effort. A study of FBI field offices to determine if some could be closed or consolidated so infuriated a senator from Montana that he put a "hold" on the confirmation hearings of Judge William H. Webster, then the FBI director who had been nominated by President Reagan to become director of the Central Intelligence Agency. The FBI field office in Montana was eventually consolidated, but it required extensive negotiations to convince the Montana senator to allow the confirmation process to proceed. Outcomes such as this are rare and should not be used as excuses for not conducting evaluations inside organizations.

CONCLUSION

Institutionalizing internal evaluation begins with understanding some of the basic assumptions about organizations that are relevant for internal evaluators, in particular, that evaluation is a nonessential component of organizations. This fundamental insight underscores the difficulty in internal evaluation and affects planning strategies. Resistance to evaluation is normal and expected, and the burden is on internal evaluators to recognize and minimize the concerns of those being evaluated.

Theoretical models of exchange, decision-making support, supply and demand, expectancy, and action research have been postulated to explain why evaluation is accepted or rejected by organizations, yet the idiosyncratic nature of organizations and the wide latitude in applying evaluation techniques pose some difficulty in prescribing a universally accepted approach to the introduction of this technique in organizations. Internal evaluation's acceptance and adoption—or even mere tolerance by an organization—hinges, to a great extent, on a reciprocal agreement between the evaluation staff and upper management on the role for evaluators and their product.

The evaluation office's reputation is built on relationships, leadership, credibility, objectivity, independence, and role definition. Internal evaluators' objectivity is attainable if appropriate training and controls are in place. Identity is an important construct for an internal evaluation office because it affects evaluation use, unequivocally the one indispensable criterion for judging internal office performance. The ability of an internal evaluation office to influence the organization is nominally based, in part, on the perception of power, which in turn is affected by location and latitude in conducting evaluative activities. The probability of significant influence on the organization increases with the proximity of the evaluation office to the senior management staff.

Advocacy evaluation is an essential component for successful internal evaluators functioning in a consultative capacity to organizations. Engaging the organization and acting as the conduit for evaluation findings to enter the decision-making processes is imperative if internal evaluators are to influence organizations.

Ethical treatment of evaluation clients and participants during evaluations and management studies is built on trust and informed consent. The credibility of the evaluation staff is dependent on consistent, reliable dealings with evaluation respondents, clients, stakeholders, and interested executive management. The organizational ethos may help or hinder internal evaluators in their quest for a fair conduct of evaluations; however, without a reputation for ethical conduct, internal evaluators will be unable to maximize their contributions.

Internal evaluation is not always the appropriate solution to organizational problems and issues. Other management techniques, including the use of external evaluators, may be more advantageous under special circumstances. It is incumbent on internal evaluators to be familiar with the cornucopia of management tools and match problems to solutions, recognizing that evaluation may not always be the correct choice.

RECOMMENDED FOR FURTHER READING

Newman, D. L., & Brown, R. D. (1996). *Applied ethics for program evaluation*. Thousand Oaks, CA: Sage.
A comprehensive treatment of ethical issues in evaluation, applicable to both internal and external evaluators.

Notes

1. These descriptions are adapted by Barkdoll from concepts presented in *Power: Its Forms, Bases, and Uses* by Dennis Wrong (1979), and "Conflict and Power" by Raven and Kruglanski in *The Structure of Conflict* edited by P. G. Swingle (1970).

2. The survey was conducted in 1991 by Michael Morris and Robin Cohn. It was a mailed survey to 700 randomly sampled members of the AEA, with a response rate of 65.6% ($N = 459$).

Chapter 6

✦

The Craft of Internal
Consulting to Organizations

KEY CHAPTER TOPICS

- ✧ Locating an internal evaluation office
- ✧ Internal consulting
- ✧ High impact model of internal evaluation
- ✧ Establishing an internal evaluation agenda
- ✧ Types of internal evaluation
- ✧ Defining and measuring evaluation use

Diligent readers, having reached this stage in the book, may be perplexed that they have not encountered more in-depth discussion about the mechanics of internal evaluation. The rationale for devoting the previous chapters to the concepts of internal evaluation is to develop an understanding of the relevant characteristics of organizations and the nature of change and their effects on internal evaluation. These concepts must be appreciated before beginning the actual discussion about internal consulting, designing evaluations, and establishing an internal evaluation office. One of the fundamental differences between internal and external evaluation is contex-

tual: Internal evaluation is inextricably conjoined to the organi-
zation. This linkage of evaluation with the organization is the
cornerstone of internal evaluation, and a clear grasp of this
association is central to the concept of high impact internal
evaluation.

This chapter begins the discussion of internal evaluation
practice, stressing how internal evaluators can organize them-
selves, establish an evaluation agenda, identify relevant issues
for evaluation, interact with clients, and increase the likelihood
that evaluation results will be used. The concept of an ex-
panded consultative role for internal evaluators will also be
reviewed. The framework and components of a high impact
evaluation model will be discussed and how it can be used to
either begin building evaluation capacity in an organization or
judge an evaluation function already in place will be shown.

Location of an Internal Evaluation Office

The location of an evaluation office or individual evaluators in the
hierarchy of an organization is prominent testimony to the value placed
on evaluation information by an organization and an indicator of the
probability of success of evaluators. Where evaluators are located affects
their role and should be dictated by their intended use. Internal evaluation can focus on service delivery at the program manager level or serve
a more strategic role, challenging programs and the direction of the
organization (Mayne, 1992a). The optimum evaluation office placement minimizes the distance from the evaluation staff to the top of the
organization. This ensures that the information gathered and processed
by evaluators will be seen by the head of the agency without alteration
or dilution. The ability of an evaluation staff to freely communicate with
the top executives is crucial if evaluation data are to be used in the
decision-making process. If there is open access, communication, and
mutual respect for the functions of both domains, evaluation will likely
be valued and used.

Isolating an evaluation unit, as an appendage to a group of mundane staff functions or to a lesser administrative office, signals indifference by the organization and indicates that evaluation is neither highly valued nor will it have a significant impact on decisions. Love (1983c) believes that the placement of evaluators at high levels in the organization is important in linking evaluation to planning and management activities and that evaluators should sit on central planning and program planning committees. The evaluation office's location is important not only to establish the relationship between the evaluation staff and senior management but also to indicate to employees the value and intended uses of evaluation. The downside to locating internal evaluation offices or individual evaluators close to top management is that it structures conflict with other organizational components that resent the perceived power imbalances between themselves and the evaluators.

Locating the evaluation function at high levels in the organization assumes that the head of the organization will be the primary client for the majority of evaluations. Both the U.S. Food and Drug Administration (FDA) and the Federal Bureau of Investigation (FBI) have used senior executives reporting to the head of the agency as directors of their internal evaluation offices (Sonnichsen, 1991). Locating evaluation offices at the executive level in the organization enhances evaluation visibility, helps ensure evaluator independence, and communicates the value of evaluation to the organization.

CENTRALIZED OR DECENTRALIZED?

Client identification and focus are the outcomes of the placement of the evaluation function. If the head of the organization is selected to be the primary client for evaluations, then placing evaluators close to that official is crucial. If, however, the evaluation function is aimed at supporting program managers, with no upward-reporting requirements, a decentralized evaluation function with evaluators close to program managers is preferred. Internal evaluation units can function successfully at both centralized and decentralized levels. The key in the location decision is the role that evaluators are expected to play. If the primary focus of evaluation is accountability, performance assessment, data collection for policy formulation, or executive decision making, then a centralized location is more appropriate and effective. If, on the other hand, the primary purpose of evaluation is support of program managers and improvement of their programs, a decentralized location may be more suitable. There are advantages and disadvantages to both.

Centralized evaluation units have greater independence, superior evaluator skills, and the ability to acquire and develop an institutional memory. Their evaluation reports receive scrutiny at the upper levels of management, increasing the probability that identified program deficiencies will be corrected. Centralizing the evaluation function benefits the organization by allowing the systematic development of a strategic evaluation plan for reviewing organizational programs. The downside to centralized units is that they can appear threatening to program managers and may be perceived as tools of the organization, used for accountability or to justify decisions. There may also be a tendency for centralized evaluation units in large organizations to acquire the "ideology" of the incumbent administration, which diminishes their independence and introduces the possibility of bias (Chelimsky, 1985).

In 1978, Canada established a centralized model of internal evaluation (McQueen, 1992). The Office of Controller General (OCG) was created as the central agency to oversee internal evaluation units in each agency of government, setting goals and procedures for the evaluation units, who reported to their own deputy ministers. Review of this model of evaluation in Canada by the OCG reveled that "some use was made of the vast majority of evaluations" and "a significant number of the evaluations lead to a reallocation of resources either within the program or within the organization" (Mayne, 1994, p. 25). However, due to new government policies implemented in 1991, the program evaluation function became a victim of government downsizing, losing status as it was decentralized, and merged with other functions, especially internal audit (Segsworth, 1994).

Decentralized evaluation units close to programs can acquire greater program expertise, appear less threatening, and experience less resistance from program managers. They may, however, lack sufficient independence from the program for the evaluation results to be viewed as credible outside the program, and the evaluators may lack the necessary methodological skills for sophisticated evaluations. The perceived lack of independence of decentralized units, based on their proximity to the program and program personnel, tends to erode the credibility of their findings and lessens the impact of evaluations as viewed by senior management officials and external stakeholders. The potential for bias that is always present in decentralized evaluation units coupled with the lack of upward information flow, if reports are not disseminated to top management, diminishes the effectiveness of this approach to evaluation from a macro-organizational perspective. The decentralized approach may, however, be appropriate for organizations wishing to monitor the implementation of programs. A requirement for program managers to periodically evaluate and report on the performance of their own programs is another decentralized approach that can produce useful information at both the program and organizational levels.

Internal Consulting to Organizations

The title of this chapter, "The Craft of Internal Consulting to Organizations," purposely substitutes *consulting* for *evaluating* to emphasize the myriad tasks and responsibilities of internal consultants in addition to the classic evaluation function. An evaluation office that focuses on its core competencies and unlocks itself from an identity as a single-mission evaluation unit can develop and market a portfolio of skills that is responsive to a broader range of organizational needs. The notion of evaluators functioning as consultants to organizations incorporates broad roles and responsibilities: correcting difficulties and implementing solutions (Sonnichsen, 1988); program consultation, knowledge building, and leadership (Fleischer, 1983); expert troubleshooter and systematic planner (Love, 1991); and consultant-mediator (Torres, 1991). By expanding its horizons beyond evaluation, an internal evaluation office enhances its utility, reduces its vulnerability during hard times, and develops a greater sensitivity to organizational needs for information. One federal government evaluation manager I interviewed told me, "We'd be down to zero [resources] if we just did evaluation."

Consulting to organizations requires not only an expansion of the "toolbox" of evaluation methodologies and techniques to accommodate additional responsibilities but also a mental reorientation to expanded service to the organization. Often, the failure of evaluation to be productive stems from the detachment of evaluation staffs from the mainstream of organizational life (Sonnichsen, 1990). Practicing internal evaluation successfully requires evaluator recognition that their world is congruous with the organization. The modern internal evaluator will become more actively engaged with the organization, recognizing that responsive service to the organization will reinforce the value of evaluative consulting.

The key to successful internal consulting in organizations is to develop the image of the evaluation office as an organizational problem-solving asset with a diversity of knowledge and skills to employ in a variety of situations. Even now, internal evaluation staffs are seldom used exclusively to conduct evaluations; ancillary responsibilities are to be expected. Management skills will be as important as evaluation skills.

> To occupy a viable and important niche in the organization, evaluation cannot often live by evaluation alone. To secure a place in the planning and decision-making processes, the evaluator may have to assume some other important organizational tasks, such as training, budgeting, finance, planning, and quality assurance. (Clifford & Sherman, 1983, p. 35)

Central to this expanded role is the notion of the organization with a need for information as the primary client and the evaluation staff as the consulting office, offering assistance and advice.

Modern internal evaluators can establish a useful niche in organizations by seeking circumstances where independent assessment is appropriate. "The evaluator's role is shifting away from a narrow analytic, objective report of facts toward an expanded role that incorporates the traditional focus with a more service-oriented, supportive problem-solving approach to evaluation" (Bellavita, Wholey, & Abramson, 1986, p. 288). An example of expanding the internal evaluator role in a nonprofit organization is the practice of the director of research and evaluation at the Salesmanship Club Youth and Family Centers in Dallas, Texas. She performs in an evaluator/managerial role during the planning and development phases of agency projects, providing input and collaborating as a full partner with senior management (Minnett, 1997). According to Minnett, when evaluators participate in leadership, evaluation research becomes routine and results in better utilization of findings.

The concept of internal evaluator consulting is also found in private industry. In 1988, in an effort to be more responsive to client needs and develop a broader skill base, Andersen Worldwide combined its management development and evaluation groups to carry out "performance consulting." By reorienting their focus to a consulting role in the organization, the internal evaluators and management development specialists expanded their services to clients, identifying business problem areas, interpreting evaluation findings, recommending corrective interventions, and assisting in implementation efforts. According to Oliver Cummings (personal communication, October 1997), managing director of the Center for Professional Education, Anderson Worldwide, developing a "consulting mind-set" adds value to the evaluative function for clients and expands evaluator service delivery beyond technical expertise to comprehensive management consulting.

Although the concept of an expanded role for evaluators has been slow to gain acceptance, it is neither a new idea nor a violation of traditional scientific neutrality. As far back as 1975, Davis and Salasin suggested that evaluators interested in increasing the use of evaluation results should consider extending their role to change consultation. They observed that

> guiding decision-makers in effective utilization of evaluation results would not seem to violate scientific values. Consideration of the determinants of utilization in designing evaluation hardly would create a value conflict at all. Even if evaluators were to extend their roles, significant benefits in the contributions of evaluators would be yielded. (p. 627)

More and more evaluation writers are championing an expanded role for internal evaluators. Internal evaluators' participation in the development of the concept of the learning organization requires an expansion of the traditional evaluator role to more active engagement with organizational members.

> An evaluator might engage organizational members in creating individual and organizational learning by expanding on the traditional role of the evaluator. This role definition requires the evaluator to become part

of the change process by blending the role of organizational development consultant and evaluator. (Preskill, 1994, p. 292)

> The practice of evaluation, in keeping with the new paradigms of change,
> will require evaluation practitioners to reconsider the nature of their
> work. This is not to suggest that evaluation of programs and personnel
> will move to the side, but rather that evaluation will need to consider its
> emerging new role in the learning organization. (Jenlink, 1994, p. 316)

The business of internal consulting to organizations sets internal
evaluators apart from other members of the organization because of
their dependent and independent roles. Internal evaluators derive their
legitimacy from the organization, depend on support for their evaluative activities, yet are obliged to seek visible and continual reaffirma-
tion of their independence. The autonomous association linking evaluators to the other organizational components is an exceptional
relationship that allows internal evaluators to critique the very organization where they are employed. This paradoxical relationship between
internal evaluators and the rest of the organization is the cornerstone
of internal consulting.

Internal evaluation consultants market both themselves and a product, in a consultative role that transcends the traditional evaluation role,
offering comprehensive consulting services to the organization. Successful internal consultants possess a variety of skills and apply those skills
fairly and independently. The notion of internal evaluators acting in a
consulting capacity is foundational to the concept of high impact
evaluation.

High Impact Model
of Internal Evaluation

Research I conducted in 1991, attempting to identify indicators of
success for internal evaluation offices, coupled with subsequent observations from consulting to internal evaluation groups, led to the identification of 12 factors that are prevalent in internal evaluation offices
where evaluators are having a high impact (Sonnichsen, 1991). The
concept of high impact evaluation in an organization explicitly incor-

porates the understanding that these impacts can be identified, measured, and demonstrated to have a positive influence on the organization. A central premise of this book is that the influence of an internal evaluation staff on an organization can be documented and quantified. In fact, it is essential for internal evaluation to have a measurable impact on an organization, or evaluation resources and expenditures will have been wasted. For valid measurement to occur, representative, unequivocal evidence needs to be accumulated to demonstrate impact.

The research approach used to assemble data for this project was to assess if evaluation data were *regularly* being used by senior decisionmakers in an organization to help formulate decisions on *major organizational issues*. If evidence was available to support this outcome, the organizational conditions and processes were examined to determine which variables were commonly present in those internal evaluation offices exhibiting *high organizational impact*.

Factors were aggregated into two classifications: (1) organizational conditions, those circumstances that affect internal evaluation practice but over which minimal control is exercised by the evaluation staff; and (2) evaluation process factors, those policies and procedures under the control of the evaluation staff that define their approach to practicing internal evaluation. Organizational conditions are those administrative practices and structural elements that exist in organizations that appear to affect the practice of evaluation. They are indicators of the organization's commitment to the concept of evaluation and the probability of utilization of results. Evaluation process factors are those administrative procedures and evaluation approaches established by and within the control of the evaluation office. They establish the tone, procedures, and policy guidance for the evaluators as they interact with the organization.

Evaluation outcomes, the third component in the model, represent the actual impact of internal evaluation practice and are derived from a combination of organizational conditions and evaluation process factors. Table 6.1 contains the organizational conditions, the evaluation process factors, and the outcomes. A Likert type scale is incorporated in the table enabling it to be used for the dual purpose of observing what factors are important for establishing an internal evaluation function and for judging the performance of an established internal evaluation office.

TABLE 6.1
Factors Associated With High Organizational
Impact Internal Evaluation Offices

	Never Achieved				Always Achieved
	1	2	3	4	5
ORGANIZATIONAL CONDITIONS					
The organization has committed sufficient staff and resources to the evaluation office.					
The evaluation office operates as an independent entity.					
The evaluation office reports to the top official in the organization.					
Agreement has been established between the director of the evaluation office and top organizational management on the goals and policies for the evaluation office.					
The head of the evaluation office has sufficient rank in the organization to be recognized as part of executive management.					
Evaluators are organizationally experienced, career employees.					
PROCESS FACTORS					
The evaluation office has defined its role and publicly announced its evaluation agenda.					
The evaluation office has the authority to self-initiate evaluations.					
The results of evaluations are incorporated in written reports and disseminated throughout the organization.					
Recommendations are issued when evaluations are completed.					
A follow-up procedure is in place to monitor the implementation status of recommendations.					

TABLE 6.1 Continued					
	Never Achieved				*Always Achieved*
	1	2	3	4	5
OUTCOMES					
Evaluation is a routine organizational function, accepted by the organization's employees and managers.					
Evaluators are accepted in the organization as credible, independent, and objective.					
The evaluation office receives requests for evaluations from top officials in the organization.					

ORGANIZATIONAL CONDITIONS FAVORABLE TO EVALUATION

An important precursor to the use of evaluation by the organizations examined was a demonstrated tolerance for organizational review. Where it was observed that organizations had a history and tradition of critical self-review, there appeared to be a greater tolerance for evaluation and subsequent use of the findings and recommendations. Organizational tolerance of evaluation results from a complex set of historical, cultural, administrative, and mission factors. Organizational needs defined the evaluator's role, but organizational culture determined evaluation existence. Commitment of resources, the use of career employees as evaluators, agreed-on autonomy, streamlined reporting to top officials, agreement on policies and procedures, and a senior official as the evaluation director were the organizational prerequisites identified for high impact internal evaluation.

PROCESS FACTORS

The internal evaluation office's role, agenda, and procedures are tangentially affected by the organization but sufficiently under the control of internal evaluators to influence the direction, style, and impact of how evaluation will be practiced and, consequently, its effect on the organization. The five process factors listed in Table 6.1—visible role definition and agenda, self-initiation of evaluations, written reports, recommendations, and implementation monitoring—represent the philosophical and administrative approaches to internal evaluation and constitute evaluation's image perceived throughout the organization. These process factors implicitly characterize the ability of an internal evaluation office to operate with independence and self-assurance, able to establish its own identity, initiate inquiry when deemed necessary, suggest changes, and monitor the status of approved and implemented changes. These process factors indicate a freedom to operate independently in the organization within the parameters previously negotiated by the evaluators and senior management. Although administrative in nature, process factors constitute the core framework that affect the outcome of evaluations.

OUTCOMES

The seven outcomes listed in Table 6.1 are symbolic of a successful internal evaluation office. They represent performance indicators that can be used to judge the impact and success of an internal evaluation office. They are also objectives to achieve for new internal evaluation offices. Recognition of these outcomes as desirable goals when establishing and institutionalizing evaluation in an organization offers guidance when evaluators negotiate with senior management over evaluation operating parameters. High impact internal evaluation occurs when evidence can be presented to reflect routine use of evaluation results on major organizational policies and issues.

There is a sequential interconnectedness between organizational conditions and process factors that leads to these outcomes. The existence of organizational conditions, listed in Table 6.1, and establishment of the evaluation processes combine to produce the outcomes. Figure 6.1 outlines the postulated relationships among the organizational

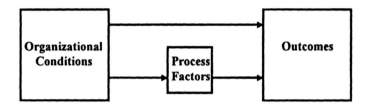

Figure 6.1. Relationships Among Organizational Conditions, Process Factors, and Outcomes

conditions, process factors, and outcomes. The arrows depict assumed causal connections.

The distinguishing characteristic that differentiates high impact internal evaluation offices from those where evaluation is not influential is the ability to affect major organizational decisions on a regular basis. In those internal evaluation offices where this is observed, there is a predominance of factors cited in Table 6.1. Every factor need not be present for high impact evaluation; however, where internal evaluation is having an influence, sufficient conditions are usually noted to suggest that they contribute to the effectiveness of the evaluation office. Obviously, there are degrees of implementation and variability of the factors. The model explicated here, based on the contributing factors listed in Table 6.1, is not proposed as a rigid, singular approach to the practice of internal evaluation but a template that can be used to guide the practice and integration of internal evaluation in organizations. Awareness of historical conditions favoring evaluation integration in internal settings can facilitate its replication in other organizations.

Aggregating the factors present in Table 6.1 creates a model of an effective or high impact internal evaluation office. This matrix can be used for determining if organizations are capable of and prepared for the establishment of an internal evaluation office or ex ante as a performance evaluation tool. Because organizations have considerable differences based on mission, culture, size, and a host of other variables, no single evaluation model can be proposed as meeting the requirements for all organizations.

Attributing causality to any single variable in the constellation of factors affecting the acceptance, use, and impact of evaluation in internal settings would be a tenuous enterprise. No single element or condition has been observed to be overwhelmingly dominant in determining the high organizational impact of an internal evaluation office. However, it can be plausibly inferred that where a preponderance of these factors are present, evaluative data will have a high probability of effectively contributing to the organization's decision-making process.

The conceptual basis for this model is grounded in commitment, an assumption of responsibility by the organization to institutionalize evaluation and a commitment by the evaluators to a publicly defined, activist evaluation role. The organizational commitment manifests itself in selecting competent, experienced employees as evaluators; assuring evaluation staff independence; reaching agreement on the evaluation role; and locating the evaluation office in the organizational structure where it reports to senior management. The evaluator role in this model requires a publicly defined mission and objectives, standardized procedures for conducting evaluations, and evaluators functioning in an advocacy mode and participating in the policy-making process in the organization.

The symbiotic relationship depicted in this model creates mutually beneficial dependencies. The organization benefits from objective, empirical information furnished by evaluators, and they in turn receive resources and support to accomplish their evaluation tasks. Withdrawing or minimizing the contributions by either senior management or the evaluators weakens the model and lessens the effectiveness of the evaluation effort. The high impact model or approach to internal evaluation builds on and uses the combined basic principles of expectancy theory and advocacy evaluation. This linkage recognizes the major significance of the communication factor for evaluators working inside organizations.

Establishing an Agenda

Having gained an understanding of the inner workings of organizations in Chapters 3 and 4, we can now turn our attention to learning how internal evaluation staffs can be established and molded to be congruent with organizations. It is incumbent on internal evaluators to be conceptually clear in their own minds, before beginning evaluative efforts in an organization, precisely what they are attempting to accomplish and how they will attain their goals.

A prerequisite for any dialogue with senior management about the role, responsibilities, and parameters of an internal evaluation office is a comprehensive understanding by evaluators of their own vision of the ideal internal evaluation office and a preconceived conception of how they wish to practice internal evaluation. Foresight by evaluators envisioning an ideal approach to practicing internal evaluation is crucial prior to any framework discussions or agreements with senior management. Without a fundamental concept in mind about the practice of internal evaluation by the internal evaluators, deliberations over integration in the organization are likely to be dominated by senior management. Without adequate prior preparation, the mechanics of any final agreements may subordinate the role of evaluation in the organization and retard its total integration.

Agenda discussions begin with remembering that the fundamental purpose, focus, and goal of internal evaluation is to influence and have a high impact on the organization by supporting the decision-making process. "In the organizational context, the evaluation process has the dual purpose of providing information and of influencing behavior, including decision-making behavior" (Love, 1983c, p. 8). Within this context, internal evaluators are challenged to represent multiple perspectives with fairness and sensitivity to promote empathic and responsible decision making (Torres, 1991). A clear notion of the evaluation agenda is critical, yet it is important to maintain flexibility and the ability to be responsive to organizational tasks. The groundwork for developing the association linking senior management to the evaluation process begins with the evaluation staff.

Polarizing frames of reference (management oriented toward stability and evaluators toward change) creates a dialectic tension between the organization's administration and the evaluators. The presence of conflicting frames of reference does not, however, preclude coexistence and a mutual endorsement of evaluation goals and operating parameters. The dualism represented by conflicting worldviews of evaluators and administrators can be mitigated over time by forging trust and understanding of each other's positions. The distinctions represented by the polarity of evaluators and senior management are not as unrelated as might be anticipated. Both parties have the success of the organization as the end goal of their efforts. The resolution of this negative dichotomy lies in trust, understanding, and a continuing dialogue. Each position tends to counterbalance the other, and the consequences of not nurturing this relationship may ultimately be injurious to the institutionalization of evaluation.

During preliminary discussions establishing the internal evaluation role, the most important issue to understand and resolve is the autonomy and independence of the evaluation staff. Senior managers should commit to allowing internal evaluative activities to take place without political interference from them or other organizational entities. Top management should not only support the autonomy of internal evaluators but also insist on their operational independence. Only by clearly establishing the parameters of the internal evaluation function will evaluative information have the opportunity to influence the organization. If program managers sense inconsistent, tepid support for the evaluation function from senior executives, they will interpret it as implicit approval to ignore or resist evaluative efforts. Major agenda issues to be resolved between management and evaluators during these discussions are the following:

- ❖ The evaluation office's mission
- ❖ Location of the evaluation office in the organization's structure
- ❖ Independence of the evaluation office
- ❖ Administrative relationship between senior management and the evaluation staff
- ❖ Access to personnel and the organization's documents
- ❖ Reporting requirements and procedures
- ❖ Evaluation personnel selection

Once logistic and administrative policies have been negotiated, the evaluators can discuss and decide on methodological alternatives.

Selecting an Evaluation Approach

Numerous approaches and variations are available to the internal evaluator beginning the quest for the ideal evaluation philosophy. Although internal evaluation is a rational and practical enterprise, internal evaluators, acting in the capacity of consultants to organizations, do not relinquish their commitment to research techniques. The collection and processing of data within organizations are adaptive procedures, adjusting social science methodological approaches to accommodate the organization's environments and needs. Like their external counterparts, internal evaluators are concerned with objectivity, internal validity, and reliability. However, they are less concerned with external validity because there is less demand to generalize internal findings to settings outside the confines of the organization. In internal evaluation, external validity is replaced by organizational relevance. The goal of internal evaluation is to produce the highest-quality information possible, given the deadlines and continually changing dynamics of organizational problems.

Selecting a methodological approach to internal evaluation begins with self-reflection and a decision on how you view the world and believe that data can be gathered from individuals and organizations to accurately portray events, issues, and opinions. Evaluator assumptions about the nature of reality tend to drive their choice of methods; therefore, it is no trivial matter for internal evaluators to become comfortable with the basic assumptions of their approaches to evaluating organizational phenomena and be able to explain and defend their methodological choices. This begins with an examination of the available alternatives.

> To understand alternative points of view it is important that a theorist be fully aware of the assumptions on which his own perspective is based. Such an appreciation involves an intellectual journey, which takes him outside the realm of his own familiar domain. It requires that he become aware of the boundaries that define his perspective. It requires that he journey into the unexplored. It requires that he become familiar with paradigms which are not his own. Only then can he look back and appreciate in full measure the precise nature of his starting point. (Burrell & Morgan, 1979, p. ix)

One conceptual framework for determining an appropriate approach to conducting internal evaluations is to ascertain the proposed use of the evaluation information. Chelimsky (1985) arranges evaluation information use into three broad areas:

❖ *Policy formulation:* To assess and/or justify the need for a new program
❖ *Policy execution:* To ensure that a program is implemented in the most cost-effective way
❖ *Accountability in public decision making:* To determine the effectiveness of an operating program and the need for its continuation, modification, or termination. (p. 8)

Although these are broad uses for evaluative information, they can also serve as guidelines for internal evaluators searching for appropriate avenues to focus their evaluation efforts.

FORMATIVE AND SUMMATIVE EVALUATIONS

There are two main categories of evaluations: (1) those with a formative/developmental emphasis, and (2) those with a summative/accountability emphasis (Boyle, 1993). Formative evaluation appraises an ongoing program to modify and improve it and is the primary and defining mode of the internal evaluator (Clifford & Sherman, 1983). Summative evaluations determine the merits of continuing or discontinuing a program. Although the predominant internal use of evaluation is formative, occasionally internal evaluators are asked to perform a summative assessment. There are also occasions when a formative evaluation will evolve into a summative evaluation. The reality is that all evaluations have formative and summative aspects, but inside organizations the primary emphasis is on program improvement, or formative evaluation.

ACCOUNTABILITY EVALUATIONS

Evaluation can be used for accountability when internal evaluators are mandated to conduct periodic assessments of organizational components to compile performance data for use by senior management for strategic planning, resource distribution, personnel assignment, equipment allocation, and budgeting decisions. Mandated accountability evaluations reporting findings to the head of the organization are the most threatening to program personnel and a challenge for evaluation personnel. Depending on cultural traditions and historical audit, inspection, and evaluation practices, mandated evaluations may be intimidating yet still yield useful management data. Mandated evaluations can be particularly helpful to senior managers when important decisions have to be made to continue, modify, or terminate programs. Accountability evaluations can be periodically mixed with other evaluation approaches when appropriate.

QUANTITATIVE AND QUALITATIVE EVALUATIONS

One common way to separate evaluation methodologies is into quantitative and qualitative approaches. Quantitative methods involve statistical analysis, random sampling, surveys, and experimental and quasi-experimental designs; qualitative methods rely on interviews, observation, document reviews, and case studies. This division establishes two alternative paradigmatic views of the nature of reality along objective and subjective dimensions. The objective and subjective worldviews have their epistemological origins in the philosophical doctrines of logical positivism and antipositivism. The quantitative versus qualitative controversy has occupied a significant academic contingent of the American Evaluation Association (AEA) during the past decade; however, the debate has recently subsided and no longer has primacy at annual AEA meetings. Patton (1997) believes the paradigm debate has "withered" and the focus shifted to "methodological appropriateness rather than orthodoxy, methodological creativity rather than rigid adherence to a paradigm, and methodological flexibility rather than conformity to a narrow set of rules" (p. 295). The relevance of this argument for the internal evaluator is to gain an understanding of the merits of the discussion to employ when methodological choices are challenged. It is a common reaction in internal evaluation for individuals unhappy with evaluation findings and recommendations to challenge the methodologies used.

The pragmatic environment of internal evaluators requires the use of mixed-method evaluation designs to be practical, responsive, useful, and result oriented. "Evaluation theory and practice today are characteristically pluralistic, embracing diverse perspectives, methods, data, and values within and across studies that aim to generate more insightful and meaningful evaluative claims" (Greene & Caracelli, 1997, p. 1). Knowing the quantitative/qualitative distinction aids in establishing a defensible methodological framework for the internal evaluator employing both methods. Reichardt and Cook (1979) believe that "using qualitative and quantitative methods in tandem, or, indeed, using any methods together, helps to correct for the inevitable biases that are present in each method" (p. 23).

Methodological decisions within organizations about analyzing problems and studying issues are pragmatic exercises in matching appropriate methods to issues and problems. Datta (1997) writes, "The qualities of the pragmatist's approach, as seen by various evaluators, include 'a paradigm of choices,' design flexibility, methodological appropriateness as the standard of quality, improved situational responsiveness, and a reliance on practical results and level of certainty as criteria of truth" (p. 34). When the Salesmanship Club Youth and Family Centers moved their headquarters to an urban, predominantly Mexican American community in Dallas, Texas, they discovered that their educational model was not effective in that impoverished environment (Minnett, 1997). After interviewing every staff member about an appropriate approach to meet the community's needs, they restructured the entire school program to serve the students and their families. In this case, a qualitative inquiry was an effective methodology to effect a programmatic change. No one, particular methodology will be the correct application to address all organizational issues, and it is common to use both quantitative and qualitative data collection methods.

CONSENSUS/CONSULTATIVE/ COLLABORATIVE EVALUATIONS

Barkdoll (1985), based on his experience directing the FDA evaluation and planning staff, developed another typology, which organizes evaluation into three "types." Type I, an accountability approach, emphasized compliance and focused on problem identification and assignment of responsibility. Type II evaluations were technical and analytical, focusing on the collection and manipulation of data. Type III evaluations evolved from the dysfunctional results generated by Type I and II evaluations and reoriented the focus within the FDA to a consensus-building, consultative engagement among all evaluation participants in a joint, cooperative effort. Type III evaluations, focusing on a supportive, problem-solving orientation, are characterized by cooperation among the participants, openness regarding the evaluation process, and a sharing of findings, conclusions, and recommendations with participants. Type III evaluations emphasized quick responses, with evaluations completed in three months and reported in both written and oral form. Moving from an inquisition orientation to a cooperative approach was successful for the FDA, but Barkdoll cautions that the applicability of the Type III approach depends on a trusting atmosphere, talented analysts, and a cooperative, consensus-building management style.

At the FDA, Barkdoll (1982) found that (1) a better working relationship between evaluators and program managers will produce a bigger, positive impact on the program manager; and (2) a study team acting in a consultant role will produce a bigger, positive impact on the program manager. A Type III evaluation of the FDA food sanitation inspection process demonstrated that a cooperative evaluation can result in a positive impact on the program (Sonnichsen, 1991). By manipulating existing program databases, an FDA evaluator discovered that food processors found to be in violation of FDA regulations during routine FDA inspections were more likely to be in violation during subsequent inspections, whereas food processors without violations tended to remain so. The evaluator recommended that FDA food inspectors concentrate their limited resources on those firms in violation. Charts and graphs were used to illustrate the evaluation findings and convince program personnel of the advantages of altering their approach to food sanitation inspections. No formal report was issued, but the evaluator traveled to field sites to explain the findings and ramifications of the evaluation.

Reinforcing Barkdoll's finding that collaborative evaluations were superior in results to accountability and technical evaluations are the results of a random survey of members of the AEA conducted by Torres, Preskill, and Piontek (1996). Analysis of the replies of 240 respondents (approximately equal representation of internal and external evaluators) showed that communication about evaluation purpose and client and audience involvement in the evaluation process enhanced understanding about evaluation and increased client/audience capacity for using the findings (Torres et al., 1996).

Another form of internal collaborative evaluation activity is *empowerment evaluation*. Empowerment evaluation is a self-reflective form of internal evaluation designed to foster improvement and self-determination (Fetterman, 1997). "It is designed to help people help themselves and improve their programs using a form of self-evaluation and reflection" (Fetterman, 1997, p. 382). Empowerment evaluation is a collaborative group activity with program participants conducting their own evaluations, sometimes using the services of an external evaluator to monitor and add credibility to the evaluation effort. According to Fetterman (1997), empowerment evaluation is fundamentally a democratic group process with each member of the group moderating the biases and agendas of other members.

CONSULTANT-MEDIATOR EVALUATIONS

The consultant-mediator evaluator is another approach to internal evaluation that recognizes the contextual and political nature of activities in organizations. Torres (1991), reacting to criticism that internal evaluation is lacking in methodological rigor, suggests viewing internal evaluation not as a poor approximation to ideal and controlled studies but as a contextual variation of evaluation that can produce high-quality evaluations if evaluators recognize their role and context within the organization. For her, the challenge for internal evaluators is not to develop new ways of knowing but to discern the nature of knowledge acquisition and local change and to develop methods consistent with and supportive of that process. Torres (1991) suggests that to avoid co-optation and habitual responsiveness to management concerns, while still addressing the larger goal of representativeness in decision making, internal evaluators can be successful if they possess the following skills for understanding and managing unique organizational contexts:

- ✧ Understanding contextual influences on the practice and use of evaluation within an organization, as well as on all other major organizational goals and operational areas
- ✧ Identifying and understanding the perspectives of stakeholders
- ✧ Working to maximize credibility and trust with all constituents

✧ Aligning methods with the epistemological orientations of the evaluation audiences

✧ Raising and representing issues to those in authority

✧ Educating those in management on the relationship between their perspectives and the perspectives of others

✧ Maintaining tolerance for ambiguity and incremental change (p. 191)

The consultant-mediator approach outlined by Torres recognizes that internal evaluators are expected to contribute to the administrative decision-making processes by collecting, interpreting, and reporting information that provides leaders with opportunities to reflect critically on the organizational context and the individuals who comprise it.

These taxonomies and examples of evaluations portray the spectrum of evaluation approaches, from imperious accountability to benevolent collaboration. These antipodal boundaries should not be interpreted as superior or inferior but illustrative of the latitude of approaches evaluators have at their disposal to address problems within organizations. Evaluators can serve organizations through the application of all varieties of evaluation methodologies: formative, summative, accountability, collaborative, analytical, consensus building, consultative, and problem solving. Slavish adherence to any one evaluation methodology or inquiry approach constrains the opportunities available to the evaluators and does a disservice to the organization. Each evaluation request or problem-solving exercise requires internal evaluators to examine all available alternatives and select the approach that offers the highest probability of success.

Evaluation Issue Identification

Critical to the successful practice of internal evaluation is the concentration of evaluative efforts on activities that are considered relevant to the organization. One of the major distinctions between internal and external evaluators is that external evaluators are usually called on to address specific, identified problems that are determined to be beyond the scope and ken of the organization's staff. Internal evaluators, on the other hand, have an ongoing responsibility, as well as an advantage over external evaluators, to detect and identify issues and problems, preferably in their incipient stages. Examining the nature, magnitude, scope, and relevance of issues and problems confronting the organization is a strategic task for internal evaluators if they are to focus their resources on meaningful work. Evaluation activities will have minimal impact if evaluators are operating at the periphery of mainstream organizational issues. Each request for evaluation should be measured against a relevance criterion before undertaken. Occupying an internal evaluation staff with trivial matters dilutes their potential benefit, resulting in a bland, ineffectual evaluation effort. What should be evaluated is the chronic dilemma for internal evaluators. Many issues in organizations can benefit from evaluative activities, but evaluation resources are usually limited and priorities have to be established. A systematized approach to issue identification is a prerequisite for internal evaluators monitoring the organization to detect and identify appropriate issues for evaluative activity.

ORGANIZATION SURVEYS

Several methodologies are suitable for evaluation issue identification, particularly those that also incorporate the marketing of evaluation's benefits, thereby aiding the institutionalization process. The inclusion of as much of the organization as possible in the issue identification process publicizes the existence and work of the evaluation staff as well as detects topical evaluation issues. Systematically surveying the entire organization is one of the most effective approaches to issue identification that incorporates both the marketing aspect of evaluation and the quest for data on relevant organizational questions. Requesting senior managers of regions, field offices, divisions, sections, programs, and specific units to identify what they see as significant issues affecting the organization that would benefit from evaluation not only identifies relevant issues but also creates interest and ownership in evaluative activity. Suggesting that respondents involve as many employees as possible in their search for issues broadens the input base for the survey. This approach to issue identification has the advantage of being nonthreatening because there is no requirement to identify problems in one's own area of responsibility. The survey process simply isolates and identifies those problem areas confronting the organization that are deemed important by the majority of respondents.

A variation of this survey approach enumerates problems previously identified by the evaluation staff and requests a priority ranking by respondents. However, the more productive, less biased approach, mentioned above, is to simply ask respondents to record, succinctly describe, and prioritize what they believe are the most salient problem areas in the organization. This open-ended methodology eliminates the inherent bias in any evaluation staff enumeration and may uncover heretofore unknown problem areas. A simple frequency weighting of identified issues generates a prioritized list of important problems that can benefit from evaluative activities.

Following the initial gathering of survey data, the next step in the organization survey process is submission of the prioritized results of the survey, along with condensed problem descriptions, to the management hierarchy for their enlightenment and input. (Note: This submission should not identify respondents by name, because the intent of the survey is to confidentially identify organizational concerns.) Asking the organization's hierarchy for priority ranking of the identified issues, plus their own additions and deletions, legitimizes the issues as a basis for the evaluation agenda. A by-product of this process is the opportunity to present senior management with the concerns and perspectives of the organization. The final step in this survey process is to provide feedback to the original respondents summarizing the results of the survey, the final priority ranking, senior management's input, and a tentative evaluation schedule. Annual surveys involving the entire organization alert management to potential problem areas in the organization, establish an agenda for the evaluation staff, and help institutionalize the evaluation ethic. The evaluation staff can then commence work on the prioritized list, constrained only by available resources.

The attraction of the survey approach to evaluation topic identification is fourfold:

1. It affords opportunities to a members of a significant portion of the organization to confidentially express their concerns with minimal threat to themselves or their programs.
2. It builds a broad-based consensus for the evaluation agenda.

3. It minimizes the bias inherent in any agenda development by the evaluation staff.
4. It advertises the existence and capabilities of the evaluation staff and the benefits of evaluation, thereby contributing to the institutionalization process.

To ensure the integrity of the process, subsequent annual iterations of surveys should provide feedback on evaluation results to the respondents, the value placed on respondent input, and the effectiveness of the evaluation process.

Modifications of the survey approach to issue identification are personal interviews with leaders in the organization, telephone interviews with field managers, and random surveys of employees. The appeal of the survey approach to solicitation of evaluation topics is its efficiency and effectiveness. Not only does this approach incorporate a significant portion of the organization in establishing an evaluation agenda, but it is also a facile methodology to initiate. It is inexpensive, consumes minimal time, and generates an invaluable database for use by the evaluation staff and the organization's hierarchy. Important topics identified but not evaluated during one year can be carried over and included in the next annual agenda.

ROUTINE PROGRAM REVIEWS

Contrary to this conspicuous, inclusive strategy for relevant issue identification are planned, predictable, routine reviews of the organization's programs. Internal evaluators should resist the temptation to initiate standardized approaches to evaluating programs. A methodical review process can become monotonous for both evaluators and program managers, with findings minimally affecting the program. The efficacy of the evaluation technique lies in its application to relevant yet intractable organizational dilemmas. Routinization of evaluation procedures restricts the availability of scarce evaluation resources for application to important organizational problems, lessens expectations of evaluation outcomes, and contributes to a somniferous atmosphere around evaluation efforts. For many years, the FBI, reacting to a General Accounting Office (GAO) recommendation to periodically review all major investigative programs, conducted in-depth reviews of these programs on a recurring five-year basis. These evaluations were time-consuming, expensive, and generally ineffectual. Without specific focus on relevant issues and problem areas, they simply became descriptions of program activities, lacking meaningful analysis. Although these evaluations affected some aspects of the program, the expansive nature of the reviews precluded in-depth examination of individual issues and resulted in recommendations that rarely had significant impacts on programs. It was eventually concluded that limiting the evaluations to one or two serious, meaningful issues in programs where there was management or program manager interest would be more productive.

SELF-INITIATED STUDIES

In addition to systematized approaches to issue identification, internal evaluators should be observant and alert to problems, policy defects, or organizational issues that can benefit from evaluative efforts and self-initiate studies in these areas. In 1989, the Office of Program Analysis and Evaluation (OPA&E), Office of Community Planning and Development (CPD), U.S. Department of Housing and Urban Development (HUD), recognized that HUD lacked any detailed knowledge of payback to cities from developers who received $4.6 billion in loans under the Urban Development Action Grant (UDAG) program (Sonnichsen, 1991). A study was self-initiated and a report issued approximately one year later reporting that over $2 billion in UDAG payments were due to cities and one out of every four cities with completed UDAG projects had received less money than it was due (HUD, 1989). The study resulted in the appointment of an executive task force to develop policy and procedures to more rigorously manage the UDAG payback process and to direct the use of these moneys by the cities.

MODEST BEGINNINGS

This discussion has focused attention on issue identification and effective methods for shaping an internal evaluation agenda. However, for a new internal evaluation office just beginning to formulate an agenda and commence evaluative activities in an organization, it is prudent to initially choose evaluation topics that are relevant and serve decisionmakers' immediate needs, yet are not complex and are minimally controversial. Choosing a macro, complex, core organizational issue for a beginning internal evaluation office is strategically unwise because the evaluation may become lengthy, generate controversial recommendations, and potentially damage the credibility of the evaluation office. The introduction of internal evaluation into an organization should proceed incrementally with initial efforts targeted to assist program managers. A modest evaluation topic that informs the decision-making process without emphasizing accountability and is sensitive to the needs of program personnel is prudent for beginning evaluators and has a greater probability for success. Participatory evaluation efforts including program personnel in the evaluation increases the potential for an appreciation for evaluation and begins the process of introducing the evaluation ethic into an organization. Once a credible reputation has been established, the internal evaluation office can select more elaborate and controversial evaluation topics.

Commitment of internal evaluation resources to relevant, meaningful organizational issues and problems is crucial if internal evaluators are to influence the organization. The identification of issues is an important mechanism in establishing the evaluation agenda and dictating the commitment of evaluation resources. If internal evaluators are to be effective and influence the organizations, the issue identification process must be carefully planned and executed.

Organizations as Evaluation Clients

If internal evaluation can indeed produce useful, unadulterated information, who should be the beneficiary? It is normal evaluation practice to identify clients as those who request evaluations, interested stakeholders, the head of the organization, or specific program managers. Rather than emphasizing individuals as clients, internal evaluators should focus on the organization as the primary client in all evaluative activities. (In actuality, this focus can be accomplished by viewing the head of the organization as the primary client for all evaluation, regardless of the initial requester.) In 1998, GAO reported that its survey of executive agencies in the U.S. government determined "that the primary role of program evaluation was internally focused on program improvement, rather that direct congressional or other external oversight. . . . The studies' primary audiences were reported to be program managers and higher-level agency officials" (p. 5).

Ceding primacy to the organization does not ignore the important roles and requirements for information of program managers and interested stakeholders, but rather emphasizes a holistic view of organizations as complex organisms, each component contributing to the health and success of the whole. This holistic approach to internal evaluation concentrates evaluation efforts toward optimizing organizational administration and operations. By removing the constrictive focus on individual programs or problems, internal evaluators can study the effects of specific evaluations on the organization and are free to integrate information generated by individual evaluations into a pattern of organizational improvement. If change is determined best for the organization, the evaluators need not be too concerned about its impact on a particular subunit (Oman, 1989). Optimizing organizational effectiveness as a goal of internal evaluators requires continually viewing the organization from a systems perspective when conducting evaluations and management studies. Establishing the organization as the primary client for evaluations underscores relevance and usefulness as criteria for judging the value and performance of an internal evaluation office. The consequences of this approach to internal evaluation are improved organizational and evaluation performance.

An excellent example of an evaluation with the organization as the primary client was the 1974 "Quality over Quantity" FBI evaluation (discussed in Chapter 4) that resulted in a major investigative restructuring. Another example of an evaluation with the organization as the primary client occurred in the U.S. Department of Justice (DOJ). Robert Diegelman (personal communication, July 1997), director of the DOJ Management and Planning staff, advised me that in 1996 the attorney general requested a review of the DOJ airplane fleet. A comprehensive evaluation of all aircraft operations in the DOJ resulted in a recommendation to merge the Immigration and Naturalization Service and U.S. Marshals Service aircraft operations. The recommendation was approved and effectively improved prisoner transportation in the DOJ.

Viewing the organization as the client may not be appropriate for all evaluative activities, particularly those conducted within individual programs by teams assembled by the program manager for review of a specific issue. It is always prudent, however, to be philosophically oriented to view the organization holistically and be sensitive to the effects of evaluative activities in one area affecting other components of the organization.

Internal Evaluation Utilization

A ubiquitous lament that evaluations are underutilized pervades the evaluation literature. The evaluation community has expended significant intellectual energy debating the accuracy of this observation, and numerous trees have been sacrificed so that we might write books and fill journal pages with explanations and prescriptions to remedy the situation. Patton (1988) and Weiss (1988) have staked out polar positions on the argument, Weiss arguing that evaluations have had only "indifferent" success and Patton asserting that, in his experience, evaluation has had a much greater impact. It is not a trivial matter. Why engage in evaluations if they have no effect? For internal evaluators, this is not an intellectual debate, but a pragmatic question of utility to the organization and survival of the evaluation function. If the work efforts of an internal evaluation staff are neither used by the organization nor influence the direction and function of the organization, then evaluation will be quickly determined not to have value and be discontinued. Conducting internal evaluations and producing reports is insufficient evidence of evaluation's influence on the organization. Internal evaluators must track and report outcomes of their evaluative efforts to be used to judge evaluation utility. One of the important distinctions between internal and external evaluators is the responsibility of internal evaluators to follow implementation of recommendations and document their impact for use in assessing the performance of an evaluation unit.

DEFINING THE UTILIZATION ISSUE

Evaluation use is difficult to demonstrate because it does not take place in controlled settings and numerous other factors can legitimately lay claim to causing any detected changes (Mayne, 1994). Defining utilization parallels defining beauty—a subjective endeavor in the mind of the beholder. The following are commonly accepted criteria for demonstrating utilization.

- ✧ *Instrumental use:* A directly attributable result precipitated by an evaluation
- ✧ *Conceptual use:* Evaluation influence over policy or operations increasing the understanding of program operations

Patton (1986) suggests utilization "occurs when there is an immediate, concrete, and observable effect on specific decisions and program activities resulting directly from evaluation findings" (p. 30). He has more succinctly called utilization "intended use by intended users" (Patton, 1988, p. 14). Weiss (1977), on the other hand, claims that utilization occurs when evaluation results are used for "enlightenment" purposes:

> Evidence suggests that government officials use research less to arrive at solutions than to orient themselves to problems. They use research to help them think about issues and define the problematics of a situation, to gain new ideas and new perspectives. They use research to help *formulate* [italics in the original] problems and to set the agenda for future policy actions. And much of this use is not deliberate, direct, and targeted, but a result of long-term percolation of social science concepts, theories, and findings into the climate of informed opinion. (p. 534)

Weiss believes that the enlightenment model of research "provides the intellectual background of concepts, orientations, and empirical generalizations that inform policy" (p. 544). Continuing her defense of the enlightenment concept in a debate with Patton that appeared in the pages of *Evaluation Practice* in 1988, Weiss reinforced her notion of evaluation utilization:

> What evaluators should aspire to achieve in the area of utilization is influence, not the status of philosopher-kings whose dictates determine program futures. It is presumptuous to think that one evaluation study, no matter how conscientiously done, should be the major basis for changes in program. . . . Evaluation is better advised to add to under-

standing about the program, to illuminate the range of options and likely effects. In essence, evaluation should be continuing education for program managers, planners, and policy-makers. (p. 18)

Enlightenment should be the goal and result of every evaluation; however, for internal evaluators evaluation needs to proximate action. For evaluators working in internal settings, there must be a direct, observable, and measurable linkage between their evaluative efforts and resulting changes in organizational activities. This may be one of the few times internal evaluators need to concern themselves with causality! This linkage must be perceived, not only by the evaluation staff but also by management. It would be difficult to sustain long-term commitment of resources to an evaluation function in an organization if tangible and traceable consequences of evaluation efforts could not be demonstrated. Persuasive evidence that evaluation affected the organization is the basis for judging internal evaluation performance and maintaining the evaluation function.

A less obvious, but more valuable indicator of evaluation is the effect that the *process* of evaluation activities has on clients, program personnel, and evaluation users. Labeled *process use* by Patton (1997), this utilization yardstick attempts to determine the changes effected by the learning process that occurred simply because an evaluation was conducted.

Process use refers to and is indicated by individual changes in thinking and behavior, and program or organizational changes in procedures and culture, that occur among those involved in evaluation as a result of the learning that occurs during the evaluation process. (Patton, 1997, p. 90)

Process use underscores the value of internal evaluation as an organizational mechanism that can benefit organizations by causing reflective activities on how and why organizational tasks are done.

MEASURING EVALUATION UTILIZATION

Internal evaluation utilization is a performance measurement exercise. The reality of the workplace requires some attempt, however feeble, to demonstrate that resources committed to an activity had a positive outcome that benefited the organization. This scenario does not always occur in a rigorous fashion, but for evaluators endeavoring to perform a task that is only reluctantly accepted in many organizations, it becomes crucial for survival. "In the end, the worth of evaluations must be judged by their utility" (Rossi & Freeman, 1989, p. 455). For internal evaluators, the issue of evaluation utilization is not an intellectual pursuit but a tangible, material, recurring judgment on the performance and value of the evaluation function and a justification for expenditures of evaluation resources.

Utilization of evaluation within organizations is complex and situationally dependent. Although accountability for use of evaluation results is not entirely under control of the internal evaluator, the evaluators can significantly affect the probability of the use of evaluative results. Responsibility for use of evaluation results is one of the areas separating internal evaluators from external evaluators. Internal evaluators have an advantage over external evaluators to influence utilization because of their proximity to the organization and extended involvement in the life cycle of an evaluation.

Ascertaining evaluation use requires that both outputs and outcomes be measured. Process indicators of evaluation activity will not convey the reality and impact of internal evaluation. It is insufficient to enumerate the number of interviews conducted, surveys completed, memoranda issued, reports published, and recommendations issued and approved. Without demonstrated positive effects resulting from evaluative activities, there is little value in maintaining an evaluation staff, and consequently the resources will be reassigned to other areas. (See Chapter 8 for evaluation follow-up procedures and Chapter 9 for a list of items in a computerized evaluation database, which is useful for tracking outputs and outcomes.)

HOW TO INCREASE
EVALUATION UTILIZATION

Internal evaluators can employ themselves to help maximize evaluation utilization. It should be noted that in all likelihood, once evaluation is fully integrated into an organization, the concern over utilization should vanish as the evaluation product will become a routine, expected outcome of evaluative activities. Because we have limited examples of this ideal situation, it is prudent to examine some of the techniques that may help achieve this goal.

Several methods are available to increase the use of internal evaluation results. The underlying theme of these approaches stresses the engagement of internal evaluators with personnel in the organization. It is important to remember that people are the essential elements in the utilization equation. "Use [of evaluation] is not simply determined by some configuration of abstract factors; it is determined in large part by real, live, caring human beings" (Patton, 1997, p. 47). Viewing the organization as an abstraction fails to recognize that people are the substance of organizations. This human element in organizations underscores the importance of evaluators initiating reciprocal communications with affected entities in an evaluation. During a presentation on evaluation utilization at the 1997 annual AEA meeting in San Diego, California, Mike Patton indicated that the "personal factor" was the single most important factor in predicting evaluation utilization. According to Patton (1997):

> The personal factor is the presence of an identifiable individual or group of people who personally care about the evaluation and the findings it generates. Where such a person or group was present, evaluations were used; where the personal factor was absent, there was a correspondingly marked absence of evaluation impact. (p. 44)

Other internal evaluators have encountered similar experiences. The internal evaluation staff at the Environmental Protection Agency's Office of Air Quality Planning and Standards (OAQPS) found that client recognition of a problem, unambiguous evaluation goals, positive interaction between evaluators and program staff, and client support for the evaluation were valid predictors of successful evaluation outcomes and utilization of the findings. Conversely, when reluctant clients were encountered (often as the result of an unrequested evaluation), where there was role ambiguity between evaluators and program staff, when "turf" issues developed, and no clear, agreed-on mandate for the evaluation existed, evaluation efforts were ineffectual.

Although myriad factors have the potential to affect the use of evaluation results, the three core issues surrounding the utilization issue for internal evaluators are relevancy, publicity, and advocacy. If internal evaluators concentrate their efforts on significant, relevant issues, communicate the evaluation results systematically throughout the organization, and join in the debate over findings and recommendations, utilization is almost assured.

Relevance. A major theme of this book is that for evaluation to become fully integrated in an organization and evaluation results used in the organizational decision-making process, evaluators must engage issues that are meaningful to the organization. In other words, relevancy assumes primacy among the criteria applied to evaluation efforts. "Irrelevance is perhaps a more important reason than low validity for failure of many evaluative studies to have an impact on agencies" (Attkisson, Brown, & Hargreaves, 1978, p. 62). Commonsense reflection should guide us to ascertain that evaluation efforts directed toward trivial, inconsequential issues and problems are unlikely to find a receptive audience, let alone influence an organization. Empirical evidence exists to support this position. A survey conducted in 1994 of 26 evaluation professionals employed by Arthur Anderson Evaluation Services determined that relevance had the greatest influence on the use of evaluation results (Callahan, Watkins, & Carr, 1994). They learned that the relevance issue was decided during the "preevaluation design" step through extensive contact with the client using a discovery-and-agreement process that established and prioritized all the known evaluation requirements. The preevaluation design begins with a discovery process with the client to determine needs, expectations, values, issues, and key decision-makers (Callahan et al., 1994). Matching an action plan to meet the client needs, developing an understanding of the evaluation process among participants, and designing a team effort for the evaluation completes the preevaluation design phase.

The relevance of evaluation to the needs of potential users was one of five variables enumerated by Leviton and Hughes (1981) that affected evaluation utilization. Internal evaluators should, therefore, be diligent in the evaluation selection process and ensure that sufficient interest in evaluation topics exists to warrant the commitment of evaluation resources. Failure to concentrate scarce internal evaluation staff resources to meaningful issues may attenuate the evaluative impact on the organization.

Publicity. To influence an organization with evaluative information, findings, recommendations, and supporting documentation have to be circulated among affected stakeholders and potential decisionmakers. Prior establishment of conduits for communicating evaluation results minimizes the reporting burden on evaluators and facilitates disclosure to the organization of the evaluation findings. Awareness of evaluation results among the pertinent parties is an essential step in affecting the positive utilization of evaluation. Evaluation results may be circulated through memoranda, reports, briefings, and informal conversations with affected stakeholders. Successful internal evaluation requires continuous propagation of the existence, use, and benefits of evaluation throughout the organization. (See Chapter 8 for evaluation report dissemination procedures.)

Advocacy. Advocacy evaluation (discussed in detail in Chapter 5) is one approach to increase the probability that evaluation results will be debated and influence organizations. Internal evaluators, using the concepts of advocacy to engage organizational components, can contribute to increased evaluation utilization.

CONCLUSION

This chapter examined the expanding consulting role for internal evaluators and developed some of the techniques valuable to institutionalization of the evaluation function in organizations. This process begins with a clear, conceptual vision of the role of an evaluation consultant, a viable evaluation agenda, and an understanding of the conflicting priorities between management and evaluators. Various approaches to internal evaluation, on a continuum from authoritarian mandates to cooperative efforts, are available to address organizational issues and problems and internal evaluators are required to match the appropriate methodology and style to the problem.

A high impact model of internal evaluation outlined a framework of conditions and evaluation processes that, if present in an organization, can aid in the institutionalization of internal evaluation and assist evaluators in their quest for influence. The model outlined has the dual capacity to determine the readiness of the organization for evaluation efforts and to measure the performance of an established evaluation office. The model requires commitment from the organization to the evaluation effort and a clear vision and direction by the evaluation staff.

Evaluation utilization is a complex issue that requires both proper organizational conditions and a concerted effort by the evaluators. The selection of issues important to the organization is of paramount importance for evaluators because it affects eventual utilization of evaluation results. Surveys of the organization have the advantage of identifying problems while reinforcing the evaluation ethic. Concentration on relevant issues, systematic communication with the organization, and advocacy of positive change will enhance the probability of effective utilization.

RECOMMENDED FOR FURTHER READING

Patton, M. Q. (1997). *Utilization-focused evaluation* (3rd ed.). Thousand Oaks, CA: Sage.

The "bible" for evaluators focused on a practical application of evaluation techniques that produce results used by clients. It is very relevant for evaluators working inside organizations.

Sonnichsen, R. C. (1991). *Characteristics of high impact internal evaluation offices.* Unpublished doctoral dissertation, Department of Public Administration, University of Southern California.

Additional research data supporting the concept of high impact internal evaluation.

Chapter 7

Designing High Impact
Internal Evaluations

KEY CHAPTER TOPICS

- ✧ Design issues and options
- ✧ Understanding program theory
- ✧ Rapid-response techniques
- ✧ Developing a design matrix
- ✧ Performance measurement

*I*nforming organizations through the internal evaluative process requires meticulous attention to the design phase of
evaluation to balance the need for rapid response with the
evaluator's concern for validity of findings. Managers want
quick access to information to help them make decisions,
whereas evaluators strive to collect all available data to ensure
accuracy and completeness. It is the evaluator's responsibility
to maintain a harmonious relationship between these opposing
mind-sets to ensure that the proper equilibrium is maintained.
The challenge for internal evaluators is to design evaluations
that are appropriate for the question or issue, timely in the
production of results, technically adequate, and responsive to

the information needs of management. This chapter will discuss internal design issues, procedures, and options; rapid evaluation methodologies; tools for facilitating evaluation designs; and the important relationship between program theories and effective evaluation designs. The chapter concludes with a discussion of the role of internal evaluators in measuring performance.

Dominant among the priorities to be considered when designing a high impact internal evaluation is appropriateness, which has two notable dimensions. First, given the issue, time frame, intended audience, and evaluation resources available, is internal evaluation the correct approach to the problem? Serious reflection on the merits of using evaluation as the solution to a specific problem may result in the discovery that other alternatives are more appropriate and possibly even quicker solutions to the problem.

Once it is decided that evaluation is suitable, the second important dimension to safeguard against is its inappropriate use. Occasionally, evaluators in organizations will be confronted with a request to collect data on an issue to justify a decision that has already been formulated but not yet formalized. Evaluators are also occasionally asked to conduct evaluative activities intended to delay responsible decision making, when ample data are already available and decision options are readily apparent. Internal evaluators should scrupulously but diplomatically refrain from attempts to be misused as a convenient vehicle for the organization's executives to avoid their responsibility as decisionmakers. There are no facile guidelines to prevent evaluation misuse, but pointing out the threat to evaluator credibility when evaluation is misappropriated may be a persuasive argument. Prior agreements between evaluators and management on evaluator independence and its linkage to credibility are valuable in these situations. (See Chapter 6 for discussion on setting agendas.) Once it is determined that evaluation is appropriate, the actual design considerations can begin.

Preliminary Design Issues to Consider

What does it mean to design a high impact internal evaluation? Designing a high impact internal evaluation is the process of selecting and matching the evaluation question to an appropriate methodology that is expected to answer the question, given the time frame, resources available, constraints, data availability, and intended use of results. The evaluation question is the central focus in planning and design. Who wants what information, when do they need it, and how will it be used? It is conceptually simple yet technically complex.

Internal evaluation designs have different considerations than external evaluation designs. In internal settings:

◇ Homogeneous populations are common
◇ Sample sizes are usually smaller
◇ Urgency is frequently paramount
◇ Issues are ordinarily ambiguous
◇ Multiclients are common
◇ Reporting procedures are not always clear

These conditions require evaluators to adapt traditional methodologies for use inside organizations. One excellent resource for obtaining input on design issues is EVALTALK, the American Evaluation Association's (AEA) online evaluation discussion list.[1] Invaluable information about design issues, application of evaluation in diverse organizational settings, and methodologies can be obtained by inquiring among practicing evaluators and academics.

EVALUATION QUESTIONS

There are essentially three types of evaluation questions (and three major evaluation designs to answer these questions): descriptive; normative; and impact, or cause and effect (General Accounting Office [GAO], 1991). Descriptive evaluation designs provide illustrative information characterizing specific issues or programs; normative evaluation designs compare actual program performance to an established standard or norm or to an expected performance target; and impact (cause-and-effect) evaluations determine whether observed changes in target populations can be directly attributed to program operations. Elementary to evaluation design discussions is recognition of the type of question to be answered and the proper matching of the design to the question.

The key to designing successful internal evaluations is a comprehensive, contextual understanding of the circumstances surrounding the issue or problem. Determining the proposed use of the evaluation is particularly critical because intended use has design implications, that is, level of rigor, sampling approaches, and statistical applications. Before deciding on a formal evaluation methodology, it is beneficial to approach consensus among the evaluators on answers to the following seven questions:

1. Is the issue or problem relevant to the organization?
2. Is the question to be answered by the evaluation conceptually clear?
3. Is there an explicit recognition of the decision-making environment?
4. Can the evaluation scope be narrowly focused?
5. Is a rapid response necessary? Is it possible?
6. Are quality, valid data available to answer the evaluation question?
7. Has the audience for the evaluation product been identified?

Spending adequate time planning an appropriate, comprehensive, focused evaluation design is time well spent. Lack of attention to this important phase of the evaluation process will affect the quality of the evaluation and its utility to the organization. GAO (1991) has developed the following elements to consider when contemplating evaluation designs:

kind of information to be acquired,

sources of information (e.g., types of respondents),

methods to be used for sampling sources (e.g., random sampling),

methods of collecting information (e.g., structured interviews, self-administered questionnaires),

timing and frequency of information collection,

basis for comparing outcomes with and without a program (for impact or cause-and-effect questions), and

analysis plan. (p. 7)

Attending to each of these elements, at the beginning of an evaluation, will preclude inferior quality, impractical, and nonused evaluations. Using a design matrix (presented later in this chapter) will facilitate the preliminary design process and ensure coverage of all the important design elements before commencing the actual evaluation. The initial interview with the evaluation client and preliminary interviews with program personnel are crucial in establishing the scope of the evaluation, the magnitude of the problem or issue, the time frame for completion, the intended use of the results, and the answers to other thorny design issues.

SCOPE AND MAGNITUDE

To objectively illuminate a problem or issue with evaluation data requires that evaluators reflect on the scope and magnitude of the question being asked before methodological options are examined. The two major challenges for evaluators designing an evaluation are asking the right questions and getting the right answers (Mohr, 1988). Evaluation requests are frequently vague and uncertain concerning the specific intent of the evaluation and the severity and scope of the problem. It is not uncommon for managers and executives to be unable to unambiguously define the issue or dilemma that confronts them. Of vital importance, and the responsibility of the evaluator, is penetration of the confusion and ambiguity that surround most evaluation questions with rigorous examination and clarification of the purpose, focus, and expectations for the evaluation before deciding on an appropriate methodology. Evaluation questions are normally complex; straightforward organizational issues rarely require evaluative attention. Lack of attentiveness to question clarity and inappropriate matching of evaluation methodologies to issues during evaluation planning stages will plague the evaluation throughout its life cycle.

Particular observance of four contingencies are crucial in the design phase of internal evaluation: (1) an unambiguous understanding of the question to be answered by the evaluation data, (2) the degree of precision needed in the evaluation data, (3) an explicit understanding by the evaluation staff and the primary client of the time frame for the completion of the evaluation, and (4) the intended use of the information. It is also appropriate to inquire about and reach a preliminary understanding on a format for the presentation of findings, retaining sufficient flexibility for changes that are dictated by the type of data collected, findings and proposed recommendations, and potential audience interest. At the outset of an evaluation, the establishment of rigorous parameters and time lines simplifies the process and expedites timely completion.

RIGOR VERSUS RELEVANCE

Time is one of the major dimensions that internal evaluators have to incorporate in their calculations when planning and designing an evaluation. The luxury of an open-ended time frame for the completion of an evaluation or management study is seldom available in organizations. More commonly encountered are short deadlines that significantly constrain the design and execution of a study or evaluation. This "rigor versus relevance" issue routinely confronts internal evaluators and their clients. Incumbent on the evaluators is the burden of determining the amount and quality of information that can be collected, analyzed, and presented within the appropriate time frame and communicating the available options to the client. It is important for clients to have a clear understanding of the trade-offs necessary to produce a timely product before initiating the evaluation. Methodological shortcuts may be appropriate as long is there is a clear understanding of the risks. Patton (1997) characterizes decisionmakers as preferring some information to no information. He believes that

> the effects of methodological quality on use must be understood in the full context of a study, its political environment, the degree of uncertainty with which the decisionmaker is faced, and thus his or her relative

need for any and all clarifying information. If information is scarce, then new information, even of dubious quality, may be somewhat helpful. (p. 259)

The role of the internal evaluator is to produce useful information for decisionmakers, yet with appropriate caveats regarding its quality. "Quick and dirty" is sometimes the unfortunate description of rapid responses to management concerns; it conveys a message of unreliability and inaccuracy. Quick responses do not obviate dependable data collection efforts that can be routinely accomplished by professional evaluation staffs accustomed to reacting to the requirements of organizational environments. A GAO (1998) survey of evaluation studies conducted in 1995 by the federal government determined that many of the studies "used relatively simple designs or research methods, and many relied on existing program data" (p. 13).

INITIAL CLIENT INTERVIEW

At this early point in the design exercise, client focus is a paramount issue to ensure that their expectations (see discussion on expectancy theory in Chapter 5) are explicitly discussed and appropriately matched to the evaluative effort. Adequate contact with clients and attention to client concerns minimize later misunderstandings about the conduct, direction, and outcome of the evaluation. The initial client interview is particularly important in establishing a comprehensive understanding of the evaluation context, and I believe the entire evaluation team that will work on the project should be present during this interview. In my experience, executives in an organization are neither intimidated nor uncomfortable with the presence of several persons during an interview and are often flattered at the attention their request has generated. The benefit to exposing all evaluation team members to the original musings of the requester far outweighs any downside to their presence. The attendance of the entire evaluation team precludes any potential for misunderstanding or dilution of the original message as it is interpreted for other team members not in attendance at the first meeting with the requester. Assembling the entire team affords an opportunity to employ the diversity, experience, and different insights that each team member brings to the issues. These insights are invaluable in postinterview design discussions, when an often-repeated phrase is: What did the client mean by that? Evaluation purpose, issue relevance, and time parameters are vital topics of discussion during the first interview with the client. Precision in defining the substance, boundaries, constraints, and time frame is a preeminent consideration during this first encounter.

Essential during the initial interview with the study requester is defining the purpose of the study. What is the motivation for requesting this particular study at this particular time? It is difficult if not impossible to properly design an evaluation/study without a complete understanding of the rationale precipitating the study and the agenda of the requester. These elements may not be apparent or readily discernible during the initial interview. It is important for evaluators to be alert and attempt to identify them during subsequent interviews. The evaluation focus, scope, and data collection efforts are essentially driven by the question to be answered; however, these issues are significantly affected by the conditions precipitating the evaluation. Failure to completely grasp the significance, motivation, and proposed usage of the evaluation data renders the design process a speculative venture.

> More than any other step in the whole process of planning and executing an evaluation, it is this failure to explore the background of and the motivations for the evaluation that explains for me why so many evaluation projects eventually falter along the way, why so many conflicts develop between manager and evaluator, and, ultimately, why the results of evaluation studies, rare though they may be, have so little impact on programming. (Gurel, 1975, p. 23)

Evaluator decisions about data collection, commitment of resources, research precision, and time allocations are dependent on a comprehensive understanding of the requester's purpose, motivation, and expectations for the evaluation.

PRELIMINARY INTERVIEWS

Upon completion of the initial interview with the requester and preliminary discussion of the issues among the evaluation team, it is instructive to conduct some preliminary interviews with program personnel to supplement the data from the requester interview. These should be unstructured interviews, designed to elicit unbiased, original opinions on the evaluation issue from those working in the program area. It may also be productive at this time to identify and interview subject matter experts to gain an outsider's perspective and background knowledge about the issue. Appropriate stakeholders are also good sources of input to ensure a representative cross section of program views. After digesting and discussing the details from these preliminary interviews, it is usually advantageous for the evaluation team to return to the original requester and attempt to clarify and begin building consensus on the study issues and parameters. These consultations with the original requester, program personnel, subject matter experts, and stakeholders comprise the preliminary design tasks and, if done conscientiously, should result in a tangible definition of the issue/problem/question to be addressed in the evaluation.

During these initial interviews, internal evaluators must be diligent in suppressing their own prejudices, preconceived opinions, and possible knowledge gained from prior experience in the area. Objective, open-minded attention to respondent input is indispensable to the formulation of accurate evaluation questions. When these preliminary interviews are completed, the evaluation team should have a well-defined issue, clear role expectations, and some preliminary data to provide the basis for beginning evaluation design discussions.

Understanding Program Theories of Operation

Upon completion of the question clarification phase of evaluation, the second step before beginning actual design efforts is the acquisition of program knowledge. A prerequisite to effective evaluation design is program understanding at both the micro and macro levels: not simply a vague awareness that designated program activities are intended to produce some anticipated outcome, but a comprehensive conception of the structure, underlying theory, and predicted cause-and-effect linkages. The micro level of understanding focuses internally on the program activities and a comparison of actual results with anticipated results.

Developing program theories of action is the heart of Patton's (1997) user-focused evaluation approach. Patton believes that it is important for evaluators to understand the program's theory of action from the point of view of the primary stakeholders and the decision-makers because their perceptions about the activities of the program and intended outcomes have consequences affecting their behavior and thinking about the program. He believes evaluators have a golden opportunity during evaluations to interact with program personnel, examining and making explicit their assumptions about expected program outcomes and their linkages with program activities. Chen and Rossi (1987) also stress the necessity for understanding program theory before undertaking the evaluation and attempting causal statements concerning program linkages.

McWeeney (1995) believes that many organizations lack a clear understanding and widespread communication of what he calls their concept of operations. For McWeeney, an organization's concept of operations is a statement of the strategic direction and goals and the theoretical foundation that links the problems and issues to be addressed with the nature of activities the organization intends to pursue, along with its performance expectations. Whether the organization has been established to address problems in law enforcement, public health, social services, foreign policy, national security, or the production of goods and services, the existence of the organization is expected to have a certain impact on the problem being addressed. Figure 7.1 uses a law enforcement example to show how to increase program understanding by illustrating the parts of an organizational concept of operations and their linkages.

The exercise of inserting appropriate program material into each box begins the process of dissecting and understanding program theory and is the one of the first steps in evaluation design. Detailing the resources available and their allocation to program activities is foundational before discovering outputs and outcomes. Recording program results (actual outputs and identified outcomes) allows evaluators to look for gaps and discrepancies among outputs, outcomes, and goals and to trace the linkages between outputs and outcomes, and inputs and activities. Are the inputs and activities properly designed to produce the

Elements	Purpose	Inputs	Activities	Results
Description	Issues or problems the organization intends to address	Total resources required for program activity	The work performed by the organization	The results anticipated from the resources invested and the work performed
Example	Mission statements, organizational charters	Total funding, program funding, work hours	Investigations, reports, training, liaison activities	Arrests, seizures, reduced crime, increased public support

Figure 7.1. Elements of a Concept of Operations: An Example From Law Enforcement
SOURCE: McWeeney (1995).

expected results, and if not, why not? A rigorous application of this design heuristic to the program being evaluated aids the internal evaluator in the program discovery and understanding process.

The use of theory in program evaluation is infrequent (Bickman, 1989; Chen, 1989) and may not be immediately evident or conceptually clear to either program personnel or evaluators. Because internal evaluation focuses primarily on practical management issues (Love, 1991), the use of theory in internal settings is routinely overlooked. However, this lack of appreciation of the theory-driven perspective of evaluation (Chen, 1989; Chen & Rossi, 1987) does not obviate its utility for internal evaluators seeking to improve programs. A comprehensive grasp of the nature of the construction and implementation of program activities, actual and theoretical relationships connecting program activities with outputs and outcomes, and a knowledge of the intended effect of the program on the identified problem it was designed to solve are necessary ingredients in the design algorithm.

Design Options

Internal evaluators have at their disposal the same methodological design strategies and evaluation approaches as external evaluators. The major differences are the frequency of use of some designs and the adaptation of these approaches to the internal environment. Whichever design or approach is chosen, however, the fundamental issue for both external and internal evaluators is matching the appropriate design to the appropriate question (Rist, 1990). The goal for the internal evaluator is to produce, within the appropriate time limits, a valid, relevant answer to the specific question of the requester. This requires internal evaluators to be familiar with all available evaluation methodologies, their strengths and weaknesses, and their application to evaluation questions. The evaluation literature generally recognizes the following seven categories of design options: front-end analysis, evaluability assessment, formative evaluation, impact evaluation, program monitoring, meta-evaluation, and meta-analysis.

FRONT-END ANALYSIS

This evaluation approach is the unfulfilled wish of most evaluators: to be asked to examine relevant issues before organizations commence program interventions. Front-end analysis is similar to policy analysis and involves reviewing available program data, examining historical outcomes of similar programs, estimating needs, providing guidance on implementation, identifying performance indicators, and speculating on program consequences and anticipated outcomes. Even those enlightened executives with some knowledge of evaluation are generally unaware of the benefits of using evaluation as a vital part of the policy and program development process. It is incumbent, as part of the internal evaluation marketing process, to continue to engage executives in the expanded use of evaluation to maximize the contribution of evaluation to the organization's operations. The training and experience of evaluators in the rigorous application of scientific tools to solve problems can clarify nascent policy processes and help ensure that new programs have appropriate and measurable goals, reasonable and attainable objectives, valid indicators of performance, and logical linkages between activities and expected outcomes. To be able to conduct front-end analysis is a goal worth seeking for a mature internal evaluation office that has established itself in an organization.

EVALUABILITY ASSESSMENT

This evaluation approach, prominently espoused by Wholey (1979, 1983, 1994) in the United States and Rutman (1980) in Canada, has as its central theme examining program activities with a truncated evaluation to determine current program reality and decide if evaluation has the potential to contribute to improving program performance. Evaluability assessment has both a retrospective and prospective outlook, determining congruence between program activities and expected outcomes and suggesting program modifications where deficiencies are detected. It is a cursory look at program goals and objectives, activities implemented to attempt to attain these goals and objectives, and the plausibility of the linkages between activities and goals. Additionally, a determination is made if quality data are available for analysis and, if the evaluation was conducted, would the program manager use the results to improve the program. In other words, evaluability assessment is a minievaluation designed to determine the probability of a full-scale evaluation improving a program. Evaluability assessment is an excellent tool for internal evaluators. It can be accomplished quickly with limited resources and often no travel. In many instances, the information gained during the evaluability assessment is sufficient to answer the study question and no additional work is required. In some cases, a small expansion of the assessment will garner the necessary information to satisfy the requester's needs.

FORMATIVE EVALUATION

Sometimes referred to as process evaluation, formative evaluation is a retrospective view of a program that focuses on internal program dynamics, describing and analyzing program activities in an effort to determine if they have a rational linkage with intended outcomes. It is an evaluation strategy that seeks to analyze program implementation to determine if modifications and improvements are necessary. Formative evaluation is used to improve program performance and is the most frequently used design by internal evaluators. This problem-solving approach has universal application in internal settings because it eschews accountability in favor of cooperative identification of program deficiencies and options to increase operating efficiency and effectiveness. Often referred to as *management studies,* these formative evaluation efforts are fundamental to the practice of internal evaluation. Caution should be exercised, however, when reporting the results of formative evaluation studies. Rist (1990) points out that one of the primary abuses of formative evaluation efforts is the attribution of causal impacts from descriptive data. Process description is an insufficient basis from which to draw judgments on program impact. Rist also cautions about a second abuse of formative evaluation when conclusions are drawn about a program on the basis of insufficient or poor quality data. The temptation to quickly review program activities and suggest recommendations for improvement that are not fully supported by data can weaken the credibility of formative evaluations and, over time, damage the reputation of the evaluation office for high-quality and impartial evaluations.

IMPACT EVALUATION

Program results are the focus of this type of evaluation in an attempt to determine how well a program works. Sophisticated evaluation designs are employed to isolate causal factors and determine if unequivocal statements can be rendered showing linkages between program activities and program results. Experimental and quasi-experimental research designs compare program outcomes with similar programs or control groups to attempt to determine the actual effects of the program. Impact evaluations are uncommon in internal settings due to time constraints and normally the lack of requirements for rigorous causal inference.

PROGRAM MONITORING

This category of evaluation has effective application in internal settings because it puts the evaluator in continuing contact with the program and program personnel. Contact with the program can be personal or via computer systems, reviewing computerized data to monitor program performance. Program monitoring is appropriate for internal evaluators due to its lack of intrusiveness yet powerful ability over time to demonstrate performance trends. Providing periodic analyses of program data, evaluators can show progress toward program goals. Although program monitoring is appropriate for determining efficiency and effectiveness, it is highly dependent on the availability of quality program data. The probability of successful program monitoring is greatly enhanced when evaluators are invited to participate during the program design phase, identifying appropriate program indicators and data collection strategies.

META-EVALUATION

Meta-evaluation is an evaluation of an evaluation or a review of the conduct of an evaluation. It can and should be done by evaluators on their own work but is more valid if conducted by another independent evaluator (Scriven, 1991). Meta-evaluation should be routinized into internal evaluation procedures because it increases the validity of evaluation findings and enhances the credibility of the evaluators. One approach is to use the Key Evaluation Checklist (KEC) (Scriven, 1991, p. 230) as an instrument for reviewing an evaluation. It also has value as a training vehicle for evaluators when external evaluators periodically review the work of an internal evaluation unit. (See Chapter 9 for additional discussions on training internal evaluators.)

META-ANALYSIS

Meta-analysis, or evaluation synthesis, is an evaluation of other evaluations previously conducted to determine if similar programs are having an effect and, if so, under what conditions and with what degree of success. It is a sophisticated mathematical process used to combine effect sizes from different programs to determine an aggregate assessment of program performance from different settings, under different conditions, and with different designs. Due to the degree of expertise needed to conduct these types of evaluations, they are usually not encountered in any number in internal settings. However, the use of meta-analysis can be valuable when initiating new programs to avoid "reinventing the wheel." External consultants can be contracted to conduct a review of the results of similar programs in an effort to discover effective interventions before new programs are initiated.

Rapid-Response Techniques

Each of these seven design options has applicability in internal settings, yet they are formal and time-consuming evaluation approaches that may not always be sufficiently responsive to client requests for information to be useful in exigent circumstances. Pressing demands on internal evaluators for rapid production of quality information are not uncommon, and inadequate responses diminish the reputation of the evaluation staff in the eyes of management. Urgency is the ubiquitous, restrictive annoyance confronting internal evaluators. Decisionmakers are under pressure to act, with or without comprehensive information. When confronted with exigent circumstances, internal evaluators can furnish rough approximations in lieu of precise, detailed data without compromising their credibility.

> The emphasis on speed, rough approximations, and relevant performance measures need not adversely affect the quality of the evaluation product. An evaluation whose findings are timely, relevant, and approximate is more useful to a decisionmaker than an evaluation that is precise but late or that looked at the wrong question. (Bellavita, Wholey, & Abramson, 1986, p. 291)

To effect a rapid evaluation response to organizational questions requires a structured framework, matching tasks and time in a systematic way. Compromise is inevitable, with trade-offs between breadth and depth, data availability and quality, and rigor and responsiveness. Simple methodologies, reliance on existing data, and briefings instead of written reports can speed up the evaluation process without jeopardizing the quality of the evaluation. Experienced internal evaluators will recognize those dilemmas when time is of the essence and devise methods to balance their reliability and validity concerns with management's urgent information production concerns.

Joseph Wholey (1983) has long championed the idea that evaluators and public managers can work together to demonstrate the effective management of public programs when evaluators focus their skills and energies on management-oriented activities. By incrementally providing quick and timely assessment data to managers about how programs work, evaluators can contribute to improved program outcomes. Iterative evaluative efforts at determining program performance may often be more beneficial than one single major evaluation effort and may even obviate a large-scale evaluation. This strategy of "sequential purchase of information . . . breaks evaluation into a series of stages, each stage being initiated only when the likely usefulness of the new information outweighs the costs of acquiring it" (Wholey, 1983, p. 119). This "sequential purchase of information" concept captures the trade-offs among timeliness, cost, and quality of information that have plagued evaluators for over two decades:

> The sequence Wholey prescribes—deciding if it [a program] is worth evaluating, providing a rapid assessment of the program to get a sense of how it is doing, troubleshooting the program on an ongoing basis by monitoring performance and outcome, and testing causal assumptions that seem particularly critical—is sequentially logical in evaluation of program effects, and reasonably comprehensive in the kinds of information it provides about effects. (Shadish, Cook, & Leviton, 1991, p. 266)

Because of their location inside the organization, internal evaluators have an advantage over external evaluators because they can rapidly respond to management requests for information. "Internal evaluators can quickly develop evaluation designs that are feasible and cost-effective because they know so much about logistical routines within the organization" (Torres, Preskill, & Piontek, 1996, p. 52). Very often, controversial issues in organizations can be promptly resolved with independent assessment by soliciting data with a few interviews and reviewing supporting program documentation. Quickly accomplished, these short projects can develop unbiased information that counter emotional program perspectives and aid decisionmakers. *Rapid-feedback evaluation,* the *90-day evaluation framework,* and *evaluative assessment* are three approaches to accommodating the pressures from managers to quickly produce program performance information. *Focus groups* and *reverse-site visits* are two other techniques for rapid data collection that complement these rapid-assessment methods.

RAPID-FEEDBACK EVALUATION

Rapid-feedback evaluation can provide managers and policymakers with quick, preliminary assessments of program performance as well as a design for more valid and reliable full-scale evaluations (Wholey, 1983). The rapid-feedback process uses existing data, preliminary interviews with program personnel, and pilot tests with small data samples. Rapid-feedback evaluation is a five-step process:

1. Collection of existing data on program performance
2. Collection of new data on program performance
3. Preliminary evaluation
4. Development and analysis of alternative designs for full-scale evaluation
5. Assisting policy and management decisions (Wholey, 1983, p. 121)

The rapid-feedback evaluation process recognizes the necessity for quality information to assist decisionmakers, yet acknowledges the collision course of evaluators and managers when negotiating time allocations for the production of the information. As with other evaluations, the results of rapid-feedback evaluations are "presented in reports and briefings outlining the preliminary evaluation findings, the remaining uncertainties regarding program performance, options for immediate use of the preliminary evaluation data, and options for additional data collection and analysis" (Wholey, 1983, p. 123).

Rapid-feedback evaluations are not quick-and-dirty evaluations but merely quick. Rapid-feedback evaluations explicitly acknowledge the quality of the data collected and the areas of uncertainty and suggest options for further inquiry. It is one more technique in the internal evaluator's toolbox permitting rapid responses to client requests without sacrificing credibility. In many instances, the information gathered during rapid-feedback evaluations may be sufficient to answer client questions and no additional evaluation will be necessary. If additional evaluative efforts are required, both the clients and the evaluators have a more enlightened vision of the requirements for a full-scale evaluative effort.

TABLE 7.1 90-Day Evaluation Framework	
Evaluation Tasks	*Allocated Time (in days)*
Interview with evaluation requester	1
Preliminary interviews with program personnel and subject matter experts	7
Literature search	5
Data collection	22
Data analysis	16
Report writing (briefing preparation)	15
Total	66

90-DAY EVALUATION FRAMEWORK

To accommodate continuous requests to internal evaluators for responses to urgent organizational questions, a 90-day time allocation framework can be used. Table 7.1 contains an outline for a 90-day evaluation to guide internal evaluators required to quickly respond to organizational requests for information. (This framework assumes 66 working days in a 90-day period.) Establishing and adhering to explicit, rigorous time frames for evaluation tasks increase the probability that the evaluation will be expeditiously completed. Organizing an evaluation around time parameters compels evaluators to synthesize evaluation tasks, eliminating nonessential components and retaining and modifying only those key elements material to the issue in question. Due to the variability in requests in internal environments, I recognize that strict application of this timetable is neither feasible nor desired. However, the concept presented here is adaptable to most situations in an organization and can guide internal evaluators as they attempt to quickly furnish quality information to decisionmakers.

The purpose of this guide is to outline the essential tasks for a competent evaluation and establish practical time allocations. Specific application will be dependent on the nature of the request, availability of evaluation resources, and organizational environment. Robert Diegelman (personal communication, November 1994), director of the Management and Planning staff in the U.S. Department of Justice, told me that he believes his decision-making environment requires that evaluation and management studies be completed within 120 days. According to Diegelman, lengthier studies lose their relevance as issues revolve in a dynamic political environment.

Winberg (1991) suggests that a "phased approach" concept is useful for rapid responses to management requests for evaluative information. He defines *phased approach* as the reporting of findings as soon as they become available. This frequent and incremental sharing of data with clients as the study proceeds may allow evaluations to be shortened when clients believe they have sufficient information on which to base a decision. An example of this phased approach, reported by Winberg, is the Indian Minerals program designed to promote the development of mineral resources on Canada's Indian reserves. Program managers, interested in improving program performance within the existing budget, requested an evaluation. Reviewing program documents, interviewing key program staff, and conducting a two-day focus group with industry and government participants generated sufficient information for decision making that no further evaluation was necessary (Winberg, 1991).

The key to successful completion of a management study within 90 days is rapid acquisition of data through selective individual interviews, focus group panels, and document reviews. Concentration on narrowly defined issues and highly selective data collection strategies can produce reliable data within very short time frames.

EVALUATIVE ASSESSMENT

In 1986, Chris Wye, then the director of the Office of Program Analysis and Evaluation in the Office of Community Planning and Development (CPD) at the U.S. Department of Housing and Urban Development (HUD), was requested by a newly appointed assistant secretary to conduct a comprehensive evaluation of CPD management so the secretary would have a basis for establishing his direction for the organization (Wye, 1989). Because of the new assistant secretary's high-level interest in the project, coupled with his evaluation inexperience and impatience, he imposed a three-week deadline and the requirement that the evaluation report be a consensus document that had been circulated and commented on before final presentation to him. Concluding that traditional evaluation methodologies were not appropriate or workable and given the time frame and unique stipulations, Wye and his staff brainstormed a unique and novel approach to solving the problem. Concluding that the term *evaluation* created expectations that could not be met, they proposed to call the project an *evaluative assessment,* thereby establishing a more realistic standard for judging the quality of the final report. The essential key to successfully completing the evaluative assessment was to structure the process to obtain concurrence from both lower- and upper-level staff in the CPD on major management performance issues. To accomplish this task, Wye and his staff developed a three-tiered structure of one-and-one-half-hour brainstorming meetings, held separately with staff experts, division directors, and office directors. To ensure the protection of lower-level staff input, each meeting was structured to allow participants to comment on or add to, but not delete or modify, the previously expressed opinions. Two evaluators who recorded participants' comments verbatim on flip charts conducted the meetings. To supplement the information collected at the three meetings, other evaluators assembled data from planning and management documents and conducted a telephone survey with field CPD personnel.

The final report combined the individual meeting report topics arranged under appropriate headings but without analysis. It was circulated for comment (none was received) 24 hours before an oral briefing of the assistant secretary and the CPD hierarchy. As reported by Wye (1989), the evaluative assessment successfully met the deadline and developed a consensus agenda of major management issues confronting CPD with little debate or compromise. Its impact on the CPD was its use by the assistant secretary in managing the department.

Commenting on its potential applicability in other situations, Wye believes the technique has both strengths and limitations. On the positive side, it is inexpensive, can be easily and rapidly implemented, and provides a consensus report. On the negative side, the technique will work only where it has the clear support of the head of the organization. The technique tends to assign responsibility and it lacks independent analysis and third-party verification. One drawback to its use is its focus on consensus as the threshold for acceptability of a conclusion. Wye speculates that the technique may have application in organizational planning processes as a positive, nonthreatening introduction to evaluative thinking. This clever approach to an evaluative dilemma, devised by Chris Wye and his internal evaluation staff at HUD, demonstrates one flexible and innovative service that internal evaluators can perform for organizational management.

The essence of rapid response to urgent requests for information is to focus on securing the needed data with the least expenditure of effort. Two time-consuming chores that occupy internal evaluators are travel to data collection sites and personnel interviews. To expedite these two important phases of many evaluations, evaluators can take advantage of two simple, flexible, and efficient techniques for data collection: focus groups and reverse-site visits. Combining these two techniques makes them particularly efficient. Assembling respondents in a centralized location, in lieu of evaluators traveling to multiple sites, and interviewing them in groups instead of individually, eliminates much of the time-consuming logistical frustration that encumbers normal evaluation procedures.

FOCUS GROUPS

Focus groups are informal, small-group discussions designed to obtain in-depth qualitative information (Dean, 1994). Focus groups allow internal evaluators working under short-deadline pressures to quickly garner opinions from large numbers of people. Assembling focus groups of 10 to 12 persons and conducting two or three sessions per day for one or two days produces a substantial body of knowledge about an issue or program that would ordinarily take one or two weeks using two evaluators on one-person interviews. The keys to success when using this technique are the careful crafting of a set of core questions rigorously focused on the issue in question, and the accurate identification and assembly of participants who are knowledgeable about the issue. The focus group technique can be either exploratory or confirmatory in nature (Duffy, 1993). It is well suited to develop issues when beginning an evaluation, or it can be used to validate data collected through surveys or document reviews. When site travel cannot be avoided, the use of focus groups can help reduce the time spent on data collection sites and the attendant travel costs.

REVERSE-SITE VISITS

Travel is almost always time-consuming and expensive, adding unproductive time to short-time frame evaluations. It is in the best interest of evaluators whenever travel can be avoided or curtailed. The concept of reverse-site visits brings the potential respondents to a central location in lieu of evaluators traveling to several sites for interviews and data collection. The most efficient use of this technique occurs when a conference or other event is already scheduled and coincides with the necessity for evaluators to conduct evaluation interviews. By coordinating with conference organizers, evaluators can conduct individual or focus group interviews after conference sessions or during breaks. This approach is particularly efficient and cost-effective when field personnel are recalled to headquarters locations for periodic conferences and the evaluators work at the headquarters locations. When no conferences are coincidentally scheduled and money is available, it still may be more efficient to invite appropriate respondents to the evaluators' location rather than schedule travel for the evaluation team. A variation of the reverse-site approach is for evaluators to travel to one location where relevant respondents are assembled for regional conferences or meetings and conduct the necessary interviews and data collection at that single site. Combining reverse-site visits with the use of focus groups allows evaluators to solicit substantial information about a program with minimal expenditure of time or money.

Design Matrix

Creating a useful evaluation design is essentially a clarification exercise to produce an unambiguous, explicit depiction of the methodology intended to answer the evaluation question. The final design should be sufficiently precise to answer the evaluation question but no more

Issue Question	Developmental Question	Methodology	Sources Of Information	Analysis	Comments
What are the steps in the hiring program?	Are they the same for professional and clerical employees? Are the required steps always followed? Are all the steps necessary?	Interviews	Personnel department executives, company policy documents	Qualitative analysis of interviews and document reviews	Compare steps in hiring program with other corporative hiring programs

Figure 7.2. Design Matrix: An Example From a Corporate Hiring Program
SOURCE: Adapted from General Accounting Office (1991).

complex than necessary. One of the tools available to the internal evaluator to assist in defining issues and creating evaluation designs is a design matrix.[2] A design matrix requires that evaluators specifically define the evaluation questions, the data collection process, the sources for the data, and the analytical techniques to be applied to the data. Completing a design matrix clarifies the evaluation issues in the minds of the evaluators and serves as a useful tool for supervisory review before beginning the evaluation. Figure 7.2 illustrates the design matrix. The example shown is one issue in the evaluation of a corporate hiring program.

The following are the procedures for completion of the design matrix:

Issue question. This column contains client question(s) and any additional questions developed to accurately portray the evaluation issue. Individual questions should be very specific, using direct quotes from the client where appropriate.

Developmental question. The information in this column contains all of the questions necessary to expand and answer the issue question. Who? What? Why? When? Where? How much? To what extent? In what way?

Methodology. What techniques will be used to obtain the answers to the evaluation questions, for example, interviews, document searches, computer database searches, surveys?

Sources of information. Where can the information be obtained to answer the question? Are the appropriate personnel, records, and data available and accessible?

Analysis. What analytical techniques will be used to examine the data? Will the data be qualitative, quantitative, or mixed; randomly or purposefully collected; and what statistical manipulations are anticipated to analyze the data?

Comments. This column contains cost data, staff allocation, information not available, skills needed for this evaluation, and so on.

Using a design matrix adds rigor to the evaluation process and forces evaluators to be conceptually clear on their evaluation strategy before beginning data collection. Using the matrix affords supervisory personnel an opportunity to review and comment on the evaluation design prior to approval. The design matrix document, with its preliminary evaluation strategy, is an excellent framework for beginning discussions between the evaluation team and evaluation managers. Meticulous attention to the evaluation questions and the anticipated approach to learning the answers imparts a systematic clarity to the design process and minimizes frustration during the analytical and writing stages of the evaluation. Additionally, use of the design matrix focuses the evaluation and delimits the parameters, preventing evaluators from following up on "interesting" but nonrelevant research topics.

Evaluation Sequence

Internal evaluation design is both an intellectual and administrative exercise. Enthusiastic evaluators, anxious to begin the intellectual challenge of designing an evaluation, may neglect mundane but important administrative tasks that are essential, complementary components to the design process. Evaluation design is only one facet in a complete evaluation strategy. Project funding, resource availability, administrative paperwork, notification procedures, and computer database updating are fundamental constituents of a complete evaluation plan. In their eagerness to begin an evaluation, internal evaluators may fail to properly plan and organize the entire evaluation, relying on later periodic adjustments to correct deficiencies in the original evaluation strategy. This approach is inefficient and ineffective and has the potential to impede prompt completion of the project. Data collection is particularly expensive, and failure to properly plan for this phase of the evaluation may affect the ability to accurately document and adequately support findings. Commencing the reporting phase of an evaluation always seems to clarify any deficiencies in the data collected but, unfortunately, comes too late for corrective action. Lamentations over a flawed data collection scheme serve little purpose except as a learning experience for future evaluations. To preclude unproductive or ineffectual evaluations, it is prudent to follow a systematized approach. Table 7.2 illustrates a methodical sequence of the significant components required for an internal evaluation.

Rigorous attention to all phases of the evaluation from the initial conception to delivery of the final product will prevent overlooking essential steps in the process. Insistence on adherence to established evaluation procedures by evaluation team leaders and executive management will pay dividends during the evaluation and contribute to the professional image of the evaluation office.

Validity

Utility has been proposed as the ultimate criterion for judging the worth of an internal evaluation. Closely allied to utility and the foundation on which utility is built is the concept of validity. Scriven (1997) writes that "validity is the highest professional imperative of the evaluator" (p. 483). An invalid evaluation has little worth and no utility. The usual approach to defining validity is to confirm that a measure is valid if it measures what it was designed to measure. The criteria for measuring design quality are generally internal and external validity (Cook & Campbell, 1979). Invalid designs have weaknesses in these two areas.

TABLE 7.2
Evaluation Sequence

1. **Study initiation**
   Opening memorandum. Contains sufficient information to convey to interested stakeholders and the evaluation staff, the commencement of the evaluation
   - Authority
   - Purpose
   - Deadlines
   - Team members
   - Administrative requirements
   Computerized control log entries
   Meetings with affected executives and managers
   Notification of department heads and appropriate stakeholders
   Contacts with subject matter experts

2. **Literature search**
   Review both organizational policies and paperwork and the substantive literature

3. **Formulation phase**
   Develop issues and frame evaluation questions

4. **Evaluation plan**
   Prepare workplan
   Design evaluation
   Prepare design matrix

5. **Data collection and analysis**
   Determine quality and availability of data
   Ascertain precision needed in evaluation data
   Resolve quantitative and qualitative data collection strategies
   Decide on random or purposeful sampling methodologies
   Plan and match appropriate statistical and analytical tools to anticipated data

6. **Communicating evaluation results (see Chapter 8)**
   Determine if report will be written
   Prepare appropriate briefings
   Resolve dissemination procedures for evaluation findings

7. **Write recommendations (see Chapter 8)**
   Identify options if appropriate

8. **Closing procedures (see Chapter 9)**
   Workpaper preparation
   Retention and disposition of workpapers
   Report annotation
   Classified material handling (if necessary)
   Control log updating

9. **Follow-up**
   After six months, determine the status of suggested changes, approved recommendations, and attempt to measure impact of the evaluation

For internal evaluators, who are generally concerned with complex issues that defy precise definitions, a more appropriate definition of validity incorporates a broader sense of the attendant condition surrounding the evaluation. Scriven's (1991) definition falls in this category when he describes valid evaluations as those "that take into account all relevant factors, given the whole context of the evaluation (particularly including the client's needs) and weight them appropriately in the synthesis process" (p. 372). Because the category of evaluative activity undertaken by most internal evaluators is better described as management inquiry and not research, the approach to validity issues also differs. The primary judges of the validity of an internal evaluation effort are those that participate in and review the evaluation. If an evaluation effort is judged by program experts to be valid then it probably is valid. Using multiple sources of evidence, establishing a chain of evidence, and having key informants review draft evaluation reports are tactics that can be employed to increase the rigor of evaluations (Yin, 1984).

Patton (1989a) uses the criterion of reasonableness to replace the criterion of rigor in the internal evaluation environment. For him, the essence of validity is face validity:

> In this situation, given what we know about what the program did, and given what we know about the impact of the program, is it reasonable to assume that there was some significant amount of linkage between what the program did and what resulted? (p. 376)

Do the evaluation results appear to those interested stakeholders to be plausible and convincing? The concept of validity in internal settings is both driven and constrained by a fluid issue environment that varies even as the evaluation is conducted. For internal evaluators, the emphasis is on production of quality information within the allocated time frame. The pragmatic reality of the internal environment causes internal evaluators to be preoccupied with time constraints, data availability, and data quality. Causality and generalizability are not ignored, but neither are they emphasized. Because most internal evaluative activity is by definition for use by the organization where it was conducted, minimal attention is devoted to external validity. In the internal environment, external validity is replaced by organizational relevance.

Data Dependability

Elegant designs, complex methodologies, and sophisticated analytical techniques may create a facade of professional internal evaluation practice, but if flawed data have been used, the final evaluation product will lack credibility when presented to clients and will encounter minimal acceptance among major stakeholders. "Perhaps the major methodological obstacle to the acceptance of internal evaluations is data dependability—how to control the potential for bias and bolster the credibility of evaluations undertaken by internal staff" (A. J. Love, personal communication, March 1997).

The cornerstone of reliable organizational data rests on a trusting relationship between the organization's front-line staff data creators and management users. An ethos of data reliability flows from an explicit understanding between data creators and users on how data will be collected, used, manipulated, and applied to meet the organization's information needs. In the absence of a clear understanding by data creators about the data's eventual use, or in those organizations where data are perceived by the front-line collector to have a potential punitive value, data quality and dependability will be severely diminished.

Developing an ethos of data accuracy at the initial collection point requires continuous communication between users and front-line staff, an understanding of the need for accuracy and integrity in collection procedures, an empathy for the difficulties encountered by front-line staff, and a reciprocal confidence between collectors and end users that data will be used for support and improvement of programs and not for disciplinary purposes. However, even under optimum standards of data integrity, there may be circumstances when inaccurate reporting occurs, with both legitimate and illegitimate rationalization. D. Wilson (personal communication, April 1997) suggests three areas where this might occur:

1. *Historical changes in criteria.* Historical changes may occur when data elements are redefined or reconceptualized by the front-line staff. Changes in data criteria may not be evident to evaluators, and any analysis of data from extended time frames needs to address this issue.
2. *Performance data.* Performance data may be continually required by the organization, yet occasionally difficult or impossible to obtain and

report. If no provisions for these situations are incorporated into performance data collection procedures, front-line staff may be tempted to submit fake data to fulfill reporting requirements.

3. *Client eligibility.* When data affect client eligibility for service, there may be a temptation by front-line staff to "fudge" the data to maintain eligibility for deserving clients or to maintain sufficient clientele to sustain continued program funding.

In those instances where data dependability is in question, internal evaluators will be better served to collect original data to maintain their credibility.

Performance Measurement

Skills developed in designing evaluations have application in other consultative roles for internal evaluators. Wholey and Newcomer (1997) believe that evaluators possess the requisite technical expertise, knowledge, and communication skills to support managers in defining and clarifying realistic goals, designing performance measurement systems, measuring outputs and outcomes, and communicating program performance results. Unfortunately, evaluation and performance measurement are usually thought of as two different management applications, when in fact they should be considered as complementary. Zapico-Goni and Mayne (1997) also suggest that performance monitoring and evaluation have complementary roles with three different aspects: (1) Elements of performance that are difficult or expensive to monitor can be more appropriately monitored with periodic evaluations; (2) the converse of the first aspect is that where evaluations are too expensive or intrusive, performance measurement systems can be used to track and provide reasonably reliable signals on program activities; and (3) program evaluations can be used to develop relevant and useful performance measures.

If the essence of internal evaluation is improved organizational performance, then it logically follows that measuring organizational performance is an integral component of internal evaluation. The commonality that links evaluation and performance measurement is the use of data, in both cases, to determine program performance. The major distinction is that performance measurement indicates what is happening but not why, whereas evaluation examines the causal connections between program activities and outcomes to answer the "why" question. One of the potential weaknesses of performance measurement systems is the use of program data for budget and management decisions without a complete understanding of the meaning of the data. Supplementing performance measurement data with evaluative interpretations answers program effectiveness questions that are important to decision-makers.

One approach to understanding the evaluation-performance measurement relationship is to view evaluation activity as bookends to performance measurement. When new programs are in their implementation stage, evaluators can assist program managers to develop and clarify program theory; select practical, valid, and measurable performance indicators; and set realistic goals and objectives. The use of evaluators when developing performance measurement systems takes advantage of the evaluator's analytical skills and experience in testing causal linkages between program activities and program outcomes. Some of the difficulties encountered when evaluating programs are vagueness of program theory, lack of logic between program activities and program intentions, and insufficient or poor quality data to determine program effectiveness. Employing evaluators at the initiation point in program development tends to clarify these issues and to facilitate subsequent evaluative assessments. After a program is fully implemented and mature, evaluation can examine linkages between program activities and outcomes and ascertain whether program activities were effective in attaining program objectives.

Much has been written about performance measurement, particularly in the public sector, and its success in that arena is open to debate. Renewed emphasis on public sector reform highlights the importance of performance measurement in these reform initiatives and its crucial role in demonstrating positive outcomes of reform strategies. The Government Performance and Results Act of 1993 (GPRA) contains language requiring the measurement and evaluation of government agency performance and reporting the findings to Congress. The increased interest by Congress in the performance of public programs affords internal evaluators an excellent opportunity to demonstrate the utility and efficacy of evaluative activities to supplement program performance measurement. Independent assessment of program performance by internal evaluators can fulfill the requirements of the GPRA while illustrating the capability of evaluation as a management tool.

Increasing pressures on organizations to not only enhance their performance but also to be able to demonstrate improvements in performance require meticulous attention to performance measurement systems that accurately appraise the organization's activities. Incorporating the concept of evaluation into performance measurement systems and using evaluator skills during program initiation and effectiveness evaluations increase the likelihood that credible program results can be reported and understood.

CONCLUSION

Internal evaluation design efforts do not eschew conventional social science principles and protocols, but adapt these canons and standards to situations encountered internally in organizations where pressures to quickly produce evaluative information are common. Internal evaluators have at their disposal the same evaluation designs and methodologies as external evaluators; however, there is greater emphasis on formative approaches and less need for experimental or causal models. Time is the overarching constraint on internal evaluators. Frequent pressures for expedient production of evaluative information are common. Successful internal evaluation design can overcome this obstacle with meticulous attention to question definition and severe limitations on the scope of the evaluation effort.

Foundational to proper evaluation design is a comprehensive understanding of the structure, theory, activities, goals, outputs, and expected outcomes of a program. A conceptual grasp of both the micro and macro functions of a program precedes design efforts. A systematic design approach, using standardized guides, matrices, and checklists, can facilitate the design process and help prevent overlooking a critical design step.

The challenge for expeditious production of quality information requires imaginative designs and methodologies for rapid yet credible responses. A framework for quick-response evaluation details evaluation tasks and allocates time frames for completion. Use of this flexible approach to internal evaluation allows internal evaluators to be responsive to urgent management requests for information while maintaining the integrity of the evaluation process. Alternative evaluative approaches to management requests for information incorporate evaluative techniques modified to conform to exigent circumstances. Focus groups and reverse-site visits are two techniques for accelerating the data collection phase of evaluative efforts. Use of evaluators and the concept of evaluation when developing performance measurement systems and initiating new programs can increase the potential for credible program assessment.

RECOMMENDED FOR FURTHER READING

Creswell, J. W. (1994). *Research design: Qualitative and quantitative approaches.* Thousand Oaks, CA: Sage.

Hedrick, T. E., Bickman, L., & Rog, D. J. (1993). *Applied research design: A practical guide.* Newbury Park, CA: Sage.
  Two valuable resources on design issues that have application for internal evaluators.

Miller, D. C. (1991). *Handbook of research design and social measurement* (5th ed.). Newbury Park, CA: Sage.
  A valuable reference source and bibliography containing digests of social science research. It contains descriptive overviews of research methodologies and approaches to basic, applied, and evaluation research.

U.S. General Accounting Office. (1991, May). *Designing evaluations.* **Program and Methodology Division. Washington, DC: Author.**
  The U.S. General Accounting Office (GAO) has periodically published technical methodological papers for use by their auditors. This publication provides valuable information on a systematic approach to matching designs to evaluation questions.

Wholey, J. S., Hatry, H. P., & Newcomer, K. E. (Eds.). (1994). *Handbook of practical program evaluation*. San Francisco: Jossey-Bass.
Contains useful, practical design and data collection procedures applicable to internal settings.

Wholey, J. S., Newcomer, K. E., & Associates. (1989). *Improving government performance: Evaluation strategies for strengthening public agencies and programs*. San Francisco: Jossey-Bass.
A useful resource for evaluators in the public sector. It contains short-term, inexpensive evaluation strategies for practical application in internal settings.

Notes

1. To subscribe to the AEA evaluation discussion list, send an e-mail message to LISTSERV@ua1vm.ua.edu with a blank subject line and the following in the body: SUB-SCRIBE EVALTALK <firstname> <lastname>

2. This design matrix has been adapted from *Designing Evaluations* (GAO, 1991).

Chapter 8

Effective Communication of Evaluation Results

KEY CHAPTER TOPICS

- ❖ Writing effective evaluation reports
- ❖ Writing effective recommendations
- ❖ Disseminating evaluation reports

*D*o internal evaluation reports make a noise when they land in executive suites?

(a) Yes
(b) No
(c) Sometimes

The correct answer is (c) Sometimes!

I suspect that the effect of many internal evaluation reports on organizations parallels the experience of kissing your sister (or brother). It is a routine, benign, perfunctory event, devoid of passion, nonmemorable, and has no lasting effects for either party involved. Ascribing these characteristics to internal evaluation reports is akin to acknowledging a lack of influence on the organization and signals a strategic flaw in the effectiveness of the evaluation office. Central to the practice of internal evaluation is the capability to cause change in the organization, and this begins with the effective communication of evaluation results.

Reporting evaluation results is the linchpin of internal evaluation. It is the initiating event during an evaluation that communicates program performance information and suggestions for change to management. The entire preliminary evaluation rubric has been necessary but insufficient if evaluation findings fail to reach and influence the appropriate audience. The reporting phase of internal evaluation is the information conduit for evaluation data and their analysis, interpretation, and recommended organizational applications. This phase of evaluation may be appropriately depicted as the most formidable portion of any evaluation because it challenges the creative communication skills of internal evaluators to both interpret the evaluative data and convey their meaning in an understandable way to the intended audience. "One of the greatest challenges that social scientists face is in translating vague program language into a workable evaluation design and then translating the results back into language that is understandable to policymakers" (Cordray, 1989, p. 381). The conceptual elegance of an evaluation design becomes irrelevant if evaluators are unable to effectively convey the message embedded in the data.

The act of transmitting evaluative information to the organization has a dual function: to provide feedback on the organization's performance and initiate necessary changes to improve performance where deficiencies are discovered. Evaluation results, in whatever forms, create an awareness of identified issues and detected performance deficiencies. Evaluation effort is largely wasted if findings and recommendations fail to attract attention, precipitate discussion, and initiate corrective action. The conceptual foundation for effective communication of evaluation results is the recognition that utility is the criterion of merit for internal evaluators. Utility requires use, which requires client knowledge, and awareness, which requires effective communication between evaluators and the organization.

This chapter will examine the rationale for devoting evaluator effort to reporting results, alternative methods for conveying evaluation results, effective and persuasive report writing, the advantages and disadvantages of reporting alternatives, and the need, logic, and style for effective recommendations. Effective report dissemination procedures are also reviewed. Written reports are not the only vehicle to convey the results of an evaluation, and this chapter will examine alternatives; however, some memorialization of evaluation efforts is vital if the organization is to be pervasively influenced by evaluation efforts over the long term.

Communicating With the Organization

For internal evaluation to effectively influence organizations, there must be a conspicuous and efficient communications conduit between the evaluators and appropriate entities in the organization. The reality of practicing internal evaluation requires that evaluators circulate the results of their efforts to clients and decisionmakers in a timely, concise, and understandable format. Effective and efficient communication with organizations obligates evaluators to investigate their audiences and match reporting procedures to audience preferences.

AUDIENCE ANALYSIS

Too often, for most of us, the act of reporting evaluation findings actually begins with the act of writing down the results of the evaluation. A more effective beginning to the task of reporting evaluation results is to devote some time to thinking before writing: thinking about the intended audience for the evaluation information; thinking about the most effective approach to present the findings; thinking about the essence of the message you are trying to convey. Audience preferences and the intended use of the findings should shape the presentation mode for evaluation results.

The target audience may be an individual, a group of individuals, an oversight board or committee, the public, or a combination of these. However, for internal evaluators the primary audience is often the head of the organization. It is productive to understand how this individual processes and uses information before crafting a data presentation strategy. Some individuals are comfortable with quantitative data, whereas others are clearly challenged by numerical presentations and prefer qualitative or descriptive data interpretations. Once preferences are identified, presentation strategies can be formulated. Quantitative data can be presented in a qualitative format and vice versa. There is increasing interest in and acknowledgment that the use of graphs can facilitate the presentation of evaluation findings. "Graphs are powerful tools for evaluators, who must compete for their audience's time. The audience can quickly retrieve information from a graph, without technical training or a particular talent with numbers" (Henry, 1997, p. 3). Sensitivity to the audience's capacity for understanding complex data will fashion the format for reporting evaluation outcomes.

ALTERNATIVES TO WRITTEN REPORTS

As noted earlier in this chapter, a written report is not the only method to effectively present evaluation findings. Imaginative means to garner the attention of decisionmakers may occasionally be necessary when more conventional approaches are unsuitable or unavailable. I once accommodated the busy schedule of the deputy director of the Federal Bureau of Investigation (FBI) by briefing him on the status of an evaluation while riding down the elevator in the FBI building, crossing Pennsylvania Avenue, and riding up the elevator in the Department of Justice building where he was scheduled to meet with the attorney general. Creative solutions help when trying to capture the attention of busy executives. Effective communication of evaluation results requires evaluator adaptation to the organizational environment and the nature of the findings. The results of a Food and Drug Administration (FDA) evaluation recommending a revised approach to inspecting food processing plants were effectively conveyed to the program manager using computer charts and graphic displays; no written report was ever prepared (Sonnichsen, 1991). Travel by the FDA evaluator to field sites helped convince program personnel of the advantages of the recommended change in inspection procedures. Systematically reviewing the options for presenting evaluation findings is the proper first step in effective communication.

BRIEFINGS

Hendricks (1994) makes the important distinction between *reports* and *reporting* and concludes that reports are not always essential for influencing a situation. An oral briefing is an effective technique for presenting evaluation findings. Briefings offer alternatives to reports and provide evaluators opportunities for face-to-face contacts with clients and decisionmakers to explain the results of the evaluation. Briefings can be used in lieu of or in conjunction with reports.

Briefings offer evaluators opportunities to visually stimulate the audience, clear up complex issues, recapitulate important points, synopsize the report, identify issues of concern, and answer pertinent questions. Whereas reports disseminated to interested stakeholders may not be read, briefings offer an occasion to ensure publicity for the results of an evaluation. Audiences assembled for briefings often bring together diverse viewpoints and varied authority and responsibility levels. Invitations to briefings should include interested stakeholders and relevant authority levels to ensure the necessary ingredients are present for action.

An optimum time allocation for briefings is one hour with only 30 minutes allocated for the evaluator presentation. The remaining time is designated for questions and discussions. Some of the most interesting and productive briefings I have attended were those where a dialogue was begun between evaluators and the audience. These discussions offer internal evaluators an opening to personalize their findings. Briefings can also be more engaging if conducted using overhead transparencies, slides, or some other visual media. Advances in computer graphics allow professional briefings to be prepared by almost anyone with access to a computer. Both Harvard Graphics™ and Microsoft PowerPoint™ are graphics software that can be used to professionalize briefings. Computer technology has made graphic presentations readily assessable and expanded the options for evaluators seeking fresh approaches to presenting findings.

The more sophisticated and professional the briefing, the greater the potential for influencing the audience. One of the dilemmas confronting evaluation office managers is the question of who should present the briefing. Not everyone is comfortable speaking in public, particularly in front of top organizational officials when controversy may be involved. Essentially, there are two options: Employ evaluation personnel with public speaking skills, or use the evaluators who conducted the evaluation. With rare exceptions, I believe the latter option is superior. Evaluators who conducted the evaluation have a more comprehensive understanding of the program and can be more responsive to questions. They will have had more contact with program personnel who may be present at the briefing, and they deserve the opportunity to demonstrate their skills in front of organizational officials who may be responsible for performance reviews and career advancement. In my experience, most evaluators can be taught briefing skills, and practice sessions with their peers will help prepare them for the task. On rare occasions, when a critical issue is involved, the evaluation is complex, and the audience is expected to be hostile, it may be prudent to have the evaluation office director or another senior evaluation staff member present the briefing. Regardless of who presents the briefing, the evaluation team should be present to answer questions.

Writing Effective Evaluation Reports

Traditionally, the option selected to present evaluation findings is a written report. Reports have the advantage that they are readily available to a large and geographically dispersed audience, they can be read on the recipient's timetable, and they memorialize the evaluation and function as an artifact to remind readers of the legitimization of the evaluation function in an organization. However, to maximize the effectiveness of an evaluation report, it must be well written, persuasive, and of course, read. Failure to connect with the intended audience renders an evaluation report ineffectual.

THE PERSUASIVE WRITING PROCESS

Too often, evaluation report writing emphasizes writing and not reporting. The evaluator becomes enamored with composing a detailed treatise on the events that transpired during the evaluation, failing to recognize that the goal of evaluation reporting is to simply elucidate and support the findings and offer solutions to the primary problem. A written evaluation report is a vehicle for conveying a message containing the important aspects of the evaluation and not the reason the evaluation was conducted. It is not uncommon for evaluators and their superiors to become infatuated with the language and phraseology in a report and devote an inordinate amount of time and energy to "wordsmithing" when what is needed is a succinctly worded identification of the problem, an explanation of the data supporting the findings, and any recommendations for change. The goal of the internal evaluator is to convert findings and recommendations into positive organizational action. The written report is a means to this end, not the end itself!

The craft of successful evaluation writing involves the writer's ability to use the evaluation findings to create vivid images in the mind of the reader, the ingenuity to convince with graphic examples, and the skillfulness to persuade with captivating language. The success in translating data to organizational action may depend on the artistry employed in interpreting evaluation study results for audiences via the written report. The proliferation of computer software and the advances in desktop publishing allow for the production of visually appealing, professional reports. Color graphics can simplify and enhance the visual presentation of complex data. Extraneous descriptive material should be eschewed in favor of concise, truly relevant evidence of the problem, the findings, and the recommended courses of action. A minimalist approach to the display of numerical statistical data is usually more effective than cluttered charts and graphs showing all the data collected.

Effective use of representative narrative comments livens up the report and vividly portrays the meaning of obscure, uninteresting data sets. Directly quoting respondents inserts vitality into writing, which might otherwise benumb the reader. For example, following an evaluation of the effectiveness of police training courses in transitioning the Panamanian army to a civilian police force, after the U.S. military intervention in Panama with "Operation Just Cause" on December 20,

1989, verbatim quotes (translated from Spanish) extracted from respondent questionnaires were used by the FBI evaluation staff in the final report:

> Months after a crime scene investigation, I was called to the district attorney's office to discuss the case. Because I had taken good notes at the crime scene, I was able to respond.

> I broke up two citizens who were arguing by using human relations training.

> I was praised by an individual for arresting him without using violence.

> I convinced an arguing couple that their behavior was harmful to their children.

> I confronted a man with a knife and twice asked him to drop it and he did. Before [the training] I would have just shot him.

Coupling these vignettes with supporting documentation painted a vivid picture of the training effect in the reader's mind much more effectively than total reliance on available statistical data. Intelligent evaluation report writing can engage the reader with imagery rather than tedious data presentations. Recognizing that the purpose of reporting evaluation findings is to enlighten, persuade, and initiate action, internal evaluators should animate their reports with accurate yet absorbing material.

Although there is no single, most effective agenda to present the findings of an evaluation, Table 8.1 outlines a traditional approach to formatting a written evaluation report that captures the essential components in a logical sequence, providing the reader with a thorough understanding of the evaluation. This reporting format is only a guide, and any vehicle used for recording the results of an evaluation should be flexible and appropriate to the audience and the conditions encountered during the evaluation.

Most evaluators, given sufficient time, can write lengthy, detailed reports, but it takes practice, skill, and discipline to write concisely under the pressure of a short deadline and still engage and persuade the

---

TABLE 8.1
Evaluation Reporting Format

Executive summary

A brief synopsis of the major findings of the evaluation.

Introduction

Authority: Identify the basis or predication for initiating the evaluation.

Goals and objectives: Explain the purpose and objective of the evaluation (either as articulated by the requester or as developed during the initial stages of the study).

Background

Develop a brief background to enable the reader to place the study in the proper contextual framework. Identify the major issues in the evaluation.

Details

Set forth the essence of the study using subcaptions to organize the report. Remember, your goal is not only to inform but persuade the reader. Develop your positions logically, use empirical evidence when available, and base your arguments on thorough and compelling documentation. Findings should be data based. The report should be balanced with relevant opposing views.

Findings

Findings describe the evidence discovered during the evaluation that pertain to the issue areas. They explicate the issues under examination. Findings form the basis for the recommendations and should be easily traceable to the details in the report.

Conclusions

Provide a brief review of the salient issues and findings in the evaluation report.

Appendixes, exhibits, and references

These sections of the report may include details of evaluation methodology, justification for evaluation design, rationale for site selection, sampling procedures, tables, charts, and if appropriate, citations to publications or references used.

Recommendations

Recommendations may be included in the report or attached as an independent document. In many cases, it may be more efficient to circulate recommendations in a separate memorandum because during the evaluation debate the initially offered recommendations may be modified, but the report should stand on its own.

---

reader. The education and experience of many evaluators has prepared them to write for scholarly journals to communicate with fellow evaluators. The jargon and format deemed suitable for these publications may be ineffective in attracting the attention of program managers or organizational executives accustomed to personal conversations and terse memos as the basis for their decision-making deliberations. Accommodating the preferences of executives and managers for concise statements of the problems and recommended solutions may not only shorten the writing phase of the evaluation but also increase the likelihood that the evaluation will influence the organization. Long evaluation reports tend to become descriptive, masking the essential topics with superfluous verbiage not central to the core issues and relevant findings. If supervisory discipline is not exercised over the reporting phase of an evaluation, it can account for a disproportionate percentage of the allocated time frame for completion. Because excessive focus on writing evaluation reports deducts valuable time from other important facets of the evaluation, evaluators need to develop efficient strategies for curtailing this phase of evaluation. Supervisory personnel should exercise caution when reviewing evaluation reports submitted for approval to ensure they are critiquing the substance of the evaluation and not the writing style of the evaluator. Fortunately, there are procedures to assist evaluators in the writing phase. Two excellent techniques to begin and end the writing process are *cognitive mapping*, or *webbing*, to help identify the major themes before beginning the writing process, and the *writer's conference*, used to review the first draft of the report.

COGNITIVE MAPPING

Cognitive mapping, or webbing (Gladis, 1989), is a preparatory writing technique designed to develop and organize the relevant themes and major issues identified during an evaluation before beginning the actual writing process. It graphically portrays the core evaluation issue(s) and facts discovered during the evaluation, allowing the evaluators to assign priorities, organize major themes, and select the pertinent issues to be discussed in the report. Gladis (1989) describes the webbing process as particularly appealing to those who learn visually:

> Like its name indicates, webbing is a way of weaving your ideas together much as a spider would do. You spin your web by writing the main topic in the middle of a page and circling the word. Next you draw out lines to bubbles of ideas that relate to the main ideas. Pretty soon you've

developed a weblike sketch on your paper. You'll easily see where you need more research and where your ideas are highly developed. (p. 34)

Figure 8.1 shows a hypothetical "web" of a corporate computer-training program. During the webbing process, you suspend judgment as you develop ideas, issues, facts, and themes and concentrate on the major points in the evaluation. This simple and practical method to develop the salient points of an evaluation prevents tedious concentration on trivial evaluation issues. It also minimizes the potential for a verbose report that fails to engage and persuade the reader.

Table 8.2 depicts the four-step webbing process that can be done alone by the report writer or jointly with the entire evaluation team.

WRITER'S CONFERENCE

Completion of the first draft of an evaluation report is a major milestone for evaluators but hardly the completion of the report-writing process. Converting the first draft into a polished final report involves the effort and skill of several members of the evaluation staff and supervisory complement. One method to quickly critique the draft report in a tactful and professional manner is the use of a writer's conference (Gladis, 1988). A writer's conference is a useful technique for the unemotional and objective review of draft evaluation reports to improve their quality and readability. It is an orderly, formal process that brings together evaluation colleagues, with diverse backgrounds and writing skills, to improve the quality of the report and minimize the myopia that can develop when one person writes a report. A writer's conference is an appropriate review procedure for reports that are complex, address significant policy issues, or will affect broad audiences. Table 8.3 outlines the strategy for conducting a successful writer's conference.

An evaluation office supervisor, with the authority to make decisions on the report, should be present to facilitate the writer's conference so that the meeting produces positive actions and the author leaves with sufficient authoritative guidance to complete a second draft. Without the presence of an official voice to make decisions, mitigate conflict,

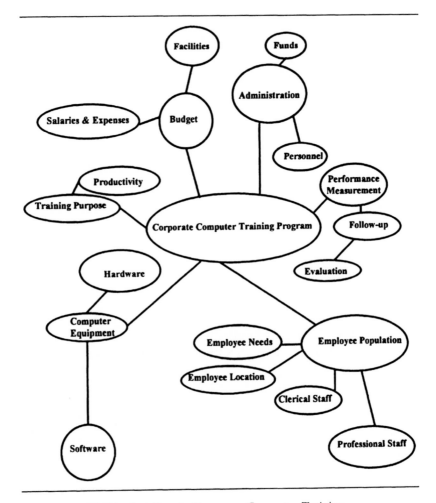

Figure 8.1. "Webbing": A Sample Corporate Computer-Training Program

and resolve controversies, the author may become confused over the direction the report should take.

It is important for the supervisor at the writer's conference to motivate the participants toward useful and productive debate. The facilitator can stimulate the writer's conference discussion by posing the following questions:

TABLE 8.2
Cognitive Mapping ("Webbing") Process

Step 1
 Write the main core issue or topic in the middle of the page and circle the word(s).

Step 2
 Draw lines off the central topic to related ideas and themes and circle.

Step 3
 Break down subideas by drawing additional lines and circled words until you have developed a weblike structure on your paper. Continue this process until you can spin your web no further.

Step 4
 Study the web and use it to develop an outline and approach to writing the evaluation report.

SOURCE: Adapted from Gladis (1989).

What worked well—what did you like about the report?

What gave you trouble?

What areas do you suggest be improved?

What parts of the report were difficult to understand?

Do the findings logically flow from the data?

Are graphics appropriate and useful? Does the report need more or less?

Is the overall strategy and format of the report designed for maximum impact and persuasion?

If necessary, each page of the report can be reviewed using this process, with the readers presenting their views and the evaluation supervisor making decisions. This collaborative writing exercise was welcomed by the FBI evaluation staff in lieu of the more traditional, isolated writing procedure.

SOME THOUGHTS ON WRITING
EFFECTIVE EVALUATION REPORTS

I have distilled the following observations on effective evaluation writing after 14 years of writing and reviewing FBI audit, evaluation,

TABLE 8.3
Writer's Conference Strategy: Procedures

The evaluation supervisor chooses appropriate evaluation colleagues to read the first draft of the report.

Readers make notations on their copy of the report in preparation for the writer's conference.

The evaluation supervisor convenes the writer's conference.

The author of the draft report presents a brief overview of the report, highlighting the strong points and areas where the author is struggling.

Report readers, in turn, present their views on the strengths of the report in a positive and constructive manner to begin the meeting in an upbeat mode and reduce the anxiety and stress of the writer. After the reviewers present their first positive observations, the second round commences the critique phase emphasizing weak points, areas for improvement, deletions, additions, and suggested changes. Comments should be limited to structure, theme, format, issues, and strategies for persuasion and impact, and not dwell on grammar or style.

The evaluation supervisor gives guidance and approval to the suggested report changes.

SOURCE: Adapted from Gladis (1988).

and inspection reports. I periodically updated these observations and distributed them to the evaluation staff for guidance.

♦ It is well to remember, when writing an evaluation report, that although the writer usually has ample preparation time, the average executive reader often hastily reviews the report, frequently not reading beyond the executive summary. The executive summary, therefore, becomes possibly the only opportunity to capture the attention of the busy executive who is expected to act on the recommendations in the report. The operative word in the executive summary is *executive* not summary; the purpose is to concisely and meaningfully convey the highlights of the evaluation and the benefits to be derived from recommended actions. It should be interesting, persuasive, and oriented around the major issues. It should not sequentially describe and summarize each section in the report, but be organized around material topics. One of the poor writing habits encountered in many internal evaluation reports is the practice of extracting descriptive selections from each section of the report, even when many of the sections are neither germane to the main point nor supportive of the significant findings.

✧ Outline the focus of the report for the audience with emphasis on prominent organizational components, individuals, or programs.

✧ The first paragraph in the executive summary should answer the question "Why was this evaluation conducted?"

✧ Format the executive summary for power and impact. Put the "good stuff" up front.

✧ Do not be afraid to include data in the executive summary.

✧ In the executive summary, "bulleted" lists may be more effective than narrative.

✧ If appropriate, use charts to depict data.

✧ Use representative, descriptive quotes that convey the essence of the data collected.

✧ Ensure that the findings and recommendations are not mixed together. These are two different components of an evaluation and should not be entwined.

✧ Be cautious with absolute statements, for example, *irreparable damage, all, every, none;* do not overstate the case.

✧ Avoid words such as *many* and *most;* be explicit; use numbers and percentages.

✧ Explain alternative views of the program if they exist and not "There is no agreed-on vision."

✧ Avoid appearing biased by including the minority viewpoint in the report. When 80% of respondents feel one way, we should be alert to set forth what the other 20% think. Statements such as "55% believe" beg for a comparative analysis: What do the other 45% think?

✧ Be careful when using means to depict data. Show ranges where appropriate and use rankings.

✧ Avoid causal-sounding statements that are unsupported by the data.

250 HIGH IMPACT INTERNAL EVALUATION

❖ Include rival data in reports. The countervailing position may even reinforce the prevailing view. A preponderance of data pointing in only one direction may be perceived as evaluator bias.

Commentaries on evaluation writing can be routinely collected and distributed to evaluation teams at the onset of the writing process to help increase the quality of reporting and reduce the amount of editing by supervisory personnel.

Using Recommendations to Convert Evaluation Findings to Organizational Action

The goal and ultimate criterion of performance for internal evaluators are to have a positive influence on the organization, usually accomplished through recommendations of remedial action to modify or correct program activities, leading to program improvement. The production of unemotional, unbiased, data-driven evaluations is a necessary but incomplete practice of internal evaluation. The indispensable element in high impact internal evaluation is the conversion of findings to positive organizational action. The pragmatic exercise of interpreting evaluation data, translating and linking the data to the reality of the workplace, and fashioning practical, effective recommendations is the key to effective internal evaluation. All four of the internal evaluation directors I contacted for input for this book commented that they "almost always" issue recommendations with their evaluation reports. One of them, George Grob (personal communication, July 1997), deputy inspector general in the Office of Inspector General (OIG), U.S. Department of Health and Human Services, commented that occasionally, when evaluation findings are overwhelmingly obvious, he will omit recommendations, leaving the client to respond to the compelling facts in the evaluation. Grob cited, as an example, a study of the costs of home use of oxygen, which discovered that Medicare was paying twice as much for oxygen as the Veterans Administration. This obvious cost imbalance did not need to be addressed by a recommendation. Another OIG study of the nationwide phenomenon of acute-care hospital closings, which generated public and congressional concern, determined that the hospitals closed were small, had low occupancy rates, and were closed for economic reasons and that patients were able to secure adequate medical care in nearby large hospitals. Neither of these studies required recommendations because the findings were indisputable and any necessary actions were obvious.

Effective transmission of evaluation data to the organization may occur through oral briefings, written reports, formal and informal meetings, casual conversations, or direct contact with interested stakeholders, organizational executives, and decisionmakers. The goal of the internal evaluator is to use the evaluation findings, converted to recommendations, as a persuasive instrument for positive change in the organization.

RECOMMENDATION FORMULATION

Evaluation recommendations, however, are not universally accepted in the evaluation community as the appropriate final step in the evaluation process. There are both philosophical and pragmatic dimensions to the argument whether recommendations are the logical concluding action in the evaluation process, with significant implications for internal evaluators. Some evaluators resolutely believe recommendations are the responsibility of the evaluator, whereas others are equally as committed to the proposition that evaluation findings should be interpreted by clients and programmatic changes initiated by them. Hendricks and Handley (1990) believe evaluators should almost always offer recommendations: "Offering recommendations is an inherent part of the responsibility of an analyst . . . evaluators, after studying a program or policy, have an obligation to convey all the information they have learned, including information on best directions for the future" (p. 110). Patton (1997), pragmatically oriented toward utility, states that "well-written, carefully derived recommendations and conclusions can be the magnet that pulls all the other elements of an evaluation together into a meaningful whole" (p. 324). Reinforcing that line of reasoning, Hendricks and Handley (1990) write that "recommendations are often the most influential product of a good evaluation, and they sometimes improve programs dramatically" (p. 109).

Tanji (1993) believes that the decision to offer or omit recommendations is based on a philosophical preference, rooted in the ontological beliefs of the evaluator. For her, the use of recommendations is centered on the attitudes of the evaluators and their subjective or objective views of reality. A preference for including recommendations in an evaluation aligns itself with a belief in an objective reality, that reality is probabilistic and courses of action are limited. The subjective approach, grounded in the belief that reality is multiple and socially constructed, shifts the emphasis and responsibility for the program to the stakeholders, avoiding evaluator-issued recommendations.

Much of the literature about the merit and validity of evaluation recommendations begins with the assumption that the evaluator is external to the program; has less than a complete understanding and grasp of the program background, history, and operational nuances; and lacks extensive knowledge of the intervening variables known only to the client, funding agency, or program manager. The following discussion will focus inside the organization. That is the arena for the internal evaluator and therefore presents a different set of criteria on which to judge the merit and practical application of evaluation recommendations. The title of this section, Using Recommendations to Convert Evaluation Findings to Organizational Action, conveys the justification for advocating recommendations as a requisite and logical end to the internal evaluation process.

Scriven (1995) has categorized program evaluators as minimalists, purists, or activists depending on their philosophical orientation to the completion of the evaluation task. Minimalists believe that evaluation consists of determining relevant facts, with the value of this information left to the interpretation of the client. Purists believe that evaluation has a responsibility to determine the merit, worth, or significance of the evaluation issue but they stop short of issuing recommendations or instructions. The activist evaluator believes that the main, or at least a very important, function of evaluation is to generate recommendations. For Scriven, the leap from empirical evaluative data to recommendations is presumptuous and "logically unsound" because most evaluators have little knowledge of the circumstances and do not possess sufficient information about the program environment to make valid recommendations. He writes: "The step to specific recommendations requires separate expertise and certification (of data and inferences) beyond the skills required for an evaluator" (p. 62). Although this may be a true circumstance for many evaluators, it does not accurately portray the situation of internal evaluators. Reichardt (1994) suggests that evaluators acquire the substantive expertise to provide sound recommendations, and he believes that this may be the future of formative evaluation.

I am convinced that the "insider" location in organizations provides experienced internal evaluators with a comprehensive knowledge base that justifies issuing recommendations at the conclusion of most evaluations. Eschewing theoretical arguments, the internal evaluator deals with the pragmatics of the workplace and the desire to influence the organization and counter the chronic inertia of the bureaucracy. Internal evaluators with long-term service in an organization are quite familiar with administrative and operational policies, decision-making procedures, internal politics, power distribution, and executive personalities and, in many cases, possess in-depth knowledge of the programs or issues being evaluated. Furthermore, over time, the variability in perspectives on organizational functions collected by experienced internal evaluators represents a comprehensive understanding of programs and procedures, creating, in effect, an evaluation staff that is a repository of collective "wisdom" on the organization. This accumulated wisdom (what Patton, 1994, p. 316, refers to as the "gray head effect") spans both time and space. It is gathered horizontally across internal structural boundaries and vertically over time and personnel changes and, in many cases, represents the only synthesizing, data-based history of organizational problem solving. Failure to engage this knowledge base through the recommendation process shortchanges the organization's return on investment (ROI) on its evaluation resource commitment.

In the internal evaluation environment, recommendations are the logical completion of an evaluation. For internal evaluators operating with a change agent philosophy and the goal of influencing the organization, recommendations are the enabling instruments of organizational change. Recommendations are opportunities for internal evaluators to summarize, focus, clarify, and explicitly interpret the evaluation findings and convert their meaning into prescriptions for program improvement. Recommendations serve to announce and disseminate what the evaluators have learned during the evaluation and their judgments about program performance and alternatives for improving the effectiveness and efficiency of the program. Recommendations function to initiate, focus, and sharpen the debate over possible new program directions. They provoke discussion and increase the awareness of the program activities and potential alterations that may improve performance. Recommendations are not set in concrete when issued by evaluators but establish one set of judgments that can be used to commence the debate over the future direction of the program.

The rationale that justifies issuing recommendations is the role recommendations have in precipitating debate over corrective action. Recommendations should not be viewed as inflexible, reified assertions about future program direction, but judgments derived from the evaluation data that can illuminate the organizational decision-making process. Recommendations are the physical end point of the evaluation but only the conceptual beginning of the discussion over future program direction. Withholding evaluators' knowledge acquired over the term of the evaluation deprives executive decisionmakers of valuable input. And decisionmakers' knowledge about the program or issues, unavailable to the evaluators, can be applied by the decisionmakers and used to modify the recommendations. Thus, recommendations represent independent, informed opinion from evaluators that can be inserted into the organizational policy-making process to expand decisionmakers' options.

Although recommendations are the logical end point for the majority of internal evaluations, internal evaluators should exercise caution when formulating conclusions from evaluative data and drafting recommendations. The objectivity argument (see Chapter 5) is again relevant to this discussion. In some cases, the act of acquiring program expertise by evaluators may compromise their independence from the program, thus diminishing the credibility of the recommendations. If evaluation expertise was acquired by previous association with the program, it may be difficult to assert unqualified independence from the program. This does not preclude assigning evaluators with program expertise to an evaluation, but any previous program relationship should be made known to the program manager. Additionally, evaluators may not always have adequate program expertise to make intelligent recommendations, particularly in highly technical areas, and should exercise appropriate judgment when deciding on recommended courses of action under these circumstances. Scriven (1995) allows that in those situations where the evaluator has program expertise at the micro level or has complete decision-related data in addition to program expertise at the macro level, evaluators can legitimately add recommendation to their evaluations. Evaluation expertise, however, does not always equal program expertise, and evaluators should refrain from acting omnipotent when it is clearly not appropriate.

WRITING EFFECTIVE RECOMMENDATIONS

Writing recommendations is not an easy task, and it is too often done in haste, at the conclusion of an evaluation. Patton (1989b) estimates that evaluators concentrate 95% of their time and effort on the evaluation and 5% on the recommendations, whereas this order is reversed for the clients. This ratio should reinforce the notion that recommendations should not be afterthoughts of evaluation efforts, but deliberate, well-crafted, empirically based suggestions for organizational action. Weiss (1988) describes the all too often encountered scenario for crafting recommendations at the conclusion of a report:

> It is not unknown for evaluators to spend so much time on data collection and analysis that they have very little time at the end to figure out the implications of their data. With two weeks left before the report is due, they scramble to find something reasonable to recommend. The cogency of their recommendations will depend heavily on how well informed they are about the field, about other programs and prior evaluations, and about individual and collective behavior. (p. 24)

Recommendations are the engine of the evaluation, converting the evaluation findings into usable information and guidance, and must be carefully constructed if they are to perform their intended task of organizational improvement. Paradoxically, recommendations are both the cornerstone and lightning rod for internal evaluations. Although prescriptive in nature and positive in outlook, they are interpreted by program managers as intrusions on their management prerogatives and usually arouse their combative spirit. The anticipated trajectory of recommendations, from formulation to implementation, as conceived by evaluators, is a path easily altered by hostile stakeholders.

Thinking about recommendations usually begins at the completion of an evaluation but more realistically should start during the first encounters with the program personnel. Recommendation domains affect evaluation design issues and should be discussed with program personnel, clients, and interested stakeholders at the front end of an evaluation (Patton, 1989a). As the evaluation develops and prospective areas for recommendations present themselves, these issues should be discussed with the program personnel and the domains expanded if necessary.

Recommendations are prescriptions for organizational improvement and normative statements about how things should be. They are grounded in the evaluation report but depart from the retrospective orientation of the report and deal with future events and assumptions about the consequences of certain recommended courses of action. Recommendations are judgments by evaluators about prescribed changes in program activities that are likely to bring about some future action. They cast the evaluator in the role of futurist suggesting alternative ways of conducting organizational business. "In effect, at the point where evaluators make recommendations, we become futurists" (Patton, 1997, p. 328).

QUALITIES OF WELL-WRITTEN RECOMMENDATIONS

Recommendations, by their nature, tend to focus attention on program deficiencies and can generate resentment by officials charged with their implementation. Program personnel can become defensive when they receive program-altering suggestions, and an empathic evaluator will craft recommendations in a manner to accomplish the intended goal without creating undue animosity. Well-written recommendations have five basic qualities: They should be timely, realistic, directed to the appropriate person or entity, comprehensible, and specific. Incorporating these characteristics into recommendations increases the probability of approval and subsequent implementation.

Timeliness has supremacy over the other four recommendation qualities. Failure to produce findings and recommendations at the appropriate time in the life cycle of a program, issue, or problem may render the evaluation effort inconsequential. Elegant, sophisticated, methodologically sound evaluations have no value if produced after decisions have already been made. From the inception of an evaluation, evaluators must be acutely sensitive to any time requirements and decision nodes that affect the production of evaluation information. Failure to grasp the significance of timely production of information renders an evaluation office ineffectual. A well-written recommendation will coincide with the decision-making schedule of the issue in question.

Profound, complex, utopian recommendations should be eschewed to avoid presenting the program manager with justification for avoidance and implementation failure. Evaluators must assess the organizational environment, weigh budget and resource constraints, and appraise any political pressures that might affect implementation. Recommendations should always be realistic and considerate of constraints and available resources. Caution should be exercised when recommending increased funding and additional resource commitments. It is a rare program that cannot be improved by allocating more money and resources and it is almost always an easy recommendation for evaluators to make. However, given the universal difficulty with finding additional money and personnel, it is wise to make this recommendation only when it has been decided that it is critical to program survival and there is a reasonable expectation that enhanced funding and personnel levels are available.

> Evaluations should be useful to managers. . . . Evaluators should aim first to provide ideas that require no new personnel, data collection requirements, or spending. Recommendations that do require new resources are more likely to be adopted if evaluators can show how existing resources can be reallocated without reducing a program or organization's effectiveness in other areas. (Bellavita, Wholey, & Abramson, 1986, p. 291)

Recommendations must be specifically directed to the individual with both the responsibility and authority for implementation. There should be no equivocation on the individual who is responsible for seeing that an evaluation recommendation is implemented. Entities do not have authority and responsibilities, people do. Failure to designate someone to oversee implementation allows the inertia of the organization to undermine the recommendations.

Recommendations should be clear in their intent, easily understood, and unequivocal in their interpretation. They should be simple, direct, very specific, and enumerated into precise tasks and actions. If there is a division in responsibility for implementing a recommendation, it should be spelled out in detail, especially if it involves crossing organizational structures.

It is helpful if recommendations focus on only one relevant issue or idea. Multistep recommendations are subject to varied interpretations and allow program personnel to claim complete compliance for partial implementation. The actual number of recommendations varies with each situation. Evaluations of complex administrative procedures may involve considerable detailed recommendations, whereas a core alteration in a program may be the subject of only one recommendation. The FBI evaluation staff once recommended 56 changes in an area involving a complex information retrieval system. There is no magical number of recommendations; however, excessive recommendations about trivial changes should be avoided in favor of fewer substantive recommendations, assuming that minor program alterations will logically follow major program adjustments.

LINKING RECOMMENDATIONS WITH FINDINGS

Successful recommendations, which result in approval and implementation, need to be explicitly linked with the findings and grounded in the empirical data in the report. Weiss (1988) observes that "in the best cases, recommendations emerge directly from the data" (p. 23). The experience of the evaluators, their observations during the evaluation, and the data collected are the essential ingredients that frame the recommendations. Evaluators reviewing program performance may gain an intuitive sense about potential avenues for program improvement, yet lack a sufficient empirical basis to issue an explicit recommendation. To avoid this dilemma, evaluators should identify tentative data collection strategies at the beginning of evaluations to ensure comprehensive coverage of all recommendation domains. Insufficient data supporting recommendations affect the credibility of the evaluation effort. Without an explicit linkage between evaluation data, findings, and recommendations, the potential for positive management action is diminished.

USE OF OPTIONS

Recommendations are not the solution for all evaluation situations. For internal evaluators wishing to change and improve organizations, recommendations at the end of an evaluation are generally suitable, but there are occasions when providing options may be more appropriate. Evaluators may identify or diagnose problems without knowing how to solve the problem (Wholey, 1986). Recommendations may distract the client's attention from the findings and excessive controversy over recommendations may reduce the credibility of the evaluator and the evaluation (Wholey, 1986). Functioning in the role of a policy analyst, evaluators can develop and compare a set of options for program change in terms of costs, implementation feasibility, likely effects on program performance, and likely important side effects (Wholey, 1986). Wholey suggests options are appropriate under the following circumstances:

There is no preponderance of evidence elevating one course of action over another.

The client is more comfortable with options and has requested them.

A political decision has to be reached and the stakeholders want to debate each alternative.

Options allow evaluators to present alternative scenarios to senior decisionmakers and are particularly germane when dealing with complex issues where the goal of the evaluators is to engender ownership of proposed major changes in the affected organizational structure or operating procedures. In 1992, the FBI evaluation office was asked to review the bureau's organizational structure and decision-making process with the goal of improving operating efficiency and reducing the number of special agent managers at FBI Headquarters in Washington, D.C. Due to the magnitude of the undertaking and the probability that radical changes might be appropriate, an advisory panel was established to review the evaluators' findings. Evaluators presented the advisory panel with several options (and the positive and negative consequences of selecting each option) for restructuring the headquarters hierarchy and reducing the number of special agent personnel needed in administrative positions. The use of options in this case was appropriate, and numerous major changes were implemented.

Presenting options can be done either without a preferred alternative or with a priority ranking based on the evaluators' judgment. The presentation of options is more conservative than offering recommendations but may precipitate a creative dialogue among evaluators and stakeholders that results in program improvements. The ultimate internal evaluation goal is organizational influence, and evaluators must match the correct strategy to each evaluation situation to meet this goal.

FOLLOW-UP PROCEDURES

It is not uncommon for program managers to have limited incentives for implementing approved recommendations, particularly when they disagree or the recommendations involve radical program alterations. Many devices, arguments, and strategies exist, including bureaucratic inertia, to thwart the implementation of evaluation recommendations. For these reasons and because evaluation office performance is based on organizational improvement, it is practical to develop procedures to routinely follow up on the implementation of approved recommendations. Appropriate time frames and notification procedures to responsible officials that a formal review of implementation status will take place should be established at the conclusion of every evaluation. An initial follow-up after six months is usually sufficient time to allow the program manager to review approved recommendation and begin the implementation process. Depending on the complexity of the recommended changes and available resources, complete or partial implementation may have occurred during that time frame. In the event implementation has not been completed, evaluators can discuss implementation problems with program personnel and exercise the options of allowing more time, negotiating a satisfactory solution, or notifying the original approval authority of the incomplete implementation status. An understanding by evaluation clients that a formal review of implementation status is an essential aspect of the complete evaluation process will aid in the implementation of change.

Recommendations are the enabling instruments of evaluative efforts that generate organizational action and lead to program improvement. Failure to include recommendations, options, suggestions, or opinions at the conclusion of evaluative efforts denies the organization the benefit of competent evaluator insights and retards the organizational learning and improvement process. Recommendations are one of the most potent weapons in the evaluator arsenal that can be used to initiate change, but they also have the potential to erode the credibility of the evaluation if not well grounded in empirical data and thoughtfully crafted, with attention to the organization's environment and the client's needs and wishes.

Evaluation Report Dissemination Procedures

After the evaluation report is written, decisions have to be made on the extent of the report circulation, proper recipients for the draft, and a time frame for responses.

DRAFT REPORT

Evaluators and clients should agree at the initiation of evaluations the extent of the circulation of the draft report. If appropriate, the details of this agreement should be included in an evaluation contract. Pertinent issues are identification of persons authorized to review and comment on the draft report, and the criteria for inclusion or exclusion of their comments in the final report. At a minimum, the primary client should be expected and encouraged to provide comments on the draft report to be included in the final report. Offering clients the opportunity to comment on recommendations (if they have not been involved in their formulation) and implementation schemes facilitates the approval process. Presenting both evaluator views and client opinions provides decisionmakers with a thorough understanding of the evaluation issues and serves as the basis for debate over challenges to evaluation findings and controversial issues. Circulation of a draft report also offers an opportunity to detect and correct any errors that may have occurred during the evaluation, thereby sparing the evaluation staff the embarrassment of having to issue a correction after a final report has been issued. During this phase of the evaluation, it is proper for evaluators and program personnel to negotiate the use of language in the report and discuss modifications, deletions, or additions. It is not improper to accommodate program personnel suggestions for changes in the report if the changes improve the quality of the report or ameliorate angst, as long as factual elements are not revised and the essence of the evaluation remains substantially unchanged.

FINAL REPORT

Final internal evaluation reports should be designed to be noticed and widely disseminated within organizations. The FBI evaluation staff used red covers with silver printing to distinguish evaluation reports from other generally circulated documents. One or two copies can be designated for each major organizational component. Extensive circulation of evaluation reports reinforces the concept of evaluation as an ongoing enterprise as well as informs the extended organization of the results of a specific evaluation. Internal evaluators should also disseminate evaluation reports to other organizational components that were not included in the evaluation but who might benefit from a review of the findings and recommendations.

CONCLUSION

Any strategy for improving organizational functions begins with effective conversion of evaluation findings to organizational action. Identifying the audience and matching the appropriate reporting procedure maximize the probability for use of evaluation findings and recommendations. Selecting the proper reporting format for a written evaluation report and establishing a systematic approach to the writing process minimize time spent on the evaluation and help ensure deadlines are met. Writing reports and reporting results are two different aspects of the communicating phase of evaluation. It is critical for internal evaluators to be cognizant that their goal is organizational action based on evaluation findings, not elegant report writing. Overemphasis on the writing phase of evaluation reporting impedes the production of useful information for organizational use and potential program improvements. Cognitive mapping and writer's conferences are two techniques to aid in the difficult writing phase of an evaluation.

Evaluation recommendations are the catalyst for organizational action. Linking the recommendations to findings and supporting documentation is imperative to preclude credibility attacks on the evaluation. Recommendation follow-up is important to document implementation status and identify performance impact for the evaluation staff.

In some cases, options may be a more appropriate means to precipitate organizational action.

Whenever possible, evaluators should supplement their reports with briefings to convey the results of their evaluations. Briefings ensure publicity for evaluation findings even when reports go unread, and they afford evaluators opportunities to clarify and explain complex material in reports. In many cases, briefings may be sufficient to convey the results of an evaluation and obviate tedious report writing.

Draft report dissemination is an important aspect of an evaluation and begins the dialogue over the results of the evaluation. Wide dissemination and comments by affected stakeholders form the basis for implementation strategy and allow evaluators to identify the breadth and magnitude of any resistance to change. Additionally, it publicizes the existence and activities of the evaluation staff.

RECOMMENDED FOR FURTHER READING

Gladis, S. D. (1989). *Process writing: A systematic writing strategy.* Amherst, MA: Human Resource Development Press.
   A good guide to basic writing skills.

Henry, G. T. (1997). *Creating effective graphs: Solutions for a variety of evaluation data* (New Directions for Evaluation, No. 73). San Francisco: Jossey-Bass.

A good discussion and guide on the use of graphs to present evaluation data.

Torres, R. T., Preskill, H. S., & Piontek, M. E. (1996). *Evaluation strategies for communicating and reporting: Enhancing learning in organizations.* Thousand Oaks, CA: Sage.

Explains the roles of evaluators in learning organizations and presents strategies for reporting evaluation results.

Chapter 9

Establishing, Administering, and Leading an Internal Evaluation Office

KEY CHAPTER TOPICS

⋄ Leading an internal evaluation office
⋄ Administration and establishment of an internal evaluation office
⋄ Administrative evaluation tools
⋄ Measuring internal evaluation performance

Evaluation leadership is a significant factor in shaping the identity of an internal evaluation office. Myth, symbolism, and tradition abound in organizations, contributing to individuals' and groups' reputations and the collective culture that identifies the whole organization. Events, crises, missions, and personalities attributed to groups create certain recognizable identities, yet evaluation offices remain enigmas. The ambiguous reputation of many internal evaluation offices results from (1) a lack of sufficient history on which to build a reputation, (2) an ill-defined and largely misunderstood mission in the organization, (3) the unappreciated and misunderstood nature of evaluation and research, and (4) the detachment from the organization based on the traditional neutrality of the research enterprise. Image creation is a crucial function of internal evaluation office directors and significantly affects the evaluation office's ability to effectively operate within an organization and influence polices and procedures.

Evaluation office directors attempting to integrate the evaluation function in an organization must be aware of the value of their own role and influence in creating and building a credible and recognizable evaluation office identity. This chapter will examine both the leadership characteristics and administrative procedures that contribute to the image and identity of a successful internal evaluation office. The chapter concludes with a discussion on measuring the performance of an evaluation office. The rationale for devoting an entire chapter to the leadership and administration of an internal evaluation office results from my research and experience demonstrating the profound effect, on the type of evaluation practiced within an organization, of the aggregate evaluation expertise, managerial orientation, competency, and behavior of the internal evaluation director. The comments in this chapter on leadership and administration are relevant to internal evaluation directors whether supervising an evaluation staff or functioning as a single evaluator.

Leadership Role

Successful internal evaluation offices are not only administered, they are led. Although the administrative policies and procedures established and followed by internal evaluators are significant to the outcome of evaluation practice, the leadership qualities of the office director are a major determinant in the ability of the evaluation office to effectively influence the organization through its evaluation activities. Internal evaluation office directors are first and foremost the interface for evaluation staff linkage with the organization. Moreover, they serve to establish and mold the image of the evaluation office as organizational executives and managers perceive it. Rank in the organization, stature among peers, managerial competence, evaluation expertise and experience, personality, and interpersonal skills all combine to create and project the persona of the evaluation office director (and the office) to the organization.

OPERATING PHILOSOPHY

One of the surprising discoveries during research I conducted in five federal government internal evaluation offices was the considerable influence evaluation directors have over the type of evaluation practiced (Sonnichsen, 1991). The director of an internal evaluation staff has great latitude and flexibility in the management and guiding philosophy of evaluation practice because evaluation is often vaguely defined and its purpose not always clearly evident. Although the five evaluation offices I studied had been structurally organized and adapted to be congruent with the administrative and decision-making apparatus of the organization, the actual practice of evaluation in all but one of the offices had been arranged to conform to the office director's management and evaluation philosophy. Unlike program offices in an organization with statutory mandates and long-accumulated histories of rules and regulations, evaluation offices commonly have freedom to develop in the direction of the leader's interests, management style, and evaluation philosophy. There are minimal impediments to prevent internal evaluation directors from fashioning their offices to reflect their own interests and experiences. Decisions on evaluator personnel, client selection, evaluation studies to be initiated, evaluation office strategies, relationships with managers and executives, reporting style, evaluation methodologies, and professional evaluation community contact and involvement are all consequential events that form the substance and appearance of the evaluation office and are substantially controlled by the evaluation office director. Whether evaluators are to function as advocates for change, act in a formative supportive role, serve in an accountability capacity, support executive decision making, conduct technical data analyses, or consult to the entire organization with technical and evaluative advice are decisions largely decided by the evaluation office director. Strong, self-assured personalities with clearly forged visions of the internal evaluator's role have the power to create, mold, and publicize the image of the evaluation office that reflects its essential constitution.

One of the major aspects of internal evaluation leadership that distinguishes it from other organizational leadership positions is its internal focus. Unlike many executive positions in organizations that continually monitor and have contact with the external environment, evaluation office directors are centripetally oriented, concentrating on the organization's needs and problems. Internal office directors are neither oblivious to the external world nor impervious from its effects on the organization and its mission; however, their main attention is focused inward. Contacts with the evaluation community, external evaluation contractors, external funding entities, regulatory agencies, and competitors are all valuable sources of input for the internal office director and contribute to evaluation office development strategies. Priority considerations, however, are given to those conditions that exist within the organization.

ROLE EXPECTATIONS

Role expectation pressures on internal evaluation office directors emanate primarily from three sources: (1) the executive management of the organization, (2) the internal evaluation staff, and (3) the personnel in the organization affected by evaluation activities. Executive management, who have a comprehensive understanding of evaluation and have committed resources to the evaluation enterprise, want useful, timely information to aid them in the process of effectively and efficiently running the organization. However, many executives may be unfamiliar with the intricacies of evaluation and require tutoring in its efficacy and use. They may fail to grasp the intricacies of research principles and require detailed explanations and interpretations of evaluation results. It is the responsibility of internal evaluation office directors to cultivate relationships with senior officials in the organization, offering constructive guidance on the value of using evaluation to expand and improve their decision making. Senior management's support for internal evaluation is an indispensable element in the integration of evaluation in organizations, and to acquire and maintain this support is one of the primary functions of an internal evaluation office director.

The evaluation staff wants and needs operational direction, job recognition, career advancement, self-fulfillment, a sense of accomplishment (i.e., an influence on the organization), and protection from retribution from other personnel in the organization. Internal evaluators view the office director in a dual role: providing supervisory policy guidance on work projects and preserving their independence by acting as a buffer between them and the organization. This bifurcated managerial and guardianship role is essential to allow internal evaluators to pursue their analytical activities without undue anxiety over reaction to their findings and recommendations.

No less important to the effective and successful implementation of evaluation in an organization is a harmonious and constructive relationship with the program managers and evaluation clients. Those who interface with the evaluators, as recipients and participants during evaluations, want assurances that evaluation will be fair, useful (to them), and nondamaging to their programs and careers. Establishing a respectful and empathic relationship with the organization's management may be the most important job of the evaluation office director. Without some support from this organizational cohort, it is unlikely that evaluation efforts will be productive. Intrinsically embedded in these managerial expectations are both complimentary and contradictory notions of evaluation. When organizational and individual program goals are in synchrony, evaluation can proceed smoothly; however, conflicts may arise when organizational and program goals do not conform. Quality evaluations may serve the needs of executive management but threaten program managers. Unhappy program managers can intimidate evaluators, refuse cooperation, frustrate recommendation implementation, and create career anxiety for the evaluators. Responding to these diverse, competing, and conflicting role expectations requires evaluation office directors to have impressive management and evaluation skills, a comprehensive understanding of the organization, and a self-assured sense of the vision and mission of the evaluation process.

Establishing and Administering an
Internal Evaluation Office

The administrative apparatus of an internal evaluation office is more than a collection of policies and procedures for evaluators to follow. The administrative practices that guide the activities of the evaluators also contribute to the public image and identity of the evaluation function perceived by other organizational components.

SELECTING INTERNAL EVALUATORS

Arguably, one of the most critical tasks in establishing an internal evaluation office is the selection of the evaluation staff. Decisions are necessary on what experience and education form the criteria for competent evaluators. The evaluators selected will be the interface with the organization, and their ability to deal with their peers and superiors when conducting evaluations is crucial to their success. The obvious qualifications sought are familiarity with the organization and its programs, interpersonal and communication skills, and an educational background in research methods. However, the absence of this combination of attributes does not preclude the development of a professional evaluation staff. Several options are available, and the one selected depends on the organization and the goals of the evaluation office. The nucleus of an evaluation staff can be developed with only five or six evaluators. An even number is preferred so that two-person teams can be assembled for conducting evaluations.

Electing to choose evaluation personnel from within the organization has the advantage of beginning the evaluation process with people who are familiar with operational programs, who understand the organization's culture and history, and who have been socialized into the organization. Optimally, social scientists with experience in organizations should be recruited, but this may not always be an option. Maturity and good judgment are also valuable attributes to identify when recruiting internal evaluators. In Ireland, an evaluation unit established to evaluate expenditures disbursed under the auspices of the European Social Fund (ESF) used work experience as the key criterion for employment in the unit (Boyle, 1993). It was determined that experience was important for the credibility of evaluators gathering field data from agencies spending the ESF money, and new college graduates lacked sufficient credibility to deal with senior managers in the agencies.

Lacking qualified personnel with research skills inside the organization may require looking outside to hire the nucleus of the evaluation staff. A combination of internal and external personnel allows the reciprocal transfer of organizational culture and program knowledge to outside personnel and training in evaluation and research skills to the on-board personnel. External evaluation consultants can be periodically contracted during the developmental stages of an evaluation staff to train personnel and assist with initial evaluations. The following examples of internal evaluation staffing in U.S. federal government agencies demonstrate the range of approaches to the staffing dilemma.

Until recently, the Federal Bureau of Investigation (FBI) selected potential evaluators from special agents with investigative experience who were willing to relocate to Washington, D.C. and serve as evaluators for three to five years. (FBI evaluators are now selected primarily from the ranks of professional support personnel, and supplemented with some agent personnel. This change in selection procedures was prompted by a decision to reduce the number of special agent personnel at FBI headquarters in administrative positions and return them to investigative roles in field offices.) The agents (and the professional support personnel) selected were trained in evaluation techniques at local universities and training seminars and paired with experienced evaluators on the job. Their prior investigative and interviewing experience provided foundational evaluation skills, which were enhanced with evaluation and methodological skills training. After service as evaluators for three to five years, they were promoted or transferred to other assignments within the FBI. This special agent rotational policy maintained fresh insights and diverse educational and background experience on the evaluation staff while expanding the awareness and appreciation of the value of evaluation within the organization. (Insufficient time has elapsed to determine the effect of the reduction of special agent evaluators.)

The Bureau of Land Management (BLM) maintains a small staff of six experienced evaluators at their headquarters in Washington, D.C., who travel around the United States training BLM field managers and professional personnel in evaluation skills. Once trained, these field personnel constitute a pool of available evaluators who are periodically assembled in four- and five-person teams for travel to other field offices where they conduct evaluations. Upon completion of an evaluation, they return to their respective field offices, resuming their regular duties until called on to conduct another evaluation. Because the BLM evaluations are conducted primarily by nonevaluators, the BLM provides a comprehensive handbook for their use, with detailed descriptions of evaluation procedures and explicit instructions to be used to conduct evaluations. A representative from the BLM headquarters evaluation staff remains on site to guide the evaluation and offer technical advice; however, the evaluation is actually supervised by one of the field managers from another office.

The Food and Drug Administration (FDA) uses permanent evaluators who have been selected from both inside and outside the FDA and hired for their analytical skills and educational background. They remain permanently on the evaluation staff, building institutional memory and enhancing their evaluation skills and their knowledge of the FDA culture and programs.

The Office of Air Quality Planning and Standards (OAQPS) in the Environmental Protection Agency (EPA) began an evaluation operation in 1994 selecting a staff with graduate degrees and scientific knowledge about air quality programs from personnel within OAQPS assigned to the operational divisions. These evaluators serve three or more years on the Program Review Group (PRG) staff and then have the option to remain in PRG or rotate back to their original assignment in OAQPS.

These four examples demonstrate the wide variety of approaches to staffing an internal evaluation office, each tailored to the individual organization and the goals of the evaluation office.

TRAINING INTERNAL EVALUATORS

Selection of evaluators from within the organization ensures knowledge of the organization but may result in a deficit of evaluation skills. This deficiency is best remedied through an ongoing training program within the evaluation office. The first two steps in an effective internal evaluation training program are the identification of the skills necessary for competent evaluators and determining the specific inadequacies of the evaluation staff. Mertens (1994) outlines an extensive list of knowledge and skills associated with competent evaluators, including not only the traditional research design, data collection and analysis strategies, and oral and written communication skills but also skills and knowledge from the disciplines of political science, economics, education, health, public administration, psychology, anthropology, philosophy, business, and government. Although this list is extensive, it underscores the diverse knowledge and skills needed by professional evaluators. Mertens further argues that evaluators need to become familiar with the philosophical assumptions underlying the positivist and postpositivist paradigms because an inquirer's philosophical assumptions and theoretical orientation influence the evaluation design process. Boyle (1993) suggests that the development of change agent evaluators requires enhancing both the theoretical and methodological "tool box" of the evaluator as well as improving the evaluators' understanding of the managerial and political context where evaluation takes place.

Although it may be impractical to initiate a formal program of study in evaluation in an internal evaluation setting, it will pay dividends to begin an educational program of evaluation topics to increase the staff's knowledge of the evaluation field. Some evaluation expertise is preferred to none, and the sequential acquisition of evaluation knowledge by the evaluators will increase their probability of success. The General Accounting Office (GAO) has developed an extensive formal training program for its evaluators delivered through its own training institute (Kingsbury & Hedrick, 1994). The GAO's curriculum emphasizes six areas: agency mission and policies, assignment planning and execution, communication skills and strategies, computers and information technology, workplace relations and management, and issue area expertise. A single evaluation course can also make a significant contribution, not only to the training of evaluators but also to the understanding of evaluation by the user community (Morris, 1994).

There are many ways to train an internal evaluation staff while continuing the work schedule. The keys to an effective learning experience are an accurate needs assessment and training opportunities that are directly relevant to work. Attendance at annual American Evaluation Association (AEA) conferences provides excellent opportunities to attend panels and listen to presentations and speeches by noted academics, consultants, and practitioners in the field. Short evaluation workshops presented the day prior to the conference afford interested participants training in a variety of evaluation-related topics. University professors and evaluation consultants are available to present short evaluation-training courses on site at internal evaluation offices. Annual training conferences sponsored by an internal evaluation office can assemble evaluation consultants and university professors as speakers for effective two-day training sessions.

The FBI evaluation office's annual training session used the services of an external evaluation consultant, who reviewed and critiqued a sample of reports written over the previous year and used this information as the basis for his presentation. Furnishing an outside professional perspective on relevant work products both engaged the evaluation staff and identified alternative approaches to conducting internal evaluations and presenting the results. There is also a rich resource of training opportunities within most organizations that can be tapped for training sessions. I found it effective to use personnel, either on the evaluation staff or elsewhere in the organization, to present training on a variety of topics. Most organizations have statisticians, psychologists, social scientists, writers, and computer experts who can easily be used periodically for skill enhancement of the evaluation staff or to temporarily participate in the evaluation itself.

Educating all the personnel in an internal evaluation office in all facets of evaluation is an unrealistic goal. It is a reasonable goal, however, to attempt to inform the evaluation staff in evaluation techniques so that they acquire sufficient knowledge about the practice of evaluation to be credible when dealing with peers and superiors in the organization and professional evaluation associates.

AUTONOMY OF EVALUATORS

One of the most important and sensitive management aspects of evaluation office leadership is the degree of autonomy afforded the evaluation staff by supervisory personnel. The tension arises between ample latitude for the evaluators to conduct their work without constant supervision and the need and desire by evaluation office management for sufficient control and accountability over evaluation activities. Evaluation managers confront the dilemma of wanting input into evaluations and ongoing feedback on evaluation progress while not hampering the initiative of competent evaluators or stifling their enthusiasm. Professional evaluators are usually well-educated, mature, competent, achievement-motivated individuals who resent excessive supervision. Recognition of the sophistication of the evaluation staff can help guide the level of supervision required. Hersey and Blanchard (1982) believe in matching leadership behavior with staff maturity (*situational leadership*) and call for leaders of mature individuals to prove their confidence and trust in their subordinates by decreasing managerial control and increasing individual responsibility. Open communication and good faith negotiation between evaluation management and staff on this issue can instill a mutual understanding of each other's needs and appropriate levels of supervision to satisfy both parties. In between total staff autonomy and stifling oversight is a compromise where professional evaluators can display their talents and fulfill personal and professional needs while supervisory personnel comfortably monitor and guide their activities without excessive management controls. A workplan, discussed later in this chapter, itemizes logical interface points during an evaluation where management and staff can gather and discuss evaluation problems and progress.

RELATIONSHIPS WITH CLIENTS

A fundamental cornerstone in establishing and building an influential internal evaluation office is the recognition that relationships with clients are a top priority. Chapter 4 discussed the views of program managers toward evaluation and evaluator responsibility to clients. Evaluation office directors also have an important obligation to interact with clients and set the tone for the evaluation environment by trying to mitigate the negative views toward evaluation expressed by the program managers in Chapter 4. It is particularly critical to establish an ongoing, positive relationship between the evaluators and internal clients because internal clients are often repeat clients, participating in many evaluations over time. Internal clients also routinely interact with other components in the organization and will quickly communicate their experiences to their peers and express displeasure over any negative contacts with evaluators. Because of this instant and pervasive diffusion of evaluators' reputations within the organization, it becomes essential that directors of internal evaluator staffs comprehend the significance of their interactions with clients and develop a professional yet empathic approach during these contacts.

A 1976 symposium jointly sponsored by the National Institute of Law Enforcement and Criminal Justice and the MITRE Corporation examined the success of program evaluation in U.S. federal government agencies and discovered that although it was agreed that evaluation was the best method for producing reliable information on the effects of social programs, concern was expressed by managers that their viewpoints were not always accommodated on the use of evaluation findings (Chelimsky, 1977). Four areas identified at the symposium underscore the polarization between evaluators and program managers:

◇ The difficulty of using the social science research model to address agency requirements for relevance, responsiveness, and timeliness in the evaluation product
◇ The failure of current agency incentive structures to reward managers for the effectiveness of their programs or for their efforts to improve effectiveness via evaluation
◇ The arduousness of reconciling different evaluation perspectives, expectations, and information needs among different evaluation users, so that information produced for one user can satisfy the needs of another
◇ The awkwardness of selecting implementation mechanisms that simultaneously reduce threats to managers and increase knowledge (Chelimsky, 1977)

Evaluators' recognition of the expectations and concerns of program managers can minimize hostile confrontations during evaluations and increase the probability of evaluation's success. Much of the perception of evaluation is the result of the ability of the evaluation office director to establish a positive image for the process.

MARKETING EVALUATION

Chapter 1 introduced the concept of evaluation as a "product" to be "sold" to an organization. Developing a positive image for evaluation and attempting to minimize the negative views of program managers toward evaluation are essentially a marketing obligation of the office director. Because the purpose, necessity, and practice of evaluation within organizations is not always clearly understood, one basic and indispensable task of the evaluation office director is to communicate the concept, value, and appropriate application of evaluation. Unlike traditional organizational functions, which are plainly evident and their purpose more accurately described by their title, for example, budget, personnel, and training, evaluation suffers from a lack of recognition and understanding and therefore must be marketed and its efficacy sold to the organization. Mayne (1992a) encapsulates the need for stressing the value and use of the evaluation function:

> Good evaluation products will not sell themselves. Getting evaluation established in an organization is first and foremost a marketing job. People in the organization will not know what you are there to do, how you are supposed to do it, nor [will they know] when they might be affected. If anything, they will assume that you are there to check up on them—to eliminate their program, if not their job. What is needed is a well-thought out communication strategy, whereby the various parties in the organization are made aware of what the evaluation unit is trying to do, how it will be done, and what role the rest of the organization should play. (p. 309)

Even though evaluation is predominantly described as an analytical management tool, for internal evaluators evaluation is a product that requires description, marketing, consumer demand, and follow-up satisfaction surveys with customers. "Success in an internal evaluation unit requires skillful marketing of planned, continuing, and completed work" (Winberg, 1991, p. 168). Stressing the value and utility of evaluation is a recurring requirement for an internal management staff, particularly the office director. Wholey (1983) enumerates some of the leadership activities that are necessary to bring evaluation to the attention of officials in the organization:

> Those in charge of evaluation can implement effective evaluation programs by setting clear evaluation objectives, by mobilizing the necessary resources, by demonstrating desired types of evaluation activities, by informally marketing their product line, and by monitoring evaluation activities and results. (p. 176)

Challenging the imagination and creativity of the evaluation office leadership is the task of selling a product that, to begin with, is only reluctantly and tenuously accepted in the organizational marketplace. Evaluation marketing has several dimensions that take place on two organizational levels. Not only must the efficacy of the evaluation technique be conveyed to the senior management of the organization, but at the same time those at the managerial level must be assured that the evaluation staff will conduct competent and fair evaluations. Conveying the notions of efficacy, competence, and fairness to both the upper- and mid-management levels in an organization is a challenging and continuous function for evaluation office directors. The bridge to acceptance of evaluation in organizations is built on a foundation of confidence and trust: confidence in the knowledge and skills of the evaluators and trust in their integrity when dealing with members of the organization. Establishing an evaluation ethic in an organization requires implanting the understanding that evaluation is impartial, conducted without prejudice, and uncompromisingly independent from political intervention by those in power.

This advertising or marketing endeavor is more effective if accomplished subtly and incorporated in some of the routine tasks of an internal evaluation office. The solicitation and identification of relevant issues for evaluation are critical tasks of the evaluation office director and can serve the dual purpose of issue identification and evaluation marketing. As discussed in Chapter 6, scanning the organization for evaluation issues can be done by memoranda, surveys, observation, personal contact with the organization's executives, attending conferences and meetings, and maintaining a list of issues generated during evaluations for follow-up evaluation. A memorandum to major components in the organization formally requesting topics suitable for evaluation both generates an evaluation topic list and broadcasts the existence and capability of the evaluation staff.

Chapter 8 suggested organization-wide dissemination of evaluation reports as one aspect of marketing an evaluation office that should be incorporated as a routine procedure. It aids in the integration of the evaluation function by maintaining a high profile of the activities of the evaluation staff. All major organizational components should receive copies of each evaluation conducted even when the evaluation topic is not particularly relevant to the component's mission. Wide dissemination of evaluation reports advertises the utility of evaluation and serves to alert the organization to evaluation activities taking place throughout the organization. Increasing the readership of evaluation reports through extensive dissemination has the added effect of reducing the perceived threat to managers by publicizing the results and recommendations occurring in other programs.

The issuance of an annual report by the evaluation office underscores the positive benefit of the evaluation function to the organization and again reminds organizational components of the value and use of evaluation to help attain the organization's goals. The annual report should contain information on all evaluations conducted, recommendations issued, recommendations implemented, and their outcomes and impact. The annual report is also an opportunity to profile and broadcast the skills available in the evaluation office and their potential applications as aids for program managers.

Toward the goal of embedding the evaluation ethic in the organization, one of the primary tasks of the evaluation office director is to maintain currency on important organizational issues, crises, problems, significant personnel changes, and strategic administrative and operational alterations to detect areas where the application of evaluation may be appropriate. Regular meetings should be scheduled with senior organizational officials to reinforce the importance attached to evaluation and to maintain an open exchange of information about the use and value of evaluation-based information. Seeking committee assignments, attending pertinent meetings, and performing tasks outside the spectrum of evaluation all contribute to reinforcing the evaluation ethic in an organization. Attendance of the evaluation director at important organizational meetings is a reminder of the evaluation function as well as an issue-scanning function.

Administrative Evaluation Tools

Establishing routine administrative procedures for an internal evaluation office not only facilitates managing the office but also conveys a message to the evaluators on processes to be followed and expectations for their activities. By maintaining guidelines for behavior during evaluations, greater efficiency and uniformity is attained and evaluator anxiety and uncertainty over expected performance is minimized. Evaluation workplans, computerized databases, client agreements, and evaluation workpapers are four administrative protocols that assist in the management of evaluation activities and help affirm the professional image of an internal evaluation office.

EVALUATION WORKPLANS

One of the important administrative techniques available to internal evaluators is the evaluation workplan. A comprehensive workplan functions both as a guide for the study team during the conduct of an evaluation and as a supervisory mechanism for evaluation office management reviewing the proposed methodology. The study team should craft it after initial interviews have been conducted and a preliminary evaluation approach formulated. Submission of the workplan to evaluation office managers initiates preliminary discussions of the evaluation plan and eventually leads to approval to begin the evaluation. The formulation of an approach to an evaluation is an iterative process, and the workplan document may be amended or revised several times before final approval. Requiring preparation of the workplan by the evaluation team commences the methodical process of defining the evaluation approach and assisting evaluators in the conceptual process of meticulously thinking through an evaluation before beginning. Table 9.1 illustrates the minimum elements that should be contained in a workplan.

The purpose of the workplan document is not to burden the evaluation team with additional paperwork but to stress the benefits of a thoughtful, methodical, and complete comprehension of the evaluation project before beginning. Incomplete understanding of an evaluation project diminishes the quality of the final product and lessens the probability that deadlines will be met.

COMPUTERIZED EVALUATION DATABASE

Maintaining an up-to-date, computerized database of information on all previous and current evaluations is essential for swift responses

TABLE 9.1 Internal Evaluation Workplan	
Title	The descriptive name for the study/evaluation.
Authority	Establish the evaluation rationale or justification and identify the original requester or source of the study, the clients, and the major stakeholders.
Background	Set forth a statement of the problem, a review of previous relevant studies, a concise profile of the program or study issue, and other pertinent information establishing the context for the evaluation.
Goals/objectives	List the study goals and objectives.
Evaluation type/format	Identify the type of evaluation to be conducted (i.e., formative or summative, program review, cost-effectiveness analysis, impact analysis), together with the anticipated format of the final product (written report, oral briefing, memorandum, etc.).
Scope	Include the issues to be addressed, any study parameters or constraints, the depth and breadth of the study, and areas that will not be included in the evaluation.
Methodology	Explain the methods to be used during the evaluation (both qualitative and quantitative), data collection procedures, expected analytical techniques, and major evaluation questions to be addressed.
Proposed travel	Show the necessity for travel, site selection, justification criteria for site selection, and a proposed travel schedule.
Required resources	Identify members of the study team; any anticipated special expertise that will be required; travel costs (if appropriate); consultant fees; and any other personnel, financial, or equipment needs that will be required for the successful completion of the study.
Timetable	Specify the starting date and expected date for completion and any time restrictions or deadlines that have to be met. Identify major milestones (literature search, site travel, data collection, data analysis, draft report, etc.) and fix time estimates for each milestone.
Other	Identify any unique characteristics of this project, unusual administrative requirements, or other pertinent data that do not fit into the above categories.

to evaluation inquiries, supervisory oversight of evaluation activities, and preparation of the annual evaluation report. Each evaluation team is responsible for initiating entries into the database, maintaining it throughout the evaluation, and ensuring its completeness before closing the evaluation. The database contains synopsized essential information pertaining to the evaluation, its status, and outcomes. Table 9.2 outlines the minimum entries the database should contain.

The availability of this type of information provides evaluation office managers immediate access to complete information on current and past studies and evaluations. Archiving this information facilitates historical analysis and rapid response to oversight entities and executive management. Furthermore, it serves as an initial source in a literature search to determine what evaluations have been previously conducted and their outcomes.

CLIENT AGREEMENTS

A critical event in the evaluation cycle is the initial meeting between the evaluation team and the program personnel. This meeting affords the evaluation office director and the evaluation team the opportunity to set the tone of the evaluation that can endure throughout the evaluation by emphasizing the positive aspects of the evaluation and attempting to ameliorate any tension or hostility exhibited by the program manager. Often, the ambient tension during evaluation results from uncertainty about the purpose and procedures of evaluation and its eventual use. One of the administrative devices to clarify the ambiguity that often surrounds the evaluation enterprise is to formally address the major evaluation issues in a "contract" or memorandum of understanding. Love (1991) views the evaluation contract as psychological rather than legal, yet binding the evaluators and manager together through a set of mutually acceptable expectations. A client agreement explicitly sets forth the terms, guidelines, expectations, parameters, and deliverables of the evaluation and establishes a relationship of trust between the contracting parties. It not only focuses issues for program managers but also requires evaluators to explicitly understand their evaluation plan before beginning evaluative activities. Client

TABLE 9.2
Computerized Evaluation Database
Title of the evaluation
Date opened
Synopsis of problem
Important milestones and their dates
Number of recommendations issued
Organizational impact

contracts or agreements should be flexible and contain whatever elements are considered appropriate for the specific evaluation that can be mutually agreed on by the client and the evaluators. Table 9.3 sets forth the minimum information that should appear in a client agreement. (See Love, 1991, p. 49, for additional items that may be appropriate for inclusion in client agreements and contracts.)

An evaluation contract is not expected to exhaust all the potentialities that will arise during the evaluation, but its use can forge an understanding on those major issues that can be anticipated at the outset of the process. It provides a framework for clarifying evaluation issues that requires both clients and evaluators to be candid and unambiguous in their expectations. However, contracts or client agreements are not always necessary or appropriate. They may be of value during the initial stages of building evaluation capacity in an organization but unnecessary after a track record has been established. If an internal evaluation group has established its credibility and built a reputation of fairness, then client agreements may be superfluous. In the OAQPS, the PRG began using contracts with clients when PRG was new to the agency, but found them unnecessary after the agency became more familiar with the mission and function of the evaluation office. Even if a formal contract is not considered necessary, it is advantageous for evaluators to informally discuss contract elements with clients during the initial interview. This precludes later misunderstandings that may impede implementation efforts of suggested changes.

TABLE 9.3
Internal Evaluation Client Contract

Purpose of the evaluation	Why is the evaluation being conducted, what will be done with the results, and what are the expectations of the client for the evaluation?
Major issues to be addressed	Identify the issues and questions the client wants answered during the evaluation.
Client(s) and stakeholders	Identify all those persons and groups that may be considered clients or major stakeholders and their roles during the evaluation.
Evaluation team	Identify evaluation team members and any program personnel or consultants who will participate in the evaluation and their roles and responsibilities.
Deadlines	Establish or negotiate time frames for milestones and evaluation completion. Clarify breadth and depth issues and be explicit about what can be accomplished within the agreed-on time frames.
Deliverables	Determine the product(s) expected upon completion of the evaluation— for example, report, briefing, memo— and if interim documents or briefings are required.
Methodology	Describe the evaluation's methodological approach, expected statistical analyses, and potential site visits.
Scope of the evaluation	Describe any constraints and parameters of the evaluation.
Draft report procedures	Explicitly agree on who will be afforded copies of the draft report, who may provide comments, and whose comments will be included in the final report.
Dissemination	Describe final distribution of the evaluation report and the anticipated briefing schedule.
Recommendations	Reach agreement on whether recommendations will be issued with the report and how they will be developed (with or without client and stakeholder participation).
Approval	Decide on approval authority for the evaluation contract.

EVALUATION WORKPAPERS

Workpapers are those formal records consolidated at the conclusion of an evaluation to document the source(s) of all statements of fact, findings, assertions, conclusions, and recommendations. They may be manually prepared or computer generated. The purpose for their preparation and retention is to document sufficient supporting data to allow interested third parties, stakeholders, clients, or auditors to independently reconstruct and authenticate the evaluation report. High-quality workpapers are complete, accurate, legible, and relevant. The preparation of quality workpapers, suitable for review by interested parties outside the evaluation staff, demonstrates professionalism by the evaluators and lends credibility to assertions of independence and objectivity.

Workpapers should contain administrative data regarding evaluation planning, interview notes, reference material, and statistical data. They are a record of work performed, a vehicle for management oversight and performance assessment, and a reference tool for planning and conducting future evaluations. Pertinent data supporting the main findings, the individuals interviewed, and the sources of information should be easily accessible and mirror the evaluation report. Controversial evaluations are often challenged, and evaluators should prepare to document the veracity and logic of their findings, interpretations, conclusions, and recommendations.

All pertinent information in the report, particularly that which is attributed to an individual source, should be annotated on one copy of the evaluation report, which is maintained with the workpapers. The annotated report functions as a guide to the location in the workpapers where supporting information and data can be found. Figure 9.1 is an example illustrating proper workpaper annotation procedures. (The annotated designations refer to locations in the workpaper storage filing system.)

Workpaper control logs can also be used in conjunction with annotation procedures to facilitate identifying and locating documents in storage. Similar documents, interviews, and data can be placed in separate files or sections and numbered or lettered accordingly. Using an annotated report in conjunction with control logs identifies where documents can be easily located and simplifies their retrieval. Figure 9.2

Statements   / *p. 31*   / *p. 33*

Individuals interviewed included current and former city managers, local city officials, local police officers, members of the state legislature, and prominent civic leaders. (List by
name.) \   \   \
        p. 40   *p. 52*   / *p. 70*   *p. 37*

Figures

Automotive Purchases

Year	Purchase Price	Discount Rate		Total
1995	$13,416	.90	=	$12.074.40
1996	$14,510	.75	=	$10,882.50
1997	$15,694	.62	=	$ 9,730.28
			Total	$32,687.18

Figure 9.1. Example of Workpaper Annotation Procedures

is an example of a workpaper control log. (Box numbers refer to boxes
where workpapers are stored.)

To safeguard identities of individuals contacted during evaluations
and ensure their continued confidentiality, workpapers should be stored
under appropriate custody, protected from theft and destruction, and
be accessible only to authorized persons. In the event that classified
national security information or sensitive proprietary business data have
been used to prepare the evaluation report, special storage arrangements should be made to protect the integrity of these documents.
Workpapers contain the original documents gathered during the evaluation and should be retained for a preestablished period of time.
Numerous approaches to workpaper preparation are available and
should be tailored to the organization's administrative procedures for
archiving documents.

Measuring Internal Evaluation
Office Performance

Internal evaluation offices may be functionally unlike most other organizational components; nevertheless, they share responsibility for assisting in the attainment of the organization's goals and therefore their

EVALUATION		City Police Automotive Purchases File # _____	

No.	Description of Item		In Box #
1.	Interview of _____	on	_____
2.	Interview of _____	on	_____
3.	Interview of _____	on	_____
4.	Interview of city manager	on	_____

Figure 9.2. Example of Workpaper Control Log

performance toward this end must be measured. It would be irresponsible for an organizational component that analyzes, critiques, and judges all other organizational operations to avoid the challenge of publicly demonstrating and documenting the quality of its work product, its performance, and its relevance and value to the organization.

In Chapter 1, *high organizational impact* was defined as the *regular use* of evaluation data in the decision-making process on *major organizational issues.* This central theme of usage is the criterion used to measure and value the contribution of internal evaluation to the organization's goals. To accurately portray the accomplishments of an internal evaluation office, it is necessary to collect and review both output and impact data. However, the efficacy of an internal evaluation office can be only partially judged by aggregating quantitative data on evaluator output. Evaluation outcome(s) and impact(s) are the ultimate standards for judging evaluation office performance, and these data need to be assembled and emphasized more than output data.

Routine output data contributing to performance assessment are the number of evaluations conducted, recommendations issued, and recommendations approved and implemented. These process and activity data allow assessments to be made pertaining to the efficient use of resources and the relevance of evaluation activities as well as providing preliminary indications of organizational impact. To complement these data, appraisal of positive organizational change attributable to evaluation activities must also be added. Documented positive organizational changes as the result of evaluation activities can be gleaned from the impact memorandum prepared six months after the completion of the evaluation. At that point, both the evaluation staff and the program staff can make assessments on the outcomes and consequences of the evaluation. For complete and equitable performance measurement, both positive and negative impacts and outcomes should be reported. The high impact model of internal evaluation discussed in Chapter 6 can be used as a guide for determining the performance of an internal evaluation unit. (see Table 6.1).

Measuring internal evaluation performance requires accumulating examples of both instrumental and conceptual use. Internal evaluators seeking instrumental performance data should also be alert for possible examples of behavioral changes, changes in thinking, or "enlightenment" that may have resulted from an evaluative effort. Notwithstanding the difficulty in detecting and documenting subtle organizational changes, occasionally instances may be encountered where the activities, findings, discussions, or recommendations (or even the evaluation process itself) may have precipitated reflection on similar issues that resulted in positive change, not only in the program evaluated but also in other organizational components. Groups or individuals in the organization may have changed their behavior and/or thinking about their activities as a result of an evaluation in another component in the organization. These behavioral modifications are exemplars of evaluation utilization and *process use,* the term used by Patton (1997) to describe changes in thinking and behavior, and program or organizational changes. (See Chapter 6 for definition of process use.) Returning to a program that has been evaluated, even after a year, may be profitable for obtaining performance data and indicators of change, because evaluation effects and implementation efforts are often gradual.

An annual, detailed, accurate internal assessment of evaluative activities not only demonstrates the contribution of the evaluation staff to the organization but also acknowledges the importance of performance assessment for each organizational component and the recognition that internal evaluation is one of many participants in achieving the organization's goals. Using both quantitative and qualitative descriptors of evaluation performance, an internal evaluation office can exhibit a leadership role by demonstrating the value of annual component performance assessments to the management of the organization. By honestly detailing the positive and negative outcomes of evaluative activities and their effect on the organization, an internal evaluation office not only publicizes the usefulness of its own work efforts but also illustrates the value of performance measurement as a management tool for determining effectiveness.

CONCLUSION

Evaluation office director roles require both administrative and leadership competencies and the ability to effectively relate to the numerous constituencies that exist in organizations. The leadership qualities, evaluation knowledge and experience, and management and interpersonal skills of evaluation office directors are major determinants in the ability of an internal evaluation office to influence an organization.

Closely following leadership, among the characteristics that determine the success of an internal evaluation office, are the selection and training of evaluators. Choosing experienced organizational employees with research skills is the optimum method for staffing an internal office, but not the only available alternative. Deficiencies in evaluation and research skills can be rectified through on-the-job experience and comprehensive, formal evaluation training. The goal is to select and train evaluators with sufficient confidence in their abilities that they can function credibly and autonomously, with minimal supervisory guidance.

Evaluation is a product, and like most products it must be "sold" to prospective clients in the organization. The development of a need for evaluation within the organization and an understanding of the benefits and value of evaluation by clients are primary tasks of the evaluation office director. Routinization, appreciation, and acceptance of the value and utility of evaluation is the goal of the internal evaluation director and is accomplished through continual communication and marketing within the organization.

Establishing routine administrative procedures for an internal evaluation office facilitates managing the office while authenticating the evaluation process within the organization. Using workplans, computerized databases, client agreements, and workpapers is an evaluation management tool serving the dual purpose of simplifying and expediting the administration of the evaluation office and professionalizing its relationships with clients.

To contribute to organizational success and establish evaluation as an asset, internal evaluators must be conscious of their responsibility to assist the organization in goal attainment and develop relevant criteria for evaluation office performance measurement. Evaluation output data need to be supplemented with evidence of organizational impact and positive outcomes to reinforce the benefit and utility of internal evaluation. Practicing professional internal evaluation extends the functions of the evaluators beyond evaluative and consultative analytical endeavors to role models of exemplary management practices.

RECOMMENDED FOR FURTHER READING

Hudson, J., Mayne, J., & Thomlison, R. (1992). *Action-oriented evaluation in organizations*. Toronto, Ontario: Wall & Emerson.
Discusses basic evaluation principles and the Canadian experience in institutionalizing evaluation in the Canadian government. It is relevant to internal evaluation because much of the evaluation conducted in Canada has been internal.

Chapter 10

❧

High Impact Internal Evaluation:
A Synthesis

KEY CHAPTER TOPICS

- ❖ Institutionalizing internal evaluation
- ❖ High impact internal evaluation conceptual framework
- ❖ Practicing high impact internal evaluation

The first nine chapters of this book outlined characteristics of the emerging new internal evaluation paradigm and presented a model of high impact internal evaluation that incorporates its features. High impact internal evaluation requires that evaluators reframe traditional approaches to conducting evaluations, adapting themselves and their evaluation techniques to the conditions encountered inside organizations. Thinking like consultants; engaging organizations in dialogues about evaluation expectations, processes, outcomes, and recommendations; and promoting the efficacy of evaluation in reducing information asymmetry will characterize effective internal evaluators. This book has advocated a practical application of evaluation and management science techniques to increase the use and consequently the impact of evaluation on organizations. The principal objective for internal evaluators is to produce evaluative information that has a positive influence or high impact on the organization. Unused evaluation results waste valuable resources, frustrate evaluators, and erode confidence in the efficacy of internal evaluation.

Internal evaluation is not a magical tool for solving all organizational ills, but it is one analytical tool for managing organizations that, if properly established and supported, can assist organizations in accomplishing their missions. Although it will remain judgmental by definition, evaluation is, nevertheless, a constructive enterprise than can support organizations in their day-to-day operations. This book has advanced the rationale and justification for internal evaluation as a prominent, useful, and necessary organizational function. It outlined the philosophy and procedures for the establishment of an internal evaluation function and offered suggestions to increase use of the evaluation product.

The three significant messages in this book are that (1) competent evaluators with senior management's support can be an effective force inside organizations, supporting the decision-making process with unbiased information; (2) there are several alternative approaches to the successful practice of internal evaluation, and the approach chosen needs to be adapted to organizational conditions; and (3) the institutionalization of evaluation will occur only when internal evaluators actively interact with the organization during the evaluation process. For internal evaluators, the implications of these messages are (1) a recognition of the impact that the environment of the host organization has on the style and process of internal evaluation practice, and (2) the necessity for evaluators to view themselves as integral components in organizations with the objective of becoming a recognized source of independent information on major issues. The pragmatic approach to internal evaluation espoused in this book is applicable to a variety of administrative circumstances and structural configurations in an organization. Successful internal evaluation can be practiced by evaluators assigned exclusively to a separate evaluation office, single individuals designated to conduct evaluations, part-time teams of evaluators conducting evaluations in addition to their regular organizational assignments, and program managers with evaluation responsibility.

Information is the fulcrum of organizations and internal evaluators can play an important role in its production and promulgation. The manipulation of information by emotional participants during organizational policy debates and competition for resources offer internal evaluators opportunities to correct information imbalances by creating and distributing unbiased empirical data to relevant stakeholders. Mitigating the destructive effects of information asymmetry with independent, empirically based evaluative information aids the decision-making process, helps integrate the evaluation function into the organization, and begins building recognition of evaluation's value. To achieve the goal of evaluation integration obligates internal evaluators to more active engagement with organizations than was previously thought acceptable for objective researchers. Institutionalization occurs when evaluation has a measurable and positive impact on an organization. This final chapter will outline a framework for institutionalizing evaluation and practicing high impact internal evaluation that incorporates and synthesizes the information in the first nine chapters of the book.

Institutionalizing Internal Evaluation

Utilization is the measuring standard for determining the degree of evaluation institutionalization in an organization. Patterns of routine evaluation use and examples of positive influence inside an organization are valid performance indicators for internal evaluation institutionalization. Evaluation institutionalization requires a collective commitment of support from senior management and program managers, a visibly defined evaluation purpose, an explicit understanding of the proposed use of evaluation results, and a clearly defined role for evaluator-consultants.

COMMITMENTS

The practice of internal evaluation requires commitment. Building evaluation capacity inside organizations commits management to support the evaluation enterprise and commits evaluators to active organizational participation in communicating evaluation processes and outcomes. Institutionalization begins when senior executives in the organization decide to critically examine and question their operations in a continuous review process that identifies and corrects deficiencies and internal evaluators commit to support that process. Senior managers and internal evaluators share responsibility for evaluation and must work together to craft the requisite administrative, environmental, and structural circumstances favorable to evaluation institutionalization.

EVALUATION ROLE AND PURPOSE

Institutionalizing evaluation in organizations first requires deciding the primary purpose for initiating evaluation and then determining an acceptable implementation process. Negotiating an agenda, identifying placement in the organization's structure and reporting channels, linking evaluation to the decision-making process, and establishing the autonomy and authority of evaluators are all significant issues to resolve before institutionalization can occur. (These topics were discussed in detail in Chapter 6.) The key to successful institutionalization is to reach agreement on expectations for these tasks between senior managers and evaluators before beginning any evaluative efforts.

EVALUATOR-CONSULTANTS

Recognition that not all organizational problems can be solved by conducting classic evaluations is one of the fundamental insights needed by internal evaluators before they can have an impact on organizations. The notion of the evaluator-consultant implies that there are myriad approaches to problem solving, only one of which is formal evaluation. Most organizational phenomena are not static and therefore do not easily lend themselves to facile measurement or quantification. However, evaluator-consultants, combining their evaluation expertise, management skills, and institutional memory, can still appropriately examine these phenomena by defining the problem and identifying the correct methodology for addressing the issue. Inadequate resources and inflexible time constraints frequently combine to prevent the use of formal, lengthy, or sophisticated evaluative techniques. On these occasions, the use of alternative methodologies to produce reasonably reliable information is generally satisfactory. Often, short file reviews, pertinent interviews with affected parties, consultation with outside program experts, comparison of programs with similar programs in other agencies or businesses, creating or clarifying mission statements, analyzing databases, or interpreting program goals and objectives will provide sufficient information for clients to solve their problems. Reducing all organizational phenomena to evaluation projects may not be in the best interests of either clients or evaluators. Approaching problems with an open mind characterizes professional evaluator-consultants working inside organizations.

High Impact Internal Evaluation Conceptual Framework

High impact internal evaluation is not a specific form of evaluation but a construct used to describe the outcomes of successful internal evaluations. High impact internal evaluation begins with a mind-set that internal evaluators can influence organizations when they perform in a consulting role and believe that evaluation is an appropriate analytical tool for instituting change. *Informed evaluators,* focusing on client needs, working with senior officials who support the evaluation enterprise, and actively linked to the organization through extensive communication channels, form the foundation of high impact internal evaluation.

High impact internal evaluation incorporates a philosophy of evaluator activism for processing and disseminating information in organizations. It does not rely on rigid methods or standardized procedures but is flexible and adaptable to ambient organizational conditions. Its basic premise is that evaluative information has a greater probability of positively affecting an organization when the information is distributed, discussed, and comprehended by appropriate stakeholders. Internal evaluation can support and influence the decision-making process in organizations when evaluation results are prominently circulated among relevant stakeholders in the organization and interpreted and advocated by evaluators during serious issue debates. High impact internal evaluation implies communication with the organization by evaluators who recognize that evaluative information generally needs a sponsor to overcome inertia and become accessible and understandable to its users. High impact internal evaluation combines a philosophical conception with a pragmatic application. Informed evaluators, with an understanding of the principles of organizational functions, managerial motivations, and information distribution dynamics, can perform successfully as agents for positive change inside organizations.

EVALUATOR PHILOSOPHY

Believing that internal evaluation is a suitable vehicle to generate an empirical basis for change is the attitude needed to successfully work inside organizations in an evaluative capacity. A basic philosophical orientation for internal evaluators to adopt to insulate themselves from traditional, conditioned reactions to existing organizational policies and procedures is to think critically, challenge assumptions, view organizations as interconnected systems, and operate autonomously. Reflective skepticism about entrenched policies, procedures, and programs offers decisionmakers alternative proposals to parochial options frequently provided by program personnel and stakeholders anesthetized by program proximity.

ADVOCACY AND EXPECTANCY

Blending together the concepts of advocacy evaluation and expectancy theory captures the essential spirit of this book: that greater intercommunication between evaluators and the organization (with both clients and senior leadership) will increase understanding of evaluation purpose, reduce uncertainty and anxiety surrounding evaluation procedures, and accelerate evaluation acceptance. Advocacy evaluation requires a philosophical migration by internal evaluators from the traditional isolation of researchers from their clients to more active communication and participation in organizational affairs. Expectancy theory is a practical explanation for increasing evaluator focus and understanding on client behavior and expectations.

As we discovered in Chapter 4, program managers want to feel more in control during evaluations. They believe that evaluation is something that should be done for them, not to them! Research evidence, opinions of program managers, and experiences of internal evaluators all demonstrate that collaborative evaluations have a greater probability of successful outcomes than those conducted in a hostile atmosphere. The reality of internal evaluation is that internal evaluators need the support of program managers, as well as support from senior executives, if evaluation is to become institutionalized. Including clients in relevant discussions throughout evaluations mitigates the stereotypical view of evaluation as an onerous burden to be avoided.

Actively engaging the organization through the advocacy process and developing explicit understandings between clients and evaluators through discussion of expectations reduce the perceived threat many clients experience and also maximizes the probability that evaluation results will be debated in organizational forums. Internal evaluators' recognition of the synergism generated by combining these two concepts forms a solid foundation for building internal evaluation capability.

INFORMATION ASYMMETRY

Internal evaluators have a responsibility not only to create quality information through their evaluative activities but also to ensure its timely distribution in the organization to appropriate individuals. Information in organizations has value: a positive value for those who possess relevant, accurate, comprehensive data on an issue; and a negative value for those who possess irrelevant, unreliable, incomplete data. Imperfect or limited distribution of factual information in organizations is common during debates over high-stakes issues. Incomplete or erroneous information offered by constituents during organizational debates deprives the organization of quality information and reduces the probability that an enlightened decision will result. These situations offer internal evaluators opportunities to introduce empirical data into the debate and compensate for information imbalances. Achieving information equilibrium among debating constituents is one of the more effective contributions of an internal evaluation staff.

INFORMED EVALUATORS

Informed evaluators are operationally experienced members of the organization as well as trained researchers. Rather than becoming contaminated from proximity to the organization, informed evaluators accumulate valuable organizational insights that complement their research skills. Insider understanding of programs, policies, and procedures is an empowering attribute of internal evaluators permitting rapid and enlightened responses to organizational requests for information. Informed evaluators constitute an institutional databank because of their awareness of the organization—its history, personalities, and operations. Due to their insider location and familiarity with the organizations, they offer organizations a quick-assessment capability.

Practicing High
Impact Internal Evaluation

High impact internal evaluation is a sufficiently flexible approach to evaluating inside organizations that practitioners can adapt it to a variety of circumstances. High impact internal evaluation combines concepts from management and evaluation science with consulting and communication skills in a continuous dialogue with the organization. Internal evaluators possess an understanding of evaluation theory, operational program theory and knowledge, institutional history, and information distribution dynamics. This provides them with a perspective unique in the organization.

The reality of practicing evaluation inside organizations requires that evaluators institute particular core practices that are indispensable for success. The following nine practices are the essence of high impact evaluation inside organizations and constitute a meaningful behavioral and procedural framework to guide the actions of internal evaluators and build internal evaluation capacity.

1. Act impartially

Internal evaluators should be competent, fair, and honest. Impartial inquiries and reporting are the standards used by clients to judge the credibility of internal evaluators.

2. Assert independence

Internal evaluators should be independent from all components in the organization and free from interference by senior executives. The optimum location for internal evaluators places them in close proximity to senior officials to eliminate dilution or alteration of evaluative information. Independence should always be stressed in conversations with senior management officials as indispensable to the production of unbiased evaluations.

3. Study relevant issues

Internal evaluators should direct their evaluative/consultative activities toward relevant organizational issues. Commitment of resources to trivial problems mars evaluator reputation and signals the organization that evaluation is not valued.

4. Be responsive and timely

Internal evaluators must develop policies and procedures that enable them to promptly respond to organizational requests for their services. Rapidly produced answers to organizational questions enhance the perceived usefulness of evaluation and contribute to institutionalization. Internal evaluators must also be alert to time lines for decision making and ensure their work product is available to decisionmakers in a timely fashion. Rough approximations that meet decision deadlines have far greater utility that precise statistics and detailed data that arrive after decisions have been made.

5. **Communicate with the organization**

Throughout this book, active participation in organizational forums where evaluation findings are discussed has been stressed as the hallmark of the high impact internal evaluator. Extensive communication with clients, stakeholders, and senior officials in the organization that acquaints them with the value and purpose of evaluation is an ongoing, critical task for internal evaluators. Advocating evaluation findings and recommendations provides organizations with valuable insights for program improvement.

6. **Focus on clients**

Attentiveness to needs, anxieties, and expectations of clients creates a more harmonious evaluation atmosphere. Collaborative evaluation endeavors have greater probability of success than do contentious undertakings.

7. **Support the decision-making process**

Internal evaluators must be philosophically oriented to the notion that the primary purpose of internal evaluation is to support the decision-making *process*. Support for the organization's decision-making process is the logical, sensible, central purpose and focus of internal evaluation and the justification for resource commitment by the organization. Decision support is not a vulnerability of internal evaluation but rather its defining characteristic. Evaluation support for decision making is neither incompatible with scientific research cannons nor does it vitiate the independence of the observer.

8. **Issue recommendations**

Internal evaluators should almost always issue recommendations or options after completion of an evaluative inquiry. Knowledge acquired during evaluations is an asset that can be used to illuminate issues and improve the decision-making process.

9. **Follow up recommendations**

All approved recommendations should be followed to ensure implementation is accomplished. The internal evaluation process is not complete until implementation of recommended changes takes place and organizational impact calculated.

Instituting and refining these practices will aid internal evaluators in achieving professional reputations inside organizations.

Final Thoughts

I have been privileged to witness firsthand the immense influence that competent internal evaluators can have on an organization. Research and the experiences of others demonstrate that internal evaluators can have a significant and positive effect on the policies and procedures of an organization. I predict that internal evaluation will continue to grow worldwide in practice and importance as its value to organizations becomes more apparent and internal evaluators are recognized as professionally competent analysts of the organizational scene. Increased pressures on managers for documented high performance and the complexity of managing modern organizations in an era of information overload will fuel the growth of internal evaluation.

Evolution of the practice of internal evaluation is still in its early stages, and developing and fostering its use and enhancing its professional image will continue to be formidable tasks facing internal evaluators. The goal is to see internal evaluation commonplace in organizations, not the exception. High impact internal evaluation is not only a possibility but a potentially universal phenomenon in modern, knowledge-based organizations. The challenges for internal evaluators are service to the organization, maintenance of professional evaluation standards, allegiance to scientific protocols, and an ethical discharge of their responsibilities as evaluators. Much of the burden of achieving these goals falls on internal evaluators themselves. Independent, credible, useful, timely assessments of relevant organizational issues will ensure progress toward this objective.

I have portrayed internal evaluation in this book as a practical, problem-solving analytical technique with a wide variety of applications for routine use inside organizations. There is no standardized approach to internal evaluation. It is an adaptation of general evaluation principles to the conditions and requirements encountered inside organizations. My own experience is that internal evaluation is successful when organizations and evaluators understand each other's motivations, expectations, and concerns. There is ample evidence that internal evaluators are having a high impact with their evaluative activities where these conditions are present. Skeptics will continue to question internal evaluators' objectivity, but the available theory and evidence suggest that independent observation and reporting by "insiders" is an attainable goal.

The future growth, impact, and success of internal evaluation will depend, to a great extent, on the development of new models, frameworks, designs, and methodologies applicable to the pragmatic needs of organizations, that is, rapid and intelligent responses to relevant questions with quality information. Internal evaluators must become innovative to reconcile basic science research tenets of methodical, independent observation with the organization's need for rapid assessment and timely production of useful information. Independence from and proximity to organizational functions are not incompatible circumstances precluding credible observations and judgments, but rather methodological, administrative, and procedural challenges to be overcome. The concepts of evaluator-consultant, evaluator-change agent, and evaluator-advocate will have to become better understood and incorporated into the repertoire of internal evaluators to facilitate their working relationships with organizational components. The focus on using evaluation products will shift from the consumer to the producer, and internal evaluators will begin to recognize and accept their responsibility for marketing their competencies and products and tailoring their services to organizational needs. An emerging internal evaluation paradigm is incorporating and refining these concepts for use inside organizations.

Last, internal evaluators must begin to record and publish their experiences, creating a literature, with not only innovative practical solutions and applications for employment inside organizations but also a theory of use that will contribute to increased acceptance and appreciation of the benefits of internal evaluation practice.

References

Adams, K. A. (1985). Gamesmanship for internal evaluators: Knowing when to "hold 'em" and when to "fold 'em." *Evaluation and Program Planning, 8,* 53-57.

American Evaluation Association. (1995). Guiding principles for evaluators. In W. R. Shadish, D. L. Newman, M. A. Scheirer, & C. Wye (Eds.), *Guiding principles for evaluators* (New Directions for Program Evaluation, No. 66). San Francisco: Jossey-Bass.

Argyris, C. (1982). *Reasoning, learning, and action.* San Francisco: Jossey-Bass.

Attkisson, C. C., Brown, T. R., & Hargreaves, W. A. (1978). Roles and functions of evaluation in human service programs. In C. C. Attkisson, W. A. Hargreaves, M. J. Harowitz, & J. E. Soresen (Eds.), *Evaluation of human service programs.* New York: Academic Press.

Barkdoll, G. L. (1982). *Increasing the impact of program evaluation by altering the working relationship between the program manager and the evaluator.* Unpublished doctoral dissertation, University of Southern California, Los Angeles.

Barkdoll, G. L. (1985). Type III evaluations: Consultation and consensus. In E. Chelimsky (Ed.), *Program evaluation: Patterns and directions.* Washington, DC: American Society for Public Administration.

Barkdoll, G. L., & Sporn, D. L. (1989). Five strategies for successful in-house evaluations. In J. S. Wholey, K. E. Newcomer, & Associates (Eds.), *Improving government performance: Evaluation strategies for strengthening public agencies and programs.* San Francisco: Jossey-Bass.

Barrados, M., & Divorski, S. (1996). Evaluation in the federal government. In *Report of the auditor general of Canada to the House of Commons.* Ottawa: Minister of Public Works and Government Services Canada.

Bartunek, J. M., & Louis, M. R. (1996). *Insider/outsider team research.* Thousand Oaks, CA: Sage.

Bellavita, C. (1986). Communicating effectively about performance is a purposive activity. In J. S. Wholey, M. A. Abramson, & C. Bellavita (Eds.), *Performance and credibility: Developing excellence in public and nonprofit organizations.* Lexington, MA: Lexington Books.

Bellavita, C., Wholey, J. S., & Abramson, M. A. (1986). Performance-oriented evaluation: Prospects for the future. In J. S. Wholey, M. A. Abramson, & C. Bellavita (Eds.), *Performance and credibility: Developing excellence in public and nonprofit organizations.* Lexington, MA: Lexington Books.

Bickman, L. (1989). Barriers to the use of program theory. *Evaluation and Program Planning, 12,* 387-390.

Blake, R. R., & Mouton, J. S. (1988). Comparing strategies for incremental and transformational change. In R. H. Kilmann, T. J. Covin, & Associates, *Corporate transformation.* San Francisco: Jossey-Bass.

Boyle, R. (1993). *Making evaluation relevant.* Dublin, Ireland: Institute of Public Administration.

Boyle, R. (1999). Professionalizing the evaluation function: Human resource development and the building of evaluation capacity. In R. Boyle & D. Lemaire (Eds.), *Building effective evaluation capacity: Lessons from practice.* New Brunswick, NJ: Transaction Publishing.

Boyle, R., Lemaire, D., & Rist, R. (1999). Introduction: Building effective evaluation capacity. In R. Boyle & D. Lemaire (Eds.), *Building effective evaluation capacity: Lessons from practice.* New Brunswick, NJ: Transaction Publishing.

Bozeman, B., & Bretschneider, S. (1994). The "publicness puzzle" in organization theory: A test of alternative explanations of differences between public and private organizations. *Journal of Public Administration Research and Theory, 4,* 197-293.

Braskamp, L. A., Brandenburg, D. C., & Ory, J. C. (1987). Lessons about clients' expectations. In J. Nowakowski (Ed.), *The client perspective on evaluation* (New Directions for Program Evaluation, No. 36). San Francisco: Jossey-Bass.

Brookfield, S. D. (1987). *Developing critical thinkers: Challenging adults to explore alternative ways of thinking and acting.* San Francisco: Jossey-Bass.

Broskowski, A., & Driscoll, J. (1978). The organizational context of program evaluation. In C. C. Attkisson, W. A. Hargreaves, M. J. Harowitz, & J. E. Sorensen (Eds.), *Evaluation of human service programs.* New York: Academic Press.

Burrell, G., & Morgan, G. L. (1979). *Sociological paradigms and organizational analysis.* Portsmouth, NH: Heinemann.

Butler, S. M., Sanera, M., & Weinrad, W. B. (Eds.). (1984). *Mandate for leadership II: Continuing the conservative revolution.* Washington, DC: Heritage Foundation.

Callahan, R. E., Watkins, J. F., & Carr, K. D. (1994, November). *Internal evaluators as change agents: An operational approach for improving organizational performance.* Paper presented at the annual meeting of the American Evaluation Association, Boston.

Chelimsky, E. (1977). *Analysis of a symposium on the use of evaluation by federal agencies* (Vol. 2). McLean, VA: MITRE.

Chelimsky, E. (1985). Old patterns and new directions in program evaluation. In E. Chelimsky (Ed.), *Program evaluation: Patterns and directions.* Washington, DC: American Society for Public Administration.

Chelimsky, E. (1992). Executive branch program evaluation: An upturn soon? In C. G. Wye & R. C. Sonnichsen (Eds.), *Evaluation in the federal government: Changes, trends, and opportunities* (New Directions for Program Evaluation, No. 55). San Francisco: Jossey-Bass.

Chelimsky, E. (1997). The coming transformations in evaluation. In E. Chelimsky & W. R. Shadish (Eds.), *Evaluation for the 21st century.* Thousand Oaks, CA: Sage.

Chen, H. T. (1989). Issues in the theory-driven perspective. *Evaluation and Program Planning, 12,* 299-306.

Chen, H. T., & Rossi, P. H. (1987). The theory-driven approach to validity. *Evaluation Review, 7,* 95-103.

Clifford, D. L., & Sherman, P. (1983). Internal evaluation: Integrating program evaluation and management. In A. J. Love (Ed.), *Developing effective internal evaluation* (New Directions for Program Evaluation, No. 20). San Francisco: Jossey-Bass.

Cook, T. D., & Campbell, D. T. (1979). *Quasi-experimentation: Design & analysis issues for field settings.* Boston: Houghton Mifflin.

Cordray, D. S. (1989). Optimizing validity in program research: An elaboration of Chen and Rossi's theory-driven approach. *Evaluation and Program Planning, 12,* 379-385.

Creswell, J. W. (1994). *Research design: Qualitative and quantitative approaches.* Thousand Oaks, CA: Sage.

Cummings, T. G., Mohrman, S. A., Mohrman, A. M., Jr., & Ledford, G. E., Jr. (1985). Organization design for the future: A collaborative research approach. In E. E. Lawler III, A. M. Mohrman, Jr., S. A. Mohrman, G. E. Ledford, Jr., & T. G. Cummings (Eds.), *Doing research that is useful for theory and practice* (pp. 275-323). San Francisco: Jossey-Bass.

Datta, L. (1997). A pragmatic basis for mixed-method designs. In J. C. Greene & V. J. Caracelli (Eds.), *Advances in mixed-method evaluation: The challenges and benefits of integrating diverse paradigms* (New Directions for Evaluation, No. 74). San Francisco: Jossey-Bass.

Davis, H. R., & Salasin, S. E. (1975). The utilization of evaluation. In E. L. Struening & M. Guttentag (Eds.), *Handbook of evaluation research* (Vol. 1, pp. 621-666). Beverly Hills, CA: Sage.

Dean, D. L. (1994). How to use focus groups. In J. S. Wholey, H. P. Hatry, & K. E. Newcomer (Eds.), *Handbook of practical program evaluation.* San Francisco: Jossey-Bass.

Derlien, H. (1990). Genesis and structure of valuation efforts in comparative perspective. In R. C. Rist (Ed.), *Program evaluation and the management of government: Patterns & prospects across eight nations.* New Brunswick, NJ: Transaction Publishing.

Downs, A. (1977). Some thoughts on giving people economic advice. In F. G. Caro (Ed.), *Readings in evaluation research.* New York: Russell Sage.

Drucker, P. F. (1986). *The frontiers of management: When tomorrow's decisions are being shaped today.* New York: Truman Talley Books/Dutton.

Drucker, P. F. (1989). *The new realities.* New York: Harper & Row.

Duffy, B. P. (1993). Focus groups: An important research technique for internal evaluation units. *Evaluation Practice, 14,* 133-139.

Evered, R., & Louis, M. R. (1981). Alternative perspectives in the organizational sciences: "Inquiry from the inside" and "inquiry from the outside." *Academy of Management Review, 6,* 385-395.

Farley, J. (1991). Sociotechnical theory: An alternative framework for evaluation. C. L. Larson & H. Preskill (Eds.), *Organizations in transition: Opportunities and challenges for evaluation* (New Directions for Program Evaluation, No. 49, pp. 51-62). San Francisco: Jossey-Bass.

Fetterman, D. M. (1997). Empowerment evaluation and accreditation in higher education. In E. Chelimsky & W. R. Shadish (Eds.), *Evaluation for the 21st century: A
handbook.* Thousand Oaks, CA: Sage.

Fishman, D. B. (1991). An introduction to the experimental versus the pragmatic
paradigm in evaluation. *Evaluation and Program Planning, 14,* 353-363.

Fleischer, M. (1983). The evaluator as program consultant. *Evaluation and Program
Planning, 6,* 69-76.

Forss, K., Cracknell, B., & Samset, K. (1994). Can evaluation help an organization to
learn? *Evaluation Review, 18,* 574-591.

General Accounting Office. (1987). *Federal evaluation: Fewer units, reduced resources,
different studies from 1980* (PEMD-87-9). Washington, DC: Author.

General Accounting Office. (1988). *Program evaluation issues* (GAO Transition Series).
Washington, DC: Author.

General Accounting Office. (1991). *Designing evaluations* (GAO/PEMD-10.1.4). Washington, DC: Author.

General Accounting Office. (1997). *The Government Performance and Results Act*
(GAO/GGD 97-109). Washington, DC: Author.

General Accounting Office. (1998). *Program evaluation: Agencies challenged by demand
for information on program results* (GAO/GGD-98-53). Washington, DC: Author.

Gladis, S. D. (1988). FBI Evaluation Workshop, Wintergreen, VA.

Gladis, S. D. (1989). *Process writing: A systematic writing strategy.* Amherst, MA: Human
Resource Development.

Greene, J. C., & Caracelli, V. J. (1997). Editors' notes. In J. C. Greene & V. J. Caracelli
(Eds.), *Advances in mixed-method evaluation: The challenges and benefits of
integrating diverse paradigms* (New Directions for Evaluation, No. 74). San
Francisco: Jossey-Bass.

Gunn, W. J. (1987). Client concerns and strategies in evaluation studies. In J. Nowakowski (Ed.), *The client perspective on evaluation* (New Directions for Program
Evaluation, No. 36). San Francisco: Jossey-Bass.

Gurel, L. (1975). The human side of evaluating human services programs: Problems and
prospects. In M. Guttentag & E. Struening (Eds.), *Handbook of evaluation
research* (Vol. 2., pp. 11-28). Beverly Hills, CA: Sage.

Hansson, F. (1997). Critical comments on evaluation research in Denmark. In E. Chelimsky & W. R. Shadish (Eds.), *Evaluation for the 21st century.* Thousand Oaks, CA:
Sage.

Hendricks, M. (1994). Making a splash: Reporting evaluation results effectively. In J. S.
Wholey, H. P. Hatry, & K. E. Newcomer (Eds.), *Handbook of practical program
evaluation* (pp. 549-575). San Francisco: Jossey-Bass.

Hendricks, M., & Handley, E. (1990). Improving the recommendations from evaluation
studies. *Evaluation and Program Planning, 13,* 109-117.

Henry, G. T. (1997). Introduction. In G. T. Henry (Ed.), *Creating effective graphs:
Solutions for a variety of evaluation data* (New Directions for Program Evaluation,
No. 73). San Francisco: Jossey-Bass.

Hersey, P., & Blanchard, K. (1982). *Management of organizational behavior: Utilizing
human resources.* Englewood Cliffs, NJ: Prentice Hall.

Hirschman, A. O. (1970). *Exit, voice and loyalty.* Cambridge, MA: Harvard University
Press.

Honea, G. E. (1992). *Ethics and public sector evaluators: Nine case studies.* Unpublished
doctoral dissertation, University of Virginia, Charlottesville.

Horst, P., Nay, J. N., Scanlon, J. W., & Wholey, J. S. (1977). Program manager and the federal evaluator. In F. G. Caro (Ed.), *Readings in evaluation research* (2nd ed.). New York: Russell Sage.

House, E. R. (1986). Internal evaluation. *Evaluation Practice, 9*, 43-46

House, E. R. (1990). An ethics of qualitative field studies. In E. G. Guba (Ed.), *The paradigm dialog*. Newbury Park, CA: Sage.

House, E. R. (1997). Evaluation in the government marketplace. *Evaluation Practice, 18*, 37-48.

Huse, E. F., & Cummings, T. G. (1985). *Organization development and change*. St. Paul, MN: West.

Indrebo, A. M. (1997, November). *The self-evaluating organization: A study of collaborative evaluation and organizational learning in schools*. Paper presented at the annual meeting of the American Evaluation Association, San Diego, CA.

Jenlink, P. M. (1994). Using evaluation to understand the learning architecture of an organization. *Evaluation and Program Planning, 17*, 315-325.

Joint Committee on Standards for Educational Evaluation. (1994). *Program evaluation standards* (2nd ed.). Thousand Oaks, CA: Sage.

Kaplan, A. (1964). *The conduct of inquiry*. New York: Harper & Row.

Katz, D., & Kahn, R. (1978). *The social psychology of organizations* (2nd ed.). New York: John Wiley.

Kennedy, M. M. (1983). The role of the in-house evaluator. *Evaluation Review, 7*, 519-541.

Kiefer, C. F., & Stroh, P. (1984). A new paradigm for developing organizations. In J. D. Adams (Ed.), *Transforming work*. Alexandria, VA: Miles River.

Kingsbury, N., & Hedrick, T. E. (1994). Evaluator training in a government setting. In J. W. Altschuld & M. Engle (Eds.), *The preparation of professional evaluators: Issues, perspectives, and programs* (New Directions for Program Evaluation, No. 62, pp. 61-70). San Francisco: Jossey-Bass.

Krathwohl, D. R. (1985). *Social and behavioral science research: A new framework for conceptualizing, implementing, and evaluating research studies*. San Francisco: Jossey-Bass.

Ledford, G. E., Mohrman, S. A., Mohrman, A. M., & Lawler, E. E. (1989). The phenomenon of large-scale organizational change. In A. M. Mohrman, S. A. Mohrman, G. E. Ledford, Jr., T. G. Cummings, & E. E. Lawler III (Eds.), *Large-scale organizational change*. San Francisco: Jossey-Bass.

Leeuw, F. L., & Sonnichsen, R. C. (1994). Evaluation and organizational learning: International perspectives. In F. L. Leeuw, R. C. Rist, & R. C. Sonnichsen (Eds.), *Can governments learn? Comparative perspectives on evaluation & organizational learning*. New Brunswick, NJ: Transaction Publishing.

Leviton, L. C., & Hughes, E. F. X. (1981). Research on the utilization of evaluations: A review and syntheses. *Evaluation Review, 5*, 525-548.

Love, A. J. (Ed.). (1983a). *Developing effective internal evaluation* (New Directions for Program Evaluation, No. 20). San Francisco: Jossey-Bass.

Love, A. J. (1983b). Editor's notes. In A. J. Love (Ed.), *Developing effective internal evaluation* (New Directions for Program Evaluation, No. 20). San Francisco: Jossey-Bass.

Love, A. J. (1983c). The organizational context and the development of internal evaluation. In A. J. Love (Ed.), *Developing effective internal evaluation* (New Directions for Program Evaluation, No. 20). San Francisco: Jossey-Bass.

Love, A. J. (1991). *Internal evaluation: Building organizations from within.* Newbury Park, CA: Sage.

Marsella, A. J., & Yang, A. L. (1983). Personality research: Anxiety, aggression, and locus of control. In R. J. Corsini & A. J. Marsella (Eds.), *Personality theories, research, & assessment.* Itasca, IL: F. E. Peacock.

Mathison, S. (1991). What do we know about internal evaluation? *Evaluation and Program Planning, 14,* 159-165.

Mayne, J. (1992a). Establishing internal evaluation in an organization. In J. Hudson, J. Mayne, & R. Thomlison (Eds.), *Action-oriented evaluation in organizations: Canadian practices.* Toronto, Ontario: Wall & Emerson.

Mayne, J. (1992b). Institutionalizing program evaluation. In J. Hudson, J. Mayne, & R. Thomlison (Eds.), *Action-oriented evaluation in organizations: Canadian practices.* Toronto, Ontario: Wall & Emerson.

Mayne, J. (1994). Utilizing evaluation in organizations: The balancing act. In F. L. Leeuw, R. C. Rist, & R. C. Sonnichsen (Eds.), *Can governments learn? Comparative perspectives on evaluation & organizational learning.* New Brunswick, NJ: Transaction Publishing.

McQueen, C. (1992). Program evaluation in the Canadian federal government. In J. Hudson, J. Mayne, & R. Thomlison (Eds.), *Action-oriented evaluation in organizations: Canadian practices* (pp. 28-47). Toronto, Ontario: Wall & Emerson.

McWeeney, T. (1995, January 30-31). Central Michigan University performance measures law enforcement seminar, Washington, DC.

Mertens, D. M. (1994). Training evaluators: Unique skills and knowledge. In J. W. Altschuld & M. Engle (Eds.), *The preparation of professional evaluators: Issues, perspectives, and programs* (New Directions for Program Evaluation, No. 62, pp. 17-27). San Francisco: Jossey-Bass.

Merton, R. K. (1972). Insiders and outsiders: A chapter in the sociology of knowledge. *American Journal of Sociology, 78*(1), 9-47.

Minnett, A. M. (1997, November). *The internal evaluator's role in self-reflective organizations: One nonprofit agency's model.* Paper presented at the annual meeting of the American Evaluation Association, San Diego, CA.

Mohr, L. B. (1988). *Impact analysis for program evaluation.* Chicago: Dorsey.

Morgan, G. (1983). *Beyond method.* Beverly Hills, CA: Sage.

Morgan, G. (1986). *Images of organization.* Beverly Hills, CA: Sage.

Morris, M. (1994). The role of single evaluation courses in evaluation training. In J. W. Altschuld & M. Engle (Eds.), *The preparation of professional evaluators: Issues, perspectives, and programs* (New Directions for Program Evaluation, No. 62, pp. 51-59). San Francisco: Jossey-Bass.

Morris, M., & Cohn, R. (1993). Program evaluation and ethical challenges: A national survey. *Evaluation Review, 17,* 621-642.

Nadler, D. A., & Tushman, M. L. (1992). Designing organizations that have good fit: A framework for understanding new architectures. In D. A. Nadler, M. S. Gerstein, R. B. Shaw, & Associates, *Organizational architecture.* San Francisco: Jossey-Bass.

Naisbitt, J. (1982). *Megatrends.* New York: Warner.

Newman, D. L., & Brown, R. D. (1996). *Applied ethics for program evaluation.* Thousand Oaks, CA: Sage.

Nicoll, D. (1984). Consulting to organizational transformations. In J. D. Adams (Ed.), *Transforming work.* Alexandria, VA: Miles River.

North, D. C. (1990). *Institutions, institutional change and economic performance.* Cambridge, UK: Cambridge University Press.

Oman, R. C. (1989). Process dimensions in program evaluation. In G. Barkdoll & J. Bell (Eds.), *Evaluation and the federal decision maker* (New Directions for Program Evaluation, No. 41). San Francisco: Jossey-Bass.

Patton, M. Q. (1986). *Utilization-focused evaluation* (2nd ed.). Beverly Hills, CA: Sage.

Patton, M. Q. (1988). The evaluator's responsibility for utilization. *Evaluation Practice, 9*(2), 5-24.

Patton, M. Q. (1989a). A context and boundaries for a theory-driven approach to validity. *Evaluation and Program Planning, 12,* 375-377.

Patton, M. Q. (1989b). FBI evaluation training workshop, Quantico, VA.

Patton, M. Q. (1990). *Qualitative evaluation and research methods* (2nd ed.). Newbury Park, CA: Sage.

Patton, M. Q. (1994). Development evaluation. *Evaluation Practice, 15*(3), 311-319.

Patton, M. Q. (1997). *Utilization-focused evaluation* (3rd ed.). Thousand Oaks, CA: Sage.

Pawson, R., & Tilley, N. (1997). *Realistic evaluation.* London: Sage.

Peters, T. (1987). *Thriving on chaos: Handbook for a management revolution.* New York: Knopf.

Peters, T. (1992). *Liberation management: Necessary disorganization for the nanosecond nineties.* New York: Knopf.

Pettigrew, M. (1996). Evaluation in the UK. *European Evaluation Newsletter, 3.*

Pfeffer, J. (1978). *Organizational design.* Arlington Heights, IL: AHM.

Pfeffer, J. (1981). *Power in organizations.* Boston: Pitman.

Phillips, D. C. (1987). *Philosophy, science, and social inquiry.* Oxford: Pergamon.

Preskill, H. (1991). The cultural lens: Bringing utilization into focus. In C. L. Larson & H. Preskill (Eds.), *Organizations in transition: Opportunities and challenges for evaluation* (New Directions for Program Evaluation, No. 49, pp. 5-16). San Francisco: Jossey Bass.

Preskill, H. (1994). Evaluation's role in enhancing organizational learning: A model for practice. *Evaluation and Program Planning, 17*(3), 291-297.

Preskill, H., & Caracelli, V. (1997). Current and developing conceptions of use: Evaluation use TIG survey results. *Evaluation Practice, 18*(3), 209-225.

Radin, B. A. (1987). The organization and its environment: What difference do they make? In J. S. Wholey (Ed.), *Organizational excellence: Stimulating quality and communicating value.* Lexington, MA: Lexington Books.

Rainey, H. G. (1991). *Understanding and managing public organizations.* San Francisco: Jossey-Bass.

Raven, B. H., & Kruglanski, A. W. (1970). Conflict and power. In P. G. Swingle (Ed.), *The structure of conflict.* New York: Academic Press.

Read, W. (1962). Upward communication in industrial hierarchies. *Human Relations, 15,* 3-16.

Reichardt, C. S. (1994). Summative evaluation, formative evaluation, and tactical research. *Evaluation Practice, 15,* 275-281.

Reichardt, C. S., & Cook, T. D. (1979). Beyond qualitative versus quantitative methods. In T. D. Cook & C. S. Reichardt (Eds.), *Qualitative and quantitative methods in evaluation research* (pp. 7-32). Beverly Hills, CA: Sage.

Richardson, E. L. (1992). The value of evaluation. In C. G. Wye & R. C. Sonnichsen (Eds.), *Evaluation in the federal government: Changes, trends, and opportunities*

(New Directions for Program Evaluation, No. 55, pp. 15-20). San Francisco: Jossey-Bass.

Rist, R. C. (1990). On the application of program evaluation designs: Sorting out their use and abuse. In R. C. Rist (Ed.), *Policy and program evaluation: Perspectives on design and utilization.* Brussels: Institute of Administrative Sciences.

Rist, R. C. (1994). The preconditions for learning: Lessons from the public sector. In F. L. Leeuw, R. C. Rist, & R. C. Sonnichsen (Eds.), *Can governments learn? Comparative perspectives on evaluation & organizational learning.* New Brunswick, NJ: Transaction Publishing.

Robertson, P. J., & Seneviratne, S. J. (1995). Outcomes of planned organizational change in the public sector: A meta-analytic comparison to the private sector. *Public Administration Review, 55,* 547-558.

Rossi, P. H., & Freeman, H. E. (1989). *Evaluation: A systematic approach* (4th ed.). Newbury Park, CA: Sage.

Rutman, L. (1980). *Planning useful evaluations: Evaluability assessment.* Beverly Hills, CA: Sage.

Rymph, D. B. (1989). Evaluation in the Department of Housing and Urban Development, 1980-1988. *Evaluation Practice, 10,* 30-39.

Rymph, D. B. (1992). Evaluation in the Department of Housing and Urban Development. In C. G. Wye & R. C. Sonnichsen (Eds.), *Evaluation in the federal government: Changes, trends, and opportunities* (New Directions for Program Evaluation, No. 55). San Francisco: Jossey-Bass.

Sanders, J. R. (1995). Standards and principles. In W. R. Shadish, D. L. Newman, M. A. Scheirer, & C. Wye (Eds.), *Guiding principles for evaluators* (New Directions for Program Evaluation, No. 66). San Francisco: Jossey-Bass.

Sanera, M. (1984). Implementing the mandate. In S. M. Butler, M. Sanera, & W. B. Weinrad (Eds.), *Mandate for leadership II: Continuing the conservative revolution.* Washington, DC: Heritage Foundation.

Schon, D. A. (1971). *Beyond the stable state.* New York: Norton.

Scriven, M. (1991). *Evaluation thesaurus* (4th ed.). Newbury Park, CA: Sage.

Scriven, M. (1993). The nature of evaluation. In M. Scriven (Ed.), *Hard-won lessons in program evaluation* (New Directions for Program Evaluation, No. 58). San Francisco: Jossey-Bass.

Scriven, M. (1995). The logic of evaluation and evaluation practice. In D. M. Founier (Ed.), *Reasoning in evaluation: Inferential links and leaps* (New Directions for Program Evaluation, No. 68). San Francisco: Jossey-Bass.

Scriven, M. (1996). The theory behind practical evaluation. *Evaluation, 2*(4), 393-404.

Scriven, M. (1997). Truth and objectivity in evaluation. In E. Chelimsky & W. Shadish (Eds.), *Evaluation for the 21st century.* Thousand Oaks, CA: Sage.

Segsworth, R. V. (1994). Downsizing and program evaluation: An assessment of the experience in the government of Canada. In R. Bernier & J. Gow (Eds.), *Un etat reduit?* [A down-sized state?] (pp. 249-259). Sainte-Foy, Quebec: University of Quebec Press.

Senge, P. M. (1990). *The fifth discipline: The art and practice of the learning organization.* New York: Doubleday.

Shadish, W. R., Cook, T. D., & Leviton, L. C. (1991). *Foundations of program evaluation: Theories of practice.* Newbury Park, CA: Sage.

Shadish, W. R., Newman, D. L., Scheirer, M. A., & Wye, C. (1995). Developing the guiding principles. In W. R. Shadish, D. L. Newman, M. A. Scheirer, & C. Wye

(Eds.), *Guiding principles for evaluators* (New Directions for Program Evaluation, No. 66). San Francisco: Jossey-Bass.

Simon, H. A. (1976). *Administrative behavior* (3rd ed.). New York: Free Press.

Sommerlad, E. (1995). The UK "voluntary" sector and the emergent role of the practitioner evaluator in NGO's [Review of *Evaluating ourselves*]. *Evaluation, 1,* 107-110.

Sonnichsen, R. C. (1988). Advocacy evaluation: A model for internal evaluation offices. *Evaluation and Program Planning, 11,* 141-148.

Sonnichsen, R. C. (1989a). Advocacy evaluation: A strategy for organizational improvement. *Knowledge: Creation, Diffusion, Utilization, 10*(4).

Sonnichsen, R. C. (1989b). An open letter to Ernest House. *Evaluation Practice, 10*(3), 59-63.

Sonnichsen, R. C. (1989c). Program managers: Victims or victors in the evaluation process. In G. L. Barkdoll & J. B. Bell (Eds.), *Evaluation and the federal decision maker* (New Directions for Program Evaluation, No. 41). San Francisco: Jossey-Bass.

Sonnichsen, R. C. (1990). Organizational learning and the environment of evaluation. In C. Bellavita (Ed.), *How public organizations work: Learning from experience.* New York: Praeger.

Sonnichsen, R. C. (1991). *Characteristics of high impact internal evaluation offices.* Unpublished doctoral dissertation, University of Southern California, Department of Public Administration.

Stame, N. (1998, October). *Evaluation in Italy: Evaluation as a tool of government* (Newsletter No. 2/98). Stockholm, Sweden: European Evaluation Society.

Stiglitz, J. E. (1994). *Whither socialism?* Cambridge, MA: MIT Press.

Tanji, J. M. (1993). Wishing for a one-armed expert: Recommendations as a philosophical attitude. *Evaluation and Program Planning, 16,* 149-152.

Tarnas, R. (1991). *The passion of the Western mind: Understanding the ideas that have shaped our world view.* New York: Ballantine.

Tate, D. L., & Cummings, O. W. (1991). Promoting evaluations with management. In C. L. Larson & H. Preskill (Eds.), *Organizations in transition: Opportunities and challenges for evaluation* (New Directions for Program Evaluation, No. 49). San Francisco: Jossey-Bass.

Toffler, A. (1981). *The third wave.* New York: Bantam.

Toffler, A. (1990). *Powershift.* New York: Bantam.

Torres, R. T. (1991). Improving the quality of internal evaluation: The evaluator as consultant-mediator. *Evaluation and Program Planning, 14,* 189-198.

Torres, R. T., Preskill, A. S., & Piontek, M. E. (1996). *Evaluation strategies for communicating and reporting: Enhancing learning in organizations.* Thousand Oaks, CA: Sage.

Treadwell, W. A. (1995). Fuzzy set theory movement in the social sciences. *Public Administration Review, 55,* 91-98.

Tushman, M. L., Newman, W. H., & Nadler, D. A. (1988). Executive leadership and organizational evolution: Managing incremental and discontinuous change. In R. H. Kilmann, T. J. Covin, & Associates (Eds.), *Cooperate transformation: Revitalizing organizations for a competitive world.* San Francisco: Jossey-Bass.

U.S. Department of Health and Human Services, Office of Inspector General. (1989). *Financial arrangements between physicians and health care businesses.* Report to Congress. Washington, DC: Government Printing Office.

U.S. Department of Housing and Urban Development, Office of Community Planning and Development. (1989). *An analysis of the income cities earn from UDAG projects.* Office of Program Analysis and Evaluation report. Washington, DC: U.S. Department of Housing and Urban Development.

Vaill, P. B. (1996). *Learning as a way of being: Strategies for survival in a world of permanent white water.* San Francisco: Jossey-Bass.

van de Vall, M., & Bolas, C. A. (1981). External vs. internal social policy researchers. *Knowledge: Creation, Diffusion, Utilization, 2,* 461-481.

Wargo, M. J. (1995). The impact of federal government reinvention on federal evaluation activity. *Evaluation Practice, 16*(3), 227-237.

Weiss, C. H. (1975). Evaluation research in the political context. In E. L. Struening & M. Guttentag (Eds.), *Handbook of evaluation research* (Vol. 1). Beverly Hills, CA: Sage.

Weiss, C. H. (1977). Research for policy's sake: The enlightenment function of social research. *Policy Analysis, 3*(4), 530-545.

Weiss, C. H. (1988). If program decisions hinged only on information: A response to Patton. *Evaluation Practice, 9*(3), 15-28.

Wheatley, M. J. (1992). *Leadership and the new science: Learning about organization from an orderly universe.* San Francisco: Berrett-Koehler.

Wholey, J. S. (1979). *Evaluation: Promise and performance.* Washington, DC: Urban Institute.

Wholey, J. S. (1983). *Evaluation and effective public management.* Boston: Little, Brown.

Wholey, J. S. (1986, October). *Options, not recommendations.* Paper presented at the meeting of the American Evaluation Association, Kansas City, KS.

Wholey, J. S. (1989). Introduction: How evaluation can improve agency and program performance. In J. S. Wholey, K. E. Newcomer, & Associates (Eds.), *Improving government performance: Evaluation strategies for strengthening public agencies and programs.* San Francisco: Jossey-Bass.

Wholey, J. S. (1994). Assessing the feasibility and likely usefulness of evaluation. In J. S. Wholey, H. P. Hatry, & K. E. Newcomer (Eds.), *Handbook of practical program evaluation.* San Francisco: Jossey-Bass.

Wholey, J. S. (1997). Trends in performance measurement: Challenges for evaluators. In E. Chelimsky & W. R. Shadish (Eds.), *Evaluation for the 21st century.* Thousand Oaks, CA: Sage.

Wholey, J. S., & Newcomer, K. E. (1997). Clarifying goals, reporting results. In K. E. Newcomer (Ed.), *Using performance measurement to improve public and nonprofit programs* (New Directions for Evaluation, No. 75, pp. 91-98). San Francisco: Jossey-Bass.

Wildavsky, A. (1979). *Speaking truth to power: The art and craft of policy analysis.* Boston: Little, Brown.

Winberg, A. (1991). Maximizing the contribution of internal evaluation units. *Evaluation and Program Planning, 14,* 167-172.

Windle, C., & Neigher, W. (1978). Ethical problems in program evaluation: Advice for trapped evaluators. *Evaluation and Program Planning, 1,* 97-108.

Worthen, B. R. (1995). Some observations about the institutionalization of evaluation. *Evaluation Practice, 16,* 29-36.

Wrong, D. H. (1979). *Power: Its forms, bases, and uses.* Key Concepts in the Social Sciences. New York: Harper & Row.

Wye, C. (1989). Stimulating change in agency management. In J. S. Wholey, K. E. Newcomer, & Associates (Eds.), *Improving government performance: Evaluation strategies for strengthening public agencies and programs* (pp. 179-194). San Francisco: Jossey-Bass.

Yin, R. (1984). *Case study research: Design and methods.* Beverly Hills, CA: Sage.

Zapico-Goni, E., & Mayne, J. (1997). Performance monitoring: Implications for the future. In J. Mayne & E. Zapico-Goni (Eds.), *Monitoring performance in the public sector.* New Brunswick, NJ: Transaction Publishing.

Index

About the Author

Richard C. Sonnichsen retired from the Federal Bureau of Investigation in 1994 after 30 years of service as a special agent investigator and senior executive. For the last 12 years, he was the deputy assistant director in charge of the Office of Planning, Evaluation, and Audits, where he managed the FBI's strategic planning efforts, financial audits, and investigative and administrative program evaluations. He currently works as an evaluation and management consultant. He is a member of the American Evaluation Association, the American Society of Public Administration, and the International Working Group on Evaluation (INTEVAL) and has taught evaluation and research at the University of Southern California Washington Public Affairs Center in Washington, D.C. as an adjunct faculty member. In 1996, he received the Alva and Gunnar Myrdal Award for Government Service from the American Evaluation Association "in recognition of his career contributions toward making internal evaluation both valued and useful." In addition to *High Impact Internal Evaluation,* he has written numerous articles on internal evaluation and chapters in eight books, and he has coedited two books, *Can Governments Learn? Comparative Perspectives on Evaluation & Organizational Learning* and *Evaluation in the Federal Government: Changes, Trends, and Opportunities.* He has served on the editorial boards of the New Directions for Program Evaluation series, *Evaluation Practice,* and *Evaluation and Program Planning.* Dr. Sonnichsen has spoken and presented papers at evaluation conferences in the United States, Canada, and Europe. He received his undergraduate degree in forestry from the University of Idaho and his master's and doctorate degrees in public administration from the University of Southern California. He resides with his wife, Sally, in Sandpoint, Idaho.